Beyond Globalism

Beyond Globalism

Remaking American Foreign Economic Policy

Raymond Vernon
Debora L. Spar

THE FREE PRESS
A Division of Macmillan, Inc.
NEW YORK

Collier Macmillan Publishers
LONDON

The Free Press
A Division of Macmillan, Inc.
866 Third Avenue, New York, N.Y. 10022

Collier Macmillan Canada, Inc.

Printed in the United States of America

printing number

2 3 4 5 6 7 8 9 10

Library of Congress Cataloging-in-Publication Data

Vernon, Raymond
    Beyond globalism.

    Bibliography: p.
    Includes index.
    1. United States—Foreign economic relations.
2. United States—Commercial policy.   3. Economic
assistance, American.   I. Spar, Debora.   II. Title.
HF1455.V47   1989   337.73   88-16299
ISBN 0-02-933161-7

Contents

Acknowledgments

AS USUAL, this book is the work of many people, notwithstanding that only two authors appear upon its cover.

Winthrop Knowlton, in his role as director of the Center for Business and Government of the John F. Kennedy School offered shelter, encouragement, and stimulation. The Ford Foundation generously provided a grant to cover the direct costs of the study.

Over the two or three years in the making of this book, the following students at Harvard contributed to the project: Kevin Barry, Victoria Bassetti, Benjamin Cohen, Claire Fleming, Andy Foose, Ya-Sheng Huang, Isabel Marshall, Allison Pugh, Qiao Yi De, and Jaikumar Ramaswamy. Eugene Salorio developed especially useful materials on agricultural trade policy. Josephine S. Vernon continued in her indefatigable role as scanner, reader, and transcriber of research materials. Miltos Catomeris was both an enthusiastic supporter and an unrelenting critic.

Moreover, a number of readers provided telling comments on earlier drafts. Michael Barzelay, in particular, persuaded us after a year into the process to abandon our initial approach and start all over again. Stephan Haggard, Brian Levy, Louis T. Wells, Heidi Vernon-Wortzel, Ethan B. Kapstein, and David Yoffie among others also suggested some helpful midcourse corrections. Grant Ujifusa performed superbly as the disinterested reader, with considerable impact on the final copy.

We have had privileged access to the recollections of many persons who were actually responsible for shaping the policies analyzed in this study. Uncertain whether to list their names, we finally decided in the negative, lest they seem to share some responsibility for our interpretations.

Finally, Kristin Kladstrup took precious days away from her all-consuming task as a writer of children's books to shepherd the manuscript through endless drafts.

To all these contributors we express our gratitude.

RAYMOND VERNON
DEBORA L. SPAR

1

A New Game

IF AMERICANS ARE confused about where their international economic policies are headed, they have a right to their confusion. The assumptions of the past four decades on which the country's policies once rested have been swept away. The United States is no longer the unchallenged economic leader of the noncommunist world, leading other nations toward an ultimate goal of open global markets. And if that is no longer the objective of the United States, where is the American economy headed?

In the decades to come, Americans will need to reassess their strengths and redefine their foreign economic goals. Indeed, the search for new options has already begun, manifesting itself in a renewed activism in international economic relations, an activism that has produced a new breed of international agreements. Such agreements are smaller in coverage and less ambitious in scope than the global aspirations of Bretton Woods and Point Four. They cover numerous functional fields, from bank safety and foreign trade to exchange rates and communication satellites. And they apply to varying players, from single countries such as Canada or Israel to larger groups such as the members of the Organization for Economic Cooperation and Development (OECD), "the rich men's club."

Some of the agreements in the new wave have been innovative and constructive, bringing benefits to the countries concerned and to the world at large. Others have been destructive and even masochistic, pushing the United States toward a set of world economic relationships that are hurtful to U.S. interests and alien to American institutions and values. But false starts are inescapable in any extended process of learning by doing; they are, in this case, a prelude to reformulating the country's basic international economic strategy around new principles and new goals.

The task we have set ourselves in these pages is to reduce those learning costs to the United States and speed the process by which the U.S. government will be able to identify a new set of goals compatible with the interests, the institutions, and the values of the nation.

AN ADDED URGENCY

Like their counterparts in other countries, American leaders over the past few decades have usually had their eyes fixed on two basic objectives: providing for an adequate national defense and raising living standards. Until just a few years ago, however, American leaders did not have to wrestle with a restraint that preoccupied leaders in most other countries, namely, the nation's ability to earn the foreign exchange necessary for achieving its ambitious goals. Until the 1970s, the vast accumulation of foreign assets in the hands of U.S. nationals, like Mama's proverbial savings account, seemed a sufficient guarantee that the United States could live for an indefinite time on the output of other countries, borrowing as necessary to finance its imports. As long as that state of mind existed among U.S. leaders, foreign economic policies were seen as secondary in importance, yielding to the needs imposed by military and political alliance building and by domestic politics.

With the more recent realization that foreign economic forces could block the achievement of basic national goals, some U.S. leaders have been tempted to cut and run, to separate the nation's economy from the rest of the world by unilateral restrictions of one kind or another. In this reaction, they have had the support of a considerable sector of the American public, many of whom profess to be willing to accept new import restrictions even if the imposition should mean higher consumer prices and retaliation by foreign countries.[1]

Our strong expectation is that this reaction will not prevail for long. The injury that such a policy would generate is far greater today than it would have been a decade or two earlier. And as we intend to demonstrate, the U.S. political system offers ample opportunity for those who would bear the injury to attack and modify the offending policy.

The spectacular decline in the cost of moving goods, people, and—especially—information across national borders has left governments with little room for unilateral action and little choice but to find changed forms of mutual accommodation.[2] With facsimile and telex facilities on tap in such far-off places as Beijing and Monrovia, with the containerization of sea and air freight available to all, international economic relations differ in kind as well as in volume from those of the 1950s. New complex business organizations have added to the intimacy of the contacts between different national economies. Today, multinational enterprises have become ubiquitous, growing out of the enterprises of many different economies from Italy to Hong Kong, and becoming a dominant vehicle for doing business in both industry and finance.

The consequences of these developments have been visible in various ways. Since 1960, for example, U.S. imports and exports of merchandise have risen at an annual average rate of about 5.8 percent in real terms, while the country's gross national product has increased at only about 3.1 percent. The difference of a few percentage points each year has given foreign trade a new meaning for the U.S. economy. Whereas U.S. imports and exports of merchandise amounted to only 14 percent of the output of goods in 1960, the figure had risen to 35 percent by 1986. Meanwhile, the other mature industrialized countries were experiencing a similar trend, finishing the period with even larger foreign trade sectors than did the United States.

Following the lead of the businessmen, investors and speculators also have lifted their sights beyond their own national economies to opportunities in other countries. The dependence of the U.S. government upon Japanese investors for help in financing the country's huge fiscal deficits in the middle 1980s was a striking illustration of the new international ties. The growth of these movements had been so overwhelming that by the mid-1980s, the world's daily foreign exchange transactions were estimated to be 25 times greater than the value of the world's daily merchandise trade. And because the new capital movements were far more mercurial than those relating directly to international trade flows, they posed a much more difficult problem for national officials attempting to maintain conditions for economic stability and growth.

Walter Wriston, former chairman of Citibank, is pushing history much faster than it is likely to go when he says, "At the end of the day, it's a new world and the concept of sovereignty is going to change."[3] Governments are not yet prepared to give up their right to pursue what Wriston regards as "dumb" policies at home or to surrender their economies to the impersonal wisdom of international financial markets. These trends have increased the measure of interdependence among countries but have also reduced the autonomy of national economies and the efficacy of independent national policies.

Developments of this sort would be disconcerting for public policymakers whenever they occurred, but they have been particularly so during the past few decades due to the nature of the demands made by national electorates on their respective governments, including that of the United States. Governments held accountable for growth, inflation, unemployment, and pollution understandably seek effective means for discharging their responsibilities. Yet with such a heavy reliance on their foreign sectors and on organizations with a multinational structure, governments have increasingly found themselves between a rock and a hard place. Any heavy-handed policy of restricting imports, for instance, could generate an unacceptable loss of exports. Any effort to stimulate growth through lower interest rates could dry up inflows of foreign capital. Any attempt to increase labor's income could precipitate a shift of production to foreign shores. Any unilateral policy, in short, would court negative international consequences and domestic repercussions.

A BENT TWIG

On first impact, the responses of the U.S. government to its changed environment seem to have produced no visible structure; hence, a picture of confusion and contradiction. On a few major issues, such as bank safety, environmental protection, energy security, the debts of developing countries, and monetary coordination, the U.S. government has joined in forms of cooperation that would have seemed novel and ambitious a few decades ago. In other areas, however, the taste of Americans for aggressive unilateral action has been growing. Recognizing that the country still has enough power to threaten even if it has lost the power to dominate, the president has been using the threat of his trade-restricting powers to persuade foreign countries to change various practices he regards as "unfair." Caught up in the same mood, congressmen have been introducing bills of a kind wholly out of keeping with traditional U.S. norms and values: to limit the right of U.S. laboratories to license their inventions to foreign firms;[4] to prevent foreign nationals from participating in mergers, acquisitions, and takeovers of U.S. firms;[5] to subsidize selected U.S. exports more widely in order to improve their chances of winning foreign markets;[6] and so on.

Yet neither those who urge retaliation nor those who counsel cooperation have given much consideration to the capacity of the United States to carry out their suggested policies. Policymakers have yet to come to grips with the fact that the United States has entered a new stage in its international economic relations. Even when they face up to the change fully, they must still deal with the fact that national institutions and values change slowly, limiting U.S. responses over the medium term to measures compatible with its history and its ideology.

For instance, while threatening foreign governments is a tempting tactic for politicians when they face difficult problems at home, it ignores the fact that U.S. values and institutions do not lend themselves very well to implementing a policy of threat. The U.S. government, as every schoolchild learns, was carefully designed to produce its decisions through a struggle among competing interests, supported and lubricated by the checks and balances among the government's three branches. As a result, the issues selected are likely to depend more on the energy and ingenuity of the special interest groups supporting them than upon the national interests of the country.

From time to time, of course, that pattern of decision making has been modified as threats such as the Civil War or the Great Depression or the two great world wars made the country willing to accept, at least temporarily, a greater concentration of power in the executive branch. Immediately after World War II, a common perception of the need for an open economic system in the noncommunist world generated a rare cohesiveness within the American body politic. The remnants of that consensus lasted through the Kennedy administration and only broke down under the divisive pressures of the Vietnam war. The U.S. decision-making system then returned to its characteristic patterns of struggle and dissent.

Meanwhile, before the unusual period of consensus had wholly evaporated, the United States enjoyed an exceptional opportunity to use its overwhelming productive capacity, its technological lead, and its military dominance to promote an American view of how the world should organize itself. The period produced a string of remarkable innovations, all directed toward the development of an open competitive system in which the objective of governments would be to create and sustain cooperation and mutual support. This was the agenda supporting the creation of a series of specialized UN agencies designed to regulate the international environment—including the World Bank, the International Monetary Fund (IMF), and the General Agreement on Tariffs and Trade (GATT)—as well as the European movement toward economic integration.

In retrospect, it seems clear that the consensus producing these institutions was remarkably fragile. The support of interest groups within the United States survived only a decade or two beyond the war's end; the unenthusiastic support of governments outside the United States grew increasingly equivocal as the years went on.

Nevertheless, although the U.S. government was beginning to lose its capacity both to develop strong positions from within and to win the cooperation of other countries, it continued to produce a stream of new approaches to meet problems as they arose. Sometimes, the new tactics entailed new unilateral measures, such as the threat of import restrictions to pry open the economies of foreign countries. Sometimes, they involved cooperative action with other governments. One example is the creation of an International Energy Agency in 1974, intended to have oil-importing countries share their oil supplies in time of shortage. Another is the so-called locomotive proposal of 1978 (repeated again in 1987), urging Germany and Japan to expand their rates of growth in order to reduce the balance-of-payment problems of the United States.

Despite that persistent record of innovation on the part of U.S. administrators, however, the U.S. government has continued to operate as a system of separate interests and divided powers. For various reasons, the officials responsible for innovations within the U.S. establishment have rarely spent much time developing a consensus within the United States before making a move in foreign economic relations. One of the factors preventing such coordination has been the constitutional separation and independence of the three branches of government; an independent Congress and an independent judiciary, guardians of the public's right to dissent from the ukases of the executive, could not easily be restructured to participate in the making of a consensus.

Another factor reducing the consensus-building propensities of U.S. administrators has been the revolving door pattern that prevails in the staffing of the topmost echelons of the executive branch. Over the decades, each new administration has swept out the occupants of three or four thousand key positions in the executive structure and replaced them with lawyers, academics, businessmen, and politicians acceptable to the winning party and eager for a brief fling at the exercise of public power. With a short public career in prospect, these officials have been far better at launching new lines of policy than at developing agreements within a sprawling, diverse bureaucracy.

Now and then, an energetic policy entrepreneur has been able to slip through the formal coordinating structures of the executive branch, avoiding the opposition and finding the ear of the president. Typical of such an initiative was the extraordinary proposal in 1986 by U.S. representatives to the GATT that governments should agree to abolish all agricultural subsidies over a ten-year period, a proposal that no consensual process in the U.S. establishment could possibly have produced.

The rest of the world has come to expect a stream of economic initiatives from the United States, and so far it has not been disappointed. At the same time, however, other countries have come to expect that following the launching of a new idea, the subsequent actions of the U.S. government might prove quite inconsistent with its initial stance. Typical of such contradictory behavior have been the many restrictive trade measures taken by the U.S. government in the years following its earnest promotion of the GATT. Typical, too, has been its chronic unwillingness to allow the IMF to frame any opinions regarding U.S. exchange-rate policy, its unilateral devaluation of the dollar in 1971, and, following devaluation, its agreement with a rump group of governments to float their various exchange rates.

Because of this record, U.S. initiatives—such as Treasury Secretary James A. Baker's 1985 proposal for helping developing countries meet their balance-of-payments problems—have been received with a certain amount of skepticism abroad; so, too, have the proposals of the United States to the assembled members of the GATT in 1986 that they should launch an ambitious program of negotiations to free up world trade in services.

It would be unwise to expect that this pattern of repeated initiatives and wobbly follow-ups can continue forever. As long as the United States was dominant in the international economy, it could easily afford the costs of inconsistent, even incoherent, policies. In the decades to come, however, this country will be much more constrained by external economic forces and will have to reconcile itself to an international system of which it is no longer the undisputed leader. Under these changed conditions, the wobbles characterizing the making of U.S. foreign economic policy in the past will become less tenable.

THE OTHER PLAYERS

Among the new conditions confronting U.S. policymakers is the increased importance of other countries' values and institutions in shaping the forms of international cooperation. Differences between the United States and other countries in values and institutions have generated differences in choice of policies from the first. For a few years following World War II, a core of Canadian bureaucrats could be counted on to promote lines of policy parallel to those of the United States. Here and there in the mix of views emanating from European states, a streak of nineteenth century liberalism would occasionally surface, with arguments for policies much like those espoused by the United States. But only a few members of the international community shared the U.S. view of a world of open borders in which governments played a highly limited role and in which nondiscrimination was the rule.

In the decades that followed World War II, the singular character of U.S. values and U.S. institutions stands out in contrast to those of other societies. The policies of most governments in the conduct of their international relations could easily be distinguished from the nondiscriminatory open market themes that the U.S. government professed as its main approach. Most countries were much readier than the United States to empower government agencies to engage in direct transactional roles in the market, much readier to single out individual industries or individual enterprises for distinctive treatment, much readier to establish state-owned enterprises and to endow them with powers to act on their own in carrying out some governmental objective.

The principal economic relations of the Europeans came to be built around a European core, including the European Community, European Monetary System, and European Patent Agreement, each composed of slightly different subsets of European countries, and a web of preferential economic arrangements that linked outlying countries to the core.

Most developing countries attached their currencies to one major currency area or another, according to their economic interests. They resisted the nondiscriminatory, nonrestrictive admonitions of the IMF and the GATT, except to the extent that their debtor status obligated them to please the bankers. When such countries have concluded that a greater degree of openness would be desirable for more rapid economic development, they have commonly found ways of increasing their imports and exports through the use of devices that keep governmental agencies very much in the picture, for example, the grant of export subsidies, the application of multiple exchange rates, and the application of penalties to enterprises that failed to meet export targets.

As for Japan, the relationship of its economic system to the norms of ethnocentric U.S. planners remained quite tenuous until the latter 1970s. For much of the postwar period, the Japanese found themselves pushed, inch by inch, to the dismantling of an economic system that had started with an almost total exclusion of foreign goods and foreign private capital. By the late 1980s, Japan had managed to bring its official regulations into line with the broad rules once supported by American planners in the hope of creating open national economies. More than that, Japanese officials were now largely persuaded that, outside of agriculture, they had a stake in persuading others to live by the early U.S. principles. For various reasons having to do with Japan's internal decision making process, however, there was no strong likelihood that the newly developed perspective would find expression in any vigorous international initiatives.

By the late 1980s, moveover, not many countries were prepared to accept the kind of world envisioned by the early postwar planners in the United States when they created their first crop of multinational institutions. To some extent that reluctance was based on a realization that the problems themselves had changed.

The planners had begun with the relatively simple idea that the most important trade restrictions imposed by governments occurred at their borders, in the form of high tariffs, discriminatory import regulations, and foreign exchange licenses. By the 1980s, however, restrictions at the borders were no longer seen as the principle problem. Instead, the focus shifted to the taut linkages between economies as a major factor in the restriction of trade; monetary policies adopted in one country for solid domestic reasons could reverberate in the economies of other countries, often with undesired results.

To the extent that restrictions were the problem, they had become more complex and more deeply embedded in the domestic institutions and domestic policies of the countries concerned. Subsidies extended to enterprises in the national economy for various social or developmental purposes were a pervasive problem, affecting competition in international markets. Restrictions on the right of enterprises to communicate some types of information across national borders also illustrate the new dimensions of the problem. Such restrictions inhibited multinational enterprises from establishing their subsidiaries in foreign countries and prevented them from being competitive in those markets. The growing complexity of the issues involved in trade restriction and the coupling of different issues in new intimate configurations has meant that the limited writ of each of the existing multinational institutions, such as the GATT in trade and the IMF in money, are proving to be handicaps for grappling realistically with problems as they arise.

Still, the fundamental goals of the United States have not greatly changed. An open competitive world market is still the preferred objective in terms of U.S. values. It is a system that places national governments in the role traditionally preferred by the United States, the role of watchman and arbiter. In contrast, other obvious alternatives, such as a system based on a policy of tit for tat—that is, a policy that each country should get only as good as it gave—would offer a serious challenge to the U.S. system. That alternative, for instance, would require placing a great deal of discretion in the hands of bureaucrats, obliging them to sort out governments according to the treatment that each had earned. In the U.S. system, an independent Congress would constantly be demanding the right to peer over the shoulder of the bureaucracy and monitor its performance, limiting the bureaucracy from exercising the discretion that such a policy requires. As a result, the bureaucracy's decisions would almost certainly consist of a string of ad hoc actions, dependent much more upon the strength of some special interest group of the moment than upon any appraisal of national needs.

If the U.S. government is to retain its objective of promoting open competitive markets, if its actions are to be more than the outcome of a series of pitched battles by special interest groups, it will need the support of international institutions reasonably capable of maintaining the rules of the road. There will always be old disputes to be settled, new problems to be faced. Existing institutional structures fall short of those needs. This is especially true in the fields of trade and investment, a fact that promises to become even more apparent as the GATT attempts to tackle the knotty issues of services and investment in the years immediately ahead. Eventually, the existing institutions will need to be considerably altered or replaced by something better.

LEARNING BY DOING

In the meantime U.S. policymakers have been hedging their bets against the limitations of multilateral institutions. Officials have engaged in a constant stream of meetings with representatives of other countries, in pairs and in groups, addressing international issues that could not have been contemplated in the 1940s when the IMF, the GATT, and the World Bank were created.

The arrangements emerging from these meetings have represented targets of opportunity rather than fixed solutions and are almost formless in their scope and content. They have reflected a growing willingness to disregard the provisions—occasionally, even the ideals—of the multilateral institutions and to rely instead on a series of small group or bilateral arrangements. Without any coherent strategy or definable structure, these agreements have resembled the actions of a blind man tapping his way over unfamiliar terrain.

Still, although lacking any obvious direction, the agreements have established many precedents for dealing with novel situations. They have created free trade areas, provided for the improved surveillance of multinational banks, harmonized some of the monetary moves of a few key countries, lightened some of the financial load of debt-ridden developing countries, developed environmental standards, and dealt with dozens of other subjects.

On the other side of the coin, the new wave of agreements has involved certain risks. One is the opportunity for the United States to play the part of bully, a posture more easily struck in small groups than in large multinational organizations. That tendency has shown up especially in connection with issues of foreign trade, with U.S. negotiators flexing their muscles in public displays aimed at impressing some special interest groups and their supporting congressmen. U.S. threats have taken various forms, such as those that withhold access to the U.S. market, to U.S. technology, or to U.S. aid. In some cases, the tactic has seemed to work, as governments have modified an existing restriction on trade or investment. Tactics of this sort have, of course, had their costs, in the form of the sullen resentment or outright indignation that the tactics provoked in foreign countries. But Americans have usually been more conscious of the short-term advantages gained than of the long-term costs incurred.

Another danger has been the creation of ineffective agreements easily disregarded by either party, even less effective, in fact, than the GATT. In fact, ineffectiveness has been the typical fate of most bilateral agreements in which the U.S. government has participated. The simple reason is that the parties have refused to set up a realistic mechanism for subsequent interpretation of the agreement and for settlement of disputes. U.S. negotiators have found it especially difficult to support an effective dispute-settling mechanism, since any such mechanism could threaten the hard-won rights of American citizens to challenge the actions taken by their own government.

A third danger, epitomized by the Organization of Petroleum Exporting Countries (OPEC), has been the tendency of small groups of nations to dump their common problems on countries outside the group. As a sure prescription for economic warfare, that is a practice flatly at odds with the U.S. long-term objective of promoting open, competitive markets.

Still, with the multilateral approach under a cloud, and with unilateral action a high-risk strategy in an interdependent world, the United States will have to continue to evaluate the opportunities for cooperation and to pursue those that seem compatible with U.S. interests, values, and institutions. The hope is that in seizing such opportunities as they arise a pattern eventually may be discerned that can lead toward the open market objective.

There will be little progress on any front, however, unless the U.S. government is prepared to deal with certain basic internal issues that affect its foreign economic policies. One such issue concerns the problems of increasing the internal flexibility of the U.S. economy in deploying its productive resources—its capital, its land, and its labor. An endless succession of public reports have made the salient points on this critical subject: that surviving in an open market system demands constant economic change; that such change can often distribute the burdens inequitably to different regions and classes of the country; and that those inequities can be mitigated somewhat by public programs of adjustment for business, labor, and local governments. In a society holding to the principle that no minority should be forced to suffer from the wishes of the majority, the possibility of making such redistributions may be the only means for preventing minorities from exercising a veto over needed measures.

Another impediment to the making of U.S. foreign economic policy is the role of the U.S. Congress. In the decades to come, other countries will be increasingly unwilling to enter into agreements that Congress may feel free to modify or to ignore. Because congressional independence is a basic component of the U.S. system of checks and balances, it presents a problem that resists easy solutions. Neither the executive nor the Congress is structured in ways making it easy for either branch of government to engage in close consultations with the other. It usually requires some manifest crisis, such as a war or a string of budgetary deficits, to produce the necessary adjustments from either side. However, some mitigating measures, already developed and adopted, have brought Congress and the executive closer in planning and negotiating some international agreements. The regular use of the so-called "fast track" provision in connection with international trade agreements since 1974 suggests that the problem of developing greater coordination between the executive and the Congress while maintaining the autonomy of the two branches can be held to manageable proportions.

Finally, responding to targets of opportunity can only be regarded as an interim approach. Eventually, the United States must draw some new coherence and new principles out of its ad hoc experiences. Such a process can only occur if U.S. policymakers are in a position to learn from experience, pushing the promising leads and avoiding the dangerous pitfalls. With the U.S. policy-making machinery in the hands of a stream of transient amateurs, however, the possibility of institutional learning is likely to be limited.

There are added reasons why the United States must soberly face the question of whether in the closing years of the twentieth century, a system of international economic relations can be fashioned and run by amateurs, even by brilliant and well-intentioned amateurs, recruited for a brief stint in positions of power. Those charged with framing the country's foreign economic policies will be asked to ride herd simultaneously on two sets of complex negotiations, one with the many organized interests clamoring to be heard inside the U.S. economy, the other with the seasoned representatives of other governments defending their national interests as vigorously as they can. If our analysis is right, the nation's policymakers will also be charged with drawing lessons from their experiences and passing on the lessons to their successors. Perhaps the time has come to recognize how demanding that challenge has become and the importance of meeting it successfully.

The most basic challenge for the American people is to understand more fully where the United States stands in the world economy, what it may be capable of achieving, and what may lie beyond its grasp. To develop that understanding, it helps to step back in time and to consider how the twig was bent.

2

Looking Back

U.S. LEADERS NOW MUST THINK of the country's foreign economic relations as a constraint on the maintenance of the country's defenses and the expansion of its living standards. This is a new experience for them that is difficult to assimilate. What is dawning even more slowly is the realization that the U.S. government cannot get very far in responding to its present problems unless it can develop much more extensive cooperative arrangements with other countries. With the United States having been both strong and independent for so many decades, the nation's leaders have found it especially hard to contemplate the possibility that they might need the cooperation of other countries in order to achieve the most basic national objectives. Furthermore, some of the institutions and values of the United States have been so distinctive as to place substantial limits on the nation's ability to cooperate with other countries, particularly if such cooperation requires modifications in the American way of doing things within the international system.

THE U.S. POLITICAL HERITAGE

"Ours is a strange system," writes Louis Henkin, distinguished constitutional scholar, "the strangest in the world. It was strange when it was conceived; it is stranger in the nuclear age."[1]

Emerging Values

It is easy to forget that the inspired men who created the U.S. Constitution were fashioning a governmental structure for purposes far more limited than those pursued today. Until the French Revolution, the governments of the Western world had been devoted mainly to a few simple objectives: defending the king's realm and amassing wealth for the sovereign treasury. With those purposes in mind, sovereigns typically sought to create strong central states, capable of raising armies and collecting taxes.

The U.S. Constitution, as an endless succession of scholars have observed, was drafted in a spirit of revulsion against those European models. The U.S. government, according to the political philosophers responsible for that extraordinary document, would be designed to play the role of watchman and arbiter, leaving the operation of the economy to the dispersed activities of its citizens. Some economic protection for the citizenry against foreign competition could be foreseen; but determining the nature and degree of that protection would be primarily a responsibility of the Congress rather than the executive.

The Constitution's founders had almost nothing to say—and probably had nothing much in mind—regarding the economic responsibilities of the state. Obviously, they did not foresee that within 150 years of the country's founding, the electorate would judge any U.S. administration as a matter of course by whether the national economy had grown at a satisfactory rate and whether the country's citizens had escaped the pain of unemployment or inflation.

In overlooking such a possibility, the drafters of the U.S. Constitution were quite in tune with their times. Before the nineteenth century, few political philosophers regarded the state as responsible in any way for the economic well-being of its population.[2] Continental philosophers had begun to emphasize the rights of individuals and the need to limit the powers of the state at the same time that men like Jefferson and Madison were drafting the Constitution, but none of them had gone so far as to hold the state accountable for the performance of the national economy.[3] Accordingly, although the contemporary emphasis on the rights of the individual was amply reflected in the U.S. Constitution and in the structure of the new government it established, the idea that the national government should assume responsibility for the economic well-being of its citizens was not a part of that intellectual package.

Nevertheless, before the nineteenth century was out, the concept that the state should accept some responsibility for its citizens' economic welfare was commonplace in Western societies. Such ideas had, of course, been implicit in the writings of Adam Smith and those who followed him in supporting a free trade policy; the ultimate justification for the adoption of a free trade policy by the state was the ability of such a policy to improve the welfare of society as a whole, rather than the welfare of the sovereign alone. Karl Marx and V. I. Lenin turned the point around and made it explicit: The object of all governmental policy, including foreign economic policy, should be to improve the welfare of the masses.

It was not until the twentieth century that governments were held accountable for the economic well-being of their people. The term "unemployment," for instance, did not come into general usage until about 1895.[4] It was later still that European governments began to move vigorously to provide their citizenry with housing, health, and education services, as well as various forms of insurance against economic risk.

The process of making the state responsible for the economic well-being of its citizens came even more slowly to the United States than to most other Western societies. The Constitution expressed the conviction of most of its drafters that a strong central government was unnecessary and undesirable. Until World War I, the U.S. economy had performed well enough so that this fundamental assumption was not often challenged. By that time, more than a century after the country's founding, its institutions and values had acquired a solidity that went with over a century of evident success. There seemed no serious reason at this stage to question the adequacy of the established institutions and values for dealing with the problems of a modern world.

The experiences of the Great Depression, however, brought U.S. attitudes toward the responsibilities of government closer to those of the Europeans. With the New Deal, Americans embraced the concepts of the welfare state, including insurance against such risks as unemployment, old age, poverty, and crop failure. The Full Employment Act of 1946 sought to codify critical elements of the changed U.S. position in national law.

Today, there is no longer any serious debate over the government's basic responsibility to ensure the economy's performing up to some minimum standards of growth and stability. Quarterly gross national product figures and the monthly consumer price index are now studied with the same care as batting averages. To be sure, there are bitter debates over the best means for achieving growth and stability, as well as endless struggles over the distribution of costs and benefits. The national government, for instance, has become the arbiter in unremitting battles between business interests attempting to improve their profits and workers attempting to increase their incomes and reduce their risks. But the principle that government is responsible for the growth and stability of the national economy is by now a settled issue.

An Evolving Structure

The United States, like other nations, has had to make large adaptations in its governmental structure to discharge its new economic responsibilities. In the case of the United States, the problems of adaptation have been particularly formidable. The original structure of the government was not designed to produce efficient decisions aimed at promoting well-defined sets of interests. Quite the contrary: The founding fathers took pains to forestall the possibility that any such capability would emerge. As they saw it, what was wrong about the governments of the Stuarts, the Tudors, and the Bourbons was not inefficiency or confusion of purpose but the goals to which they were directed. The founding fathers were determined not to re-create a government whose goals could be defined by any single interest, whether a royal house or an aggressive state government.

That dominant view shaped the U.S. Constitution, producing the much-analyzed system of divided authority, of checks and balances, among the three branches of government. The same principle lay behind the subsequent adoption of the Bill of Rights, which was designed among other things to ensure the ability of ordinary people to participate effectively in the continual political struggle that was envisaged. And that principle supported and legitimated the activities of the country's many special interest groups, whose organizations would shape the political landscape in the years to follow.

Yet, the U.S. system has managed to escape the fate of the dinosaur. With changes in the domestic and international environment, the system has managed slowly and ponderously to change the distribution of powers among the various institutions of government.

An early manifestation of a latent capacity for adaptation appeared after the Civil War when the U.S. public began to recognize the country's rapidly expanding interests in foreign markets. As acquisitive colonial powers set about dismembering China and dividing up Africa, the U.S. president was allowed to assume much stronger powers for conducting the country's foreign affairs. Responding to what many saw at the time as the country's "manifest destiny," a series of strong presidents established new precedents and new norms that altered the fundamental balance between congressional and presidential power in the area of foreign policy.

William McKinley used his role as commander-in-chief of the armed forces in uninhibited style, employing executive agreements rather than treaties in order to reduce the Senate's blocking power over critical foreign policy questions.[5] Theodore Roosevelt and Woodrow Wilson interpreted presidential powers over the use of troops and the conduct of foreign policy in very much the same spirit, broadening and deepening the relevant precedents. Although some presidents thereafter would assert their acquired rights more vigorously than others, and although every president thereafter would face repeated challenges to those rights, presidential powers in the conduct of the military and political aspects of foreign affairs were permanently enlarged.

On domestic economic issues, too, the system has displayed a certain flexibility, responding to obvious crises by deviating somewhat from its norms. In the depths of the Great Depression, for instance, the U.S. government briefly undertook an elaborate experiment, now largely forgotten, creating institutions structured on corporatist principles under a National Recovery Administration. These institutions were expected to act as instruments for the development of a national industrial policy and an incomes policy, much like those that European governments were attempting to develop at the time.

Indeed, from the New Deal's beginnings in 1933 to the Korean War's end in 1953, a generation of Americans grew accustomed to the U.S. government's exercising a strong central role in order to achieve well-defined national objectives. During those two remarkable decades, the priorities of the U.S. government were reasonably unambiguous: first, to crawl out of the deep economic rut into which the country had fallen during the Great Depression; then, to win a world war and manage its difficult aftermath. Leaders of business and labor found themselves cooperating with politicians and bureaucrats from time to time in joint efforts to respond to the emergencies confronting the nation. The role of the executive branch was greatly expanded as new agencies proliferated to regulate and administer various economic programs and activities. In the spirit of the times, the Supreme Court gave the new agencies plenty of leeway, exempting their findings from judicial review when they appeared to rest on facts that could be best determined by the agency's particular expertise. Throughout the 1950s and 1960s, the courts continued to support the position that the formulation of specific types of public policy should be left in the hands of the federal agencies created for that purpose.[6]

Nevertheless, the fundamental concept of restraint on the exercise of power by bureaucrats, so long a part of the American credo, was not greatly modified. Less than two years after the NRA was created in 1933, for example, the Supreme Court struck down the experiment as unconstitutional.

The American public's preference for holding bureaucratic powers under a very tight rein has appeared repeatedly in various other forms. The Administrative Procedures Act, adopted in 1946, held administrative agencies to various procedural standards aimed at protecting and enlarging the rights of petitioners and defendants doing business with the agencies.[7] In the decades that followed, various court decisions began to cut back the powers that the administrative agencies had acquired earlier.[8]

Finally, in the 1960s and 1970s, the American disposition to check the powers of the bureaucracy took forms that were so novel as to represent a daring experiment in practicing democracy. President Lyndon B. Johnson's conduct of the Vietnam War followed by Richard Nixon's Watergate disaster brought the American fear of strong presidents to the surface. Reacting to the perceived excesses of Johnson and Nixon, the Congress enacted a string of statutes aimed at restraining executive power.[9] Legislation such as the so-called sunshine laws gave the public at large unprecedented access to official documents, required government agencies to conduct most of their deliberations in public, and gave interested parties extensive opportunities to register their views before the agencies.[10] Other legislation vested Congress or one of its two houses with the power to delay, restrain, or strike down measures taken by the executive branch, or even to prod a reluctant executive into action. Later, the Supreme Court would strike down congressional vetoes as unconstitutional, demonstrating thereby that no branch of government was immune from the balancing process.[11] But enough of these new regulations would remain to keep the U.S. executive on a relatively short leash.

Despite periodic bursts of presidential initiative, then, Congress and the courts have vigorously upheld their prerogative to check and to balance the power of the president in the conduct of foreign relations. While the president's position as commander-in-chief has bestowed on him a certain authority in issues with a military or political cast, he has had no such authority where foreign economic policies were concerned.

The Structure in Operation

Has the system worked? Lord Keynes offered a summary judgment early in World War II, after ten weary days wandering through the Washington bureaucracy, trying to round up lend-lease aid for his country. "But you don't have a government in the ordinary sense of the word," he said in frustration.[12] It was a harsh judgment but easy to understand if one is accustomed to a parliamentary system.

Laboring to diffuse and decentralize the power of government, the founding fathers created a federal system in which the concept of checks and balances provided the grand design. As the responsibilities of the U.S. government evolved over the years, however, the disposition to diffuse power produced results that the founding fathers could not have foreseen.

When the government assumed new economic responsibilities in the 1930s and the decades that followed, it developed devices for discharging the added functions that took some cognizance of the American preference for avoiding increased power at the center. With each new function, an "independent" agency was created. Beginning with the Interstate Commerce Commission for regulating the railroads in 1887 and the Federal Trade Commission for regulating competition in 1914, Congress went on to create the Securities and Exchange Commission, the Nuclear Regulatory Commission, the Environmental Protection Agency, and so on. The prevailing assumption was that with the creation of the specialized bodies, each standing on its own statutory foundations, the bureaucracy involved would be guided by explicit standards in its decision making and would be held to a high standard of accountability for its performance.

As the independent agencies proliferated, however, the congressional committees, subcommittees, and related bodies performing oversight functions increased as well.[13] With the passage of time, the number of bodies in the executive and legislative branches that could claim an interest in any given issue involving the economy of the

United States grew spectacularly. One fundamental consequence became clear rapidly. By the beginning of the postwar period, anyone hoping to develop a coordinated view on some broad policy issue among the executive agencies and congressional committees concerned faced a near-impossible task.

It is worth noting that although U.S. legislators have been prepared to create a variety of institutions to administer the government's responsibilities, they have rarely favored the creation of state-owned enterprises. Whereas such enterprises are found by the hundreds in every other mature industrialized economy, only a handful have existed at the national level in the United States, notably including the TVA, Amtrak, Conrail, and Comsat. All told, these state-owned enterprises account for less than one percent of the output of the United States, compared with analogous figures in other mature industrialized economies on the order of 5 to 15 percent. Even in the field of agriculture, where the U.S. government has developed elaborate systems of control, there has been considerable hesitation about allowing state trading authorities to move directly into agricultural markets, even though the absence of such institutional arrangements has at times placed the agricultural sector at a disadvantage. True, in times of crisis, the U.S. government has been ready to create state-owned enterprises, as evidenced by the Reconstruction Finance Corporation in the Great Depression and the War Facilities Corporation in World War II. But unlike almost all other countries, the U.S. government quickly liquidated these organizations once the emergencies for which they were created had passed.

The reluctance of U.S. governments to create state-owned enterprises is symptomatic of the uneasiness experienced by the American public whenever U.S. bureaucrats appear able to exercise discretion and authority in the handling of individual transactions. In creating state-owned enterprises, a government could not avoid bestowing that kind of authority on public managers; indeed, the choice of the enterprise form by a government has usually reflected an intention to grant just such powers. Accordingly, the U.S. government has tended to shy away from the use of this instrumentality.

The tendency to hold the powers of the bureaucracy in check has been heightened by the transitory tenure of leaders in the executive branch. Most civil servants in the federal government, especially those making up the rank and file, are qualified careerists firmly committed to public service. But, as noted before, each change in a U.S. administration signals the departure of three or four thousand political appointees in key positions in the executive branch, to be replaced by the political appointees of the incoming administration. The new entrants characteristically expect to keep their jobs for only a few years.[14] Some of them may be familiar with the prior history and current problems of the agencies to which they are appointed, having been recruited for their jobs from the rapidly growing community of law offices, trade associations, and national media that have become part of the permanent Washington community; but most will have only a superficial knowledge of the programs that they are expected to administer or the policies they are expected to develop.

The U.S. government's reliance on so-called inners-and-outers to provide leadership in the executive branch has had complex consequences, not all of them negative. The governmental organizations that were put together to formulate and execute the New Deal's programs in the 1930s were headed largely by lawyers, professors, and other educated amateurs from private life. The wartime and postwar efforts that followed were headed by much the same type of official. Leaders of this sort occasionally displayed the kind of uninhibited brashness that is required for a creative initiative. Because they were amateurs, they sometimes refused to recognize the size of the obstacles that their proposals would have to overcome.[15] Because they were temporary occupants of their posts, they were sometimes indifferent to the long-term consequences of their inspirations. In short, they were in a position to avoid the paralysis induced by knowing too much about the problems they confronted.[16]

As issues have arisen, however, officials with limited backgrounds and brief tenures in office could not be expected to spend much time locating all the interested parties in the U.S. government and developing a broad consensus among them. The number of agencies to be contacted usually was high. Many were led by strangers with just as transitory a hold on their jobs, coming from diverse backgrounds, and operating from a limited sense of history.[17] As a result, many important U.S. initiatives during the postwar period were launched without any serious effort on the part of the initiators to develop any consensus either within the executive branch or in the country at large. Commonly, these initiatives stemmed instead from an energetic bureaucrat or two, operating from conviction or interest, skilled in broken-field running through the bureaucratic opposition, and in a position to command the ear of the president.

Where major U.S. initiatives were involved, the energetic bureaucrat usually could not move very far without securing the president's blessing. But the decision-making style of each president has proved to be an important variable in determining the ability of governmental entrepreneurs to push their favored policies through the bureaucracy. In some cases, presidents have insisted that a proposed economic initiative should have an airing among the executive agencies immediately concerned. A few have even participated directly in the process; President Kennedy, for instance, sometimes worked with his staff and departmental representatives over the details of new initiatives in foreign trade and foreign aid, such as the Trade Act of 1962 and the Alliance for Progress program.[18] In other administrations, including those of President Eisenhower and President Reagan, it was common practice for the immediate White House staff or the National Security Council to adjudicate the disputes and orchestrate the compromises between warring agencies before a recommendation reached the president's desk.

Some coordinating structures have worked better than others. From time to time, presidents have had to shake down a proliferating maze of interagency committees, whose uncertain and overlapping jurisdictions guaranteed that they would be ineffectual. But even in periods when such coordinating mechanisms were relatively well conceived and organized, the entrepreneurial proclivities of the top officials of the governmental bureaucracy have been so strong that from time to time they managed to evade the screening process on their way to the Oval Office. In each administration, a few officials have emerged whose association with the president or whose force of personality or sheer ingenuity have allowed them to sell their proposals directly to the president. Furthermore, some presidents have been quick to bypass the coordinating apparatus, preferring to reach out to one or two advisers to guide them in making the hard decisions; President Nixon's decision-making habits, for example, especially favored that approach.

In addition to overcoming the obstacles within the executive branch, officials eager to launch initiatives in foreign economic policy have had to reckon with the checking and blocking powers of Congress and other outside bodies. Congress has been deeply involved, for example, in matters involving trade policy, tax policy, and budgetary policy, reflecting the fact that various groups outside the government usually can identify where their short-run interests lie. It is true that in other policy areas just as important, such as monetary and banking policy, the disposition and capacity of Congress to check initiatives from the executive arm of government have been more limited. But even in those areas, the executive can expect some congressional involvement in any foreign economic proposals.

It is remarkable, then, that the dominant characteristic of the U.S. government in the foreign economic realm has not been either passivity or stalemate. Despite the possibility of congressional vetoes and bureaucratic infighting, initiatives emanating from the U.S. executive have been imaginative and frequent, especially in comparison with those originating in other countries. How then does one explain the persistent initiatives in international economic matters by the executive branch of the U.S. government despite the threats of congressional veto and bureaucratic impasse?

Our interpretation of the evidence produces a paradoxical conclusion. The U.S. system of checks and balances, although designed to inhibit the president from moving very far without some check on his actions, has actually contributed to the capacity of the executive branch to initiate proposals for consideration by the international community. Because each branch of the U.S. government is intended to be a force capable of checking the other two, all three have retained a degree of identity and autonomy rarely found in other governments. Each branch has jealously guarded its prerogatives and has received support from key Supreme Court decisions.[19] In short, whether or not the policies of the executive branch win approval, the president's right to initiate proposals in the name of the United States remains unquestioned.

Given the entrepreneurial proclivities of high-level policymakers in the executive branch, the president's unchallenged right to launch new initiatives has been sufficient to generate a stream of interesting proposals. What is more, despite the power of Congress to block most of these proposals, many have managed to run the gauntlet and survive.

Initiatives in some fields of policy have had a better chance of surviving the congressional process than others. Those most vulnerable to congressional check have been narrow propositions affecting well-defined special interest groups that could easily be rallied in opposition. For instance, U.S. labor unions have had no difficulty in using the Congress to kill proposals to end the preferences that each government extends to its merchant marine.

On the other hand, proposals framed by the executive branch in close collaboration with the affected special interests and the relevant congressional committees have had a much better chance of surviving. Safety-at-sea agreements, corporate disclosure issues, bank supervision agreements and international postal regulations would fall in this category. In such cases, specialists in the executive branch sometimes find it possible to make their peace with all the potential sources of opposition in the United States and to develop a coordinated view for discussions with foreign governments. Negotiations on such narrow subjects have often taken place at relatively low levels in the respective governments involved, without much involvement from the transitory leadership at the top of the U.S. agencies.[20]

If cases of that sort have presented any problem in terms of public policy, it has been the problem of capture; that is, the risk that U.S. officials and their counterparts in other governments may have drifted into the role of agents for specialized interest groups, without much regard for the national interests that they were charged with representing.[21] From time to time, situations of that sort have produced international agreements that dealt with various products and services, fixing output and dividing up markets without consideration for the broader picture. On the other hand, intimate working relationships between regulators and the regulated have sometimes produced beneficial agreements that might not have proved possible with wider participation. For example, a series of agreements were reached in the 1970s and 1980s among the supervising authorities of the principal national banking systems that strengthened their collective oversight of multinational banks and provided for stiffer capital standards. These agreements would not have been possible without the close participation of the banks themselves, a participation that rested on their conviction that the added oversight was indeed in their collective interest.

Another illustration of the power of special interest groups is provided by the history of foreign aid programs in the United States. These programs have rarely had broad-based support from the U.S. public; instead, they have survived mainly on the basis of coalitions composed of highly disparate special interests. In the case of most of the aid bills shepherded through Congress over the past three decades, for instance, an improbable coalition of humanitarian agencies, defense strategists, ethnic minorities, and commercial interests supported by long-time bureaucrats have pooled their collective power to obtain the desired appropriations. Lacking any well-defined opposition, the political strength of these coalitions has proved sufficient in most years to determine the general shape of U.S. foreign aid legislation.

The president appears to have exhibited his greatest powers as initiator of new proposals when the projects involved were broad and diffuse, touching diverse U.S. interests in ways that were unclear or complex and cutting in many different directions. Typical of such broad and diffuse initiatives have been a string of proposals in the 1970s and 1980s for collaborating with Japan and Germany over changes in interest rates and exchange rates. Some of these proposals have carried a potential economic impact for U.S. interests far greater than any conceivable proposal to negotiate over U.S. tariffs. As a rule, however, these broad projects have stirred barely any opposition from the public or Congress. Faced with complex proposals of this sort, special interest groups usually have had neither the time nor the expertise to sort out their interests, frame their reactions, and mobilize their opposition. As a result, the field has been left open to the innovators in the executive branch.

Another example of broad, diffuse proposals has been the executive's periodic demands for the right to negotiate broadly on trade issues covering a range of interests so wide as to affect all corners of the economy. Presidents have successfully demanded and secured such powers from the Congress nine times in the four decades following World War II. Because the powers demanded by the president were so broad, the debate that followed tended to highlight the general national interest and submerge narrower issues relating to individual products and services. So many special interests have been brought into play that none has been capable of dominating the outcome.

What has puzzled many other governments is the fact that the U.S. executive branch continues to be the source of a stream of initiatives for international cooperation despite the power of Congress and the courts to check, modify, or reverse those initiatives at birth or later. That the U.S. Congress would pass a new tax on oil imports, for instance, only days after the U.S. executive had agreed to a freeze on new import restrictions is a phenomenon difficult for most other governments to comprehend. It has not helped a great deal to explain that both of these actions stemmed from a common characteristic of the U.S. structure of government, namely its system of checks and balances. The gap between U.S. values and institutions and those of most other countries has been sufficiently large to make easy understanding in either direction exceedingly difficult.

COMPARISONS AND CONTRASTS

Only a few of the inspired amateurs in the U.S. government who were responsible for the U.S. leadership role during the first decade after World War II possessed first-hand knowledge of the principal foreign countries with which they had to deal. Most shared a strong ethnocentric bias, believing without much reflection that the U.S. preference for limited governments and open markets would not only benefit the United States but other countries as well. Apart from their zest for spreading the American gospel, these U.S. leaders enjoyed the overwhelming power, the unlimited self-confidence, and the towering prestige of the United States that then prevailed. These assets went a long way in securing agreements on economic matters from other nations.

Today, needless to say, the situation has changed. No longer quite as capable of achieving its objectives by the sheer weight of economic and political power, the U.S. government has a greatly increased need to understand the considerable gap between U.S. values and institutions and those of other major players in the global economic system. The need is particularly strong because although the size of the U.S. economy is no longer overwhelming in relation to that of other countries, it still occupies a space of continental proportions, a fact that fosters some strongly parochial views on the part of most Americans.[22]

It would be a hopeless task to attempt to describe the institutions and values of other countries likely to figure prominently in the foreign economic relations of the United States during the decade or two ahead. Practically every major nation has been the target of a dozen scholarly studies bearing directly on this question. Still, a few illustrations will serve to indicate the nature of the differences in institutions and values that U.S. policymakers will have to take into account as they chart a course for future U.S. economic relations.

The Europeans

If there is one European country that Americans are ready to agree they do not quite understand, it is France. They are struck by its tolerance for a strong centrist government, by the subservience of its central bank to the national administration, by its propensity to give bureaucrats almost free rein in governing the country's economic affairs, and, especially, by its acceptance of a process allowing those bureaucrats to make major economic decisions without regard for any general rules. As a result, when French bureaucrats urge their American counterparts to think seriously of developing a system of "managed" international trade, the Americans shudder, unable to picture a system in which visible rules are abandoned in favor of the ad hoc decisions of an empowered bureaucracy. Each of these tendencies runs contrary to the typical preferences of Americans.

Less obvious to the American observer is the permeability of the boundary between the public and the private sector in France. Links between the sectors manifest themselves in complex ways, above all in the financing of large enterprises and the recruitment of key personnel. A series of old boy networks bridge the public–private frontier, networks built on common attendance in a handful of prestigious professional schools, and on the mystique of membership in various specialized professional bodies: For instance, the *inspecteurs de finance* and the *inspecteurs des mines* occupy positions in French policymaking for which there is no U.S. counterpart.[23]

It may no longer be important to track down the sources of these striking differences in such basic aspects of the American and French economies. All that is certain is that the roots run very deep, going back to the era when the Bourbons were building a tight central government in Paris while the American colonists were establishing their dispersed settlements on the other side of the Atlantic ocean. What matters today is that those differences contribute to persistent rivalry and rancor between the two countries, visible in the OECD, the GATT, and various other organizations.

The rancor tends to reach a particularly high pitch where issues of technological leadership are involved. Among the distinctive values repeatedly emphasized by French leaders is the establishment of the country's dominance in industries that are the symbols of modern technological leadership, notably, aircraft, nuclear reactors, and computers.[24] The historical origins of the French concern to excel in advanced technologies are not clear, but the objective has persisted over a long period of time.[25] Although Americans share the same goals, they have been inclined to regard French ambitions as pretentious and to react with considerable impatience to the persistent efforts of French governments to establish a lead in high technology.

In Germany, some of the institutions that are employed for national decision making also lie outside of the experience of the ethnocentric American. On the surface, the German structure of government seems familiar to the American observer in some respects, with an independent central bank separated from the executive and considerable economic powers residing in the *länder,* or state governments.

What strikes an unfamiliar chord, however, is the highly concentrated economic structure of the country. For nearly a century, three or four giant banks have held a pivotal position in German industry, controlling the principal industries of the country through the direct ownership of shares or through a trustee relationship with other shareholders. These banks have been key actors in developing Germany's industrial policies and in working toward a national consensus with labor leaders and government officials over the terms of these policies.

In developing a national consensus, the German government has often made use of extraparliamentary institutions comprising representatives of business, labor, and government, who come together periodically to mull over and reach agreement on critical issues of tax policy, incomes policy, or trade policy. In those consultations, German bureaucrats have often been allowed to exercise far more authority over national economic policy than the U.S. public would tolerate. Although the U.S. government experimented with similar institutions in the extraordinary year or two of the NRA, Americans have typically reacted with hostility to national policymaking through such extragovernmental channels.

The values that German governments bring to bear in assessing matters of foreign economic policy are also somewhat strange to U.S. experience. It has sometimes been difficult to know which of the strands in Germany's complex history has been dominant in shaping the country's reactions—its persistent streak of nineteenth-century liberalism, its penchant for order and rationality, or its revulsion against the tragedies of two world wars.[26] On one issue, however, the national reaction in the past few decades has been highly predictable: Germany has consistently rejected any project entailing a significant risk of inflation.[27]

As a rule, American policymakers have had only limited patience for the German penchant for tight money and fiscal frugality, regarding this emphasis as exaggerated and neurotic. What most Americans cannot recall is the German hyperinflation in 1923, a period of months during which the national currency was literally destroyed. During that time, prices and money supplies increased so fast that bank employees were periodically allowed to cart away as much paper money from the bank vaults as their wheelbarrows could carry.

Even the United Kingdom, which many Americans think of as an older, poorer, and smaller version of the United States, displays some profound differences from the United States that deeply affect its approach to foreign economic policy. For one thing, the structure of the British government is highly centrist, containing nothing like the checks and balances that are basic to the U.S. system. For another, its internal political disputes follow much clearer ideological lines than those of the United States. Unlike the United States, for example, one of Great Britain's principal political parties is explicitly the representative of a labor class and unabashedly hostile to various aspects of open competitive markets. At the same time, the top layers of the British bureaucracy are far more professional and stable than their counterparts in the United States; and in the handling of individual cases, they need have far less concern for the checking and reviewing powers of the parliament and the courts.[28]

The Japanese

In the case of Japan, the difficulties of Americans in understanding an alien system has not been for lack of interest or attention. On the contrary: Waves of instant experts have appeared, ready to interpret Japanese behavior in terms that a U.S. audience would easily understand, overwhelming and drowning out the less primitive analyses of the real experts. William Safire, writing to several hundred thousand *New York Times* readers, describes the Japanese as "past masters at lip service," who use their monopolistic ways to promote a brand of capitalism that is unfair by U.S. standards.[29] How else, Safire asks, can one explain why on Black Monday, October 19, 1987, prices on the Tokyo Stock Exchange fell only 20 percent while prices on the New York Stock Exchange fell as much as 30 percent?

No one doubts that the brand of capitalism developed by Japan in the twentieth century since it emerged from feudalism has differed in substantial respects from that found in the United States. The founders of the capitalist institutions in the two countries responded to wholly different priorities in totally different circumstances. Whereas one of the highest priorities of the U.S. founders was to prevent the concentration of public power, the founders of modern Japan were intent on preventing the country from suffering China's fate at the time, that is, falling under the domination of the European powers and the United States. For two hundred years before breaking out of their feudal structure, Japanese leaders had been watching China's progressive dismemberment, aware that unless Japan industrialized, it was likely to experience the same fate: Not surprisingly, the clear and unambiguous goal of the new Japanese leaders, operating with the apparent concurrence of the Japanese people, was to catch up. For decades thereafter, every major policy of the Japanese government was targeted at that objective, which determined the content of its laws and the structure of its institutions. In the period of Japan's military aggression, from 1931 to 1945, those institutions were distorted by political assassinations and runaway militarists. But under the influence of a benign military occupation and of the compelling challenge to rebuild the Japanese economy, Japan's public and private institutions once again took the lead in the catch-up process.

For several decades after World War II, the genius of the Japanese model was that it combined the spur of strong competition among Japanese firms with the advantages of cooperation in facing outsiders. The measures of cooperation accompanying the uninhibited competition took various forms. They included joint planning exercises between the private sector and the government, undertaken through elaborate committee structures; risk-sharing between private and public financial institutions, designed to enlarge the capacity of individual firms to finance new modern plants; and joint importing of raw materials by rival Japanese firms, aimed at increasing their bargaining power in foreign countries. None of these measures was altogether novel, some having been practiced by other countries, including France, Germany, and even occasionally the United States. But the Japanese, with application and effort, developed cooperative measures operating at a level that no other capitalist country had previously obtained.

One added element in the Japanese structure distinguishing it sharply from that of the United States has been the role of the public bureaucrat. The instant expert's descriptions of the Japanese bureaucrat usually casts him in a role considerably larger than life, as a power dominating and directing the Japanese economy. And, indeed, one aspect of such descriptions is essentially correct. The Japanese bureaucracy as a rule has enjoyed the high respect of the Japanese public. The typical bureaucrat has usually commanded considerable public respect, evident in various subtle ways; for example, when government officials step down from their positions, usually to take post-retirement jobs in private industry, the ex-bureaucrats are referred to as *Amikudari,* "those descended from heaven."

Nevertheless, Japanese bureaucrats have usually been obliged to run their proposals through a gauntlet of critical comment inside the Japanese establishment that, in some respects, is more demanding than the gauntlet facing their American counterparts. In sharp contrast to their American counterparts, Japanese officials typically spend their entire professional careers in a single organization. Because the bureaucracies are so stable, the individuals involved in hammering out policy positions expect to be involved with one another repeatedly over the years. In such circumstances, the individual who uses hidden ball maneuvers or engages in broken field running in order to win a point courts major risks over the longer term. Accordingly, consultations within the Japanese establishment are, as a rule, more extensive than those that occur within the U.S. government.[30]

On the other hand, none of those generalizations can be taken as eternal verities. To be up-to-date in reporting Japanese practices and Japanese institutions, one has to be published with the speed of light. In the 1980s, Japan's banks and industrial enterprises were spreading their affiliates around the world at a rate unmatched in history. At the same time, foreign-owned enterprises were finally beginning to enlarge their place in Japan's domestic markets to a degree no longer trivial. The patterns of interaction between Japan's public and private sectors had always depended to a considerable degree on keeping Japanese business interests at home and holding foreign business influences at bay. With that pattern already breached extensively, it remains to be seen whether a new set of Japanese institutions and values will emerge.

The Developing Countries

Attempting to capture the range and variety of considerations that developing countries have brought to bear in the development of their foreign economic policies would be a futile undertaking. The very term *developing countries* is inadequate, as it attempts to encompass in one phrase some 120 societies reflecting vastly different conditions of development, different institutions, and different histories.

Still, when addressing issues of foreign economic policy, these disparate nations do share some elements in common. In most, the political leaders see economic sovereignty as an attribute only recently acquired, going back only 30 or 40 years. Before then, most of these countries were colonies. Those that had nominal independence were heavily dependent on Europe and North America for the sale of raw materials and the acquisition of manufactured goods. As a result, the leaders in practically all these countries have placed a heavy value on the right to choose their economic policies without the interference of outsiders. At the same time, most national leaders have felt fully entitled by history to any preferential treatment or foreign aid that they could extract from the more mature industrialized countries, measures that they have seen as small compensation for decades of economic exploitation.

Similarly, despite the wide variety of cultures and institutions encountered among the developing countries, practically all of them differ markedly from the United States in their perceptions of the normal relationship of the private sector to the government. British ex-colonies in Africa, such as Ghana and Nigeria, are conditioned by the remnants of their colonial past, carrying with it a history of trade monopolies, a roster of inefficient state-owned enterprises, hostility toward non-African expatriates, and continuing rivalry among modernizing and traditional tribes. African countries in the francophone tradition, such as Senegal and the Ivory Coast, also display remnants of a colonial past while aping the *dirigiste* tendencies of metropolitan France. Countries with a Hispanic tradition, shaped by a history in which the monarch was the licensor of all economic activity, see private enterprise as a privilege rather than a right.

The results of these differences appear in institutions and laws that differ markedly from those of the United States. Once again, ministers in developing countries characteristically have far more discretion in the handling of individual cases. Indeed, in Hispanic countries, laws enacted by legislatures characteristically are not operational until implemented by executive regulations; and such regulations commonly provide that notwithstanding the provisions of the regulation, a minister is entitled to decide any case on the merits as he perceives them. With such provisions in place, "national treatment" and "nondiscrimination," concepts precious to U.S. policymakers, lose what precision they might otherwise have.

Developing countries also have other reasons for resisting the national treatment concept, especially if it seems to guarantee rights to enterprises owned by foreign nationals. No country, not even the United States, has escaped from the ambiguities and dilemmas that foreign-owned enterprises commonly create. Established under the laws of the foreign countries in which they do business, such enterprises are almost never entitled to quite the same rights as those owned by nationals. In the case of developing countries, however, the distinctions tend to be very large.

The reasons why most developing countries are unenthusiastic about giving foreign-owned enterprises the same paper rights as domestically owned enterprises are quite compelling. For one thing, foreign-owned enterprises have commonly dominated public utilities and other basic industries in the developing countries to an extent not encountered in Europe, the United States, or Japan. That unease is exacerbated by the fact that foreign-owned enterprises are never quite free of the commands of their home governments. Conditioned by their history, therefore, most developing countries have looked on foreign-owned firms as a special class of enterprise, to be admitted to the country only with caution and restraint.

FOUR DECADES OF EXPERIENCE

The values and institutions of the United States differ sufficiently from those of other countries to substantially heighten the difficulties that normally bedevil efforts at cooperative action. However, the differences have not presented an absolute barrier to cooperation. Nor have they affected all policy areas in quite the same way. In some fields, such as that of bank safety, U.S. representatives have found it easy to work with officials from other countries. In other areas, however, differences in governmental structures and national values have presented formidable obstacles.

To develop a sense of the conditions under which U.S. economic policymakers are likely to operate, it is helpful to review the experience of the past few decades. In the chapters that follow, we explore four areas: the conduct of international trade; the operations of multinational enterprises; the problems associated with foreign exchange flows; and the administration of foreign aid.

Our focus is on the four decades following World War II, a period rich in case studies, published memoirs, and other relevant materials. In this period, as well, some of the principals in the policymaking process can still be consulted about their participation in and assessment of events. The events recounted in the chapters that follow are selective and illustrative. They enrich our various hypotheses and assumptions but without providing very powerful tests of their validity. Such tests will have to await more definitive accounts of U.S. policymaking in this era, including more searching reviews of the archives and more exhaustive analyses by historians. Meanwhile, those who are concerned with the ability of the U.S. government to formulate international economic policies in the coming decades must push ahead with their hypotheses and prescriptions, trying to understand the forces that have shaped U.S. policies in the past and sketching the general directions that seem feasible and desirable for the future.

3

The Politics
of International Trade

OF THE VARIOUS STRANDS making up the foreign economic policy
of the United States, none commands the instant attention of politicians and interest groups as much as trade policy. In the earliest days
of the Republic, trade policy was already the subject of acerbic debate between the political parties. Today, it continues to be the issue
regarded by the American public as the heart of foreign economic
policy, dwarfing such matters as the clashes among national monetary and fiscal policies, the struggles over the activities of multinational enterprises, and the debates over foreign aid.

But special interests alone have not determined the shape of U.S.
trade policy. Ideology has played its part, manifested in a persisting
national consensus that the executive powers of government should
be constrained and the discretion of the bureaucracy limited. Party
traditions, too, have been critical, often reflecting battles over issues
long since gone. The general concerns of individual congressmen for
the long-run interests of the country have also influenced the policies
adopted, as has the fortuitous presence of innovators in the bureaucracy capable of commanding the ear of the president.

In the 1980s, all the major elements in the policymaking mix were
still in evidence. But the balance among these forces had begun to
produce a somewhat different set of outcomes than in the decades
just preceding. Legislators were placing increased emphasis on protecting individual industries and exhibiting less concern over the
long-run disadvantages of a protectionist policy. This emerging posi-

tion, like the policies of earlier decades, can only be understood against the backdrop of a long, historical process.

THE ROOTS OF POLICY

Since the earliest days of the Republic, debates over U.S. trade policy have served as the occasion for adversaries to struggle over large economic issues.[1] For instance, in arguing for protection of the country's infant industries, Alexander Hamilton placed the same stress on the importance of long-term structural change as would Latin American economists in the 1950s; some U.S. economists would be repeating the argument in the 1980s.[2] And the debate between Daniel Webster and Henry Clay over the Tariff Act of 1824 echoed an ideological fervor much wider than the particular interests involved.[3]

In the decades following the Civil War, ideology also appears to have played a role in explaining the vote on the tariff, with Republicans persistently voting for higher tariffs and Democrats showing a strong preference for lower ones. Although the parties could be distinguished somewhat by the economic composition of their membership and by the geographical areas from which they drew their strength, they were not strikingly different in these respects. The consistency with which the two parties followed their traditional positions on the tariff issue suggest that the differences between their memberships were more subtle than pocketbook interests alone.[4]

The year 1930 marked a critical event in U.S. trade policy, an event whose influence is still being felt today. In that year, with the Republican party in firm control of Congress, the Smoot-Hawley Tariff Act was enacted, introducing the highest tariff rates in U.S. history. The vote as usual ran on straight party lines, appearing to represent simply one more outcome of the struggle between the low-tariff Democrats and the high-tariff Republicans; the following tally (which omits a few abstentions and independent votes) reflects the usual party division. But the extreme character of the tariff requires some added explanation.

A dramatic change in the fiscal position of the U.S. government probably accounts in part for the uninhibited lunge of the Republicans in Congress toward higher tariffs. Until the federal income tax was introduced in 1913, tariff revenues had represented nearly half of the income of the federal government.[5] Although we have found little direct evidence that congressional leaders were worried about

Table 3-1   **Tally of Votes on Smoot-Hawley Tariff By Party**

| | For | | Against | |
	House	Senate	House	Senate
Republicans	248	50	11	5
Democrats	22	8	140	30

SOURCE: Provided by E. M. Graham. His count includes paired votes as well as a few cases in which absentees later recorded their positions in the *Congressional Record*.

the fiscal implications of their actions when they altered tariff rates, we think it safe to assume that as long as tariffs represented a substantial source of revenue, some inhibitions deterred the adoption of prohibitive tariffs or zero tariffs, either of which would have reduced the revenue flow. By 1930, however, tariff revenues had fallen to about 14 percent of aggregate federal revenues, so that prohibitive tariffs were no longer as threatening to the U.S. budget.

Previously, another source of restraint on Republican support for high tariffs had been the internationalists within the party. Although they were a part of the Republican coalition, the members of this group shared the view of many Wilsonian Democrats that world peace bore a close relationship to world trade. The Republican internationalists, however, had been dismayed and dispirited by the party's repudiation in 1921 of the bid to join the League of Nations, and for the rest of the decade they had little influence in the party.[6]

In the conditions of the late 1920s, still another element that ordinarily would have curbed the Republican party's support for higher tariffs also failed to play its usual role, namely, the agricultural interests of the Midwest and Far West. As a rule, farm groups had resisted high tariffs even when they affiliated themselves with the Republican party. But the years following World War I had been catastrophic for many sectors of U.S. agriculture; wartime demands had greatly increased the production of grain, meat, and wool in the United States, Canada, Australia, and Argentina, producing a postwar glut that drove U.S. prices down and increased U.S. imports. In that kind of crisis situation, short-run pocketbook politics proved the determining factor: The agricultural interests among the Republicans were prepared to align themselves with the party's industrial interests in a common effort to obtain more protection.[7]

But such pocketbook politics was not the only factor in the picture. One of the dogs that scarcely barked at all during the enactment of the Smoot-Hawley tariff was the U.S. labor movement. In the several decades before the 1920s, labor's behavior had belied the assumption that on matters such as the tariff, labor would always respond to its obvious short-run economic interests. Instead, different factions in the labor movement struggled over the tariff issue during those years. Those for higher tariffs justified their stand in terms of familiar short-run pocketbook interests, while their opponents emphasized concern for the living standards of the poor and for the promotion of world peace. In the textile industry, two rival unions took opposing positions. At the national level, the president of the American Federation of Labor, Samuel Gompers, was an ideological free trader, while some of his vice presidents were strong protectionists. In 1924, Gompers died, making way for a protectionist successor. Even then, the AFL as an organization clung formally to its position of "neutrality," as many of its constituent labor unions refused to follow their national president's protectionist line.[8]

In 1934, however, the Trade Agreements Act radically reversed the direction of U.S. tariff legislation. By that time, after three years of disastrous economic decline, the Democrats had taken firm control of Congress. Once again, the vote followed straight party lines.

And once again, short-run pocketbook interests fail to provide an altogether satisfying explanation of the reversal. For one thing, the act was adopted at the early recovery stage of the deepest depression in the country's history, hardly a propitious time for reducing tariffs. Nor can the passage of the new trade law be explained in terms of some overall economic strategy on the part of the administration. At the time of the law's passage, the general direction of the administration's foreign economic policies was quite uncertain, the subject of violent internal debate.[9] A year earlier, President Roose-

Table 3-2   **Tally of Votes on the Trade Agreements Act of 1934 By Party**

	For		Against	
	House	*Senate*	*House*	*Senate*
Republicans	3	5	112	30
Democrats	279	52	11	6

SOURCE: Provided by E. M. Graham.

velt had refused to cooperate with other governments in a London Economic Conference. Moreover, a radical experiment that had just been introduced to control U.S. agricultural markets clearly foretold the need for effective restrictions on the importation of agricultural products; and an extensive panoply of codes for industrial products developed under the National Recovery Administration implied the existence of controls at the border for these imports as well.[10]

What, then, was the source of the political drive that produced the remarkable reversal?

In the background, influencing all U.S. tariff enactments from the middle of the nineteenth century, were echoes of the past, the bitter consequences of the Civil War. The war had stamped an image deep in the minds of southern politicians, who saw the Republican party, Abraham Lincoln's party, as the enemy. Any southerner wishing to participate in the political life of the country had no choice but to join the Democrats. Although all southern political leaders were members of the Democratic party, they typically saw themselves primarily as defenders and leaders of an agrarian south, struggling to maintain its overseas markets in cotton, tobacco, citrus fruits, apples, and peanuts. In that struggle, the villain was an industrial Republican North, bent on excluding the cheap industrial products of British and European manufacturers. That caricature would influence the policies of southern members of Congress for nearly a century, accounting in part for the Democratic party's attachment to a low tariff policy.

The Democratic victory of 1932 had placed control of the key House and Senate committees in the hands of a group of superannuated congressmen from southern states, this at a time when committee chairmen in Congress exercised much greater control over their committees than is the case today.[11] Their predisposition toward free trade, based largely on the passions and interests of an earlier century, was indispensable for the passage of the 1934 act.

Nevertheless, even more was needed to explain so radical a shift in tariff policy. What was required in addition was a policy entrepreneur within the administration, an individual prepared to push the project at a time when the administration was still altogether uncertain about the direction of its economic policies.

In this case, the entrepreneur was Cordell Hull, a senator from Tennessee who had left Congress to become secretary of state. In addition to sharing the common values of southern Democrats, Hull was a principal supporter of free trade and an adherent to the Wilsonian doctrine of peace-through-trade, a doctrine that had been rejuvenated by the Democratic victory.[12] Hull's ready access to President Roosevelt was a major factor in his taking command of the trade issue and launching an initiative that would have seemed altogether improbable on the basis of pocketbook politics alone.

One added element in the dramatic reversal of trade policy cannot be overlooked, namely, the role of the new generation of bureaucrats brought into the government by the New Deal. Although Hull's influence alone might have been decisive, he was also supported by a full contingent of bureaucratic staffers who shared his beliefs. The country's professional economists, almost without exception, had been against the enactment of the Smoot-Hawley tariff; a remarkable petition signed by 1,028 prominent economists in 1930 had vainly urged President Hoover to veto the bill. It is striking how many signers of that 1930 petition managed in the succeeding years to work their way into key governmental positions in trade policy, occupying high offices in the State Department and other agencies. Among others, Clair Wilcox, Henry F. Grady, Herbert Feis, Howard S. Piquet, Lynn R. Edminster, and Willard L. Thorp, all signers of the petition against Smoot-Hawley, had central roles in shaping the country's new economic program. These professionals, typically committed to the neoclassical free-trade approach, supported the Hull initiative and injected its spirit into all levels of the bureaucracy.

In addition, the forces that might have been moved by short-term pocketbook calculations to resist trade liberalization were quiescent for the time being. The labor unions, although still divided on the protectionist issue, had become members of the ruling political coalition. Their principal reward in the coalition was the social programs of the New Deal. Accordingly, they were prepared to tolerate the trade policy initiatives of the southerners with whom they were allied. Meanwhile, business leaders, wincing under the president's scathing indictment as "malefactors of great wealth" and mollified at the same time by the powers they had acquired under the NRA codes, were choosing their political battles with considerable caution.[13] The combination of forces proved sufficient to ensure the passage of the 1934 trade act.

Having won the battle for passage of the Trade Agreements Act, however, supporters of the program in the executive branch were under no illusions that they had a firm mandate to strike out boldly in the direction of freer trade. Their authority to reduce tariffs, valid for only a few years, was a limited grant from Congress to reduce rates to the extent required for carrying out the terms of a trade agreement. Acutely conscious of Congress's capacity to reverse itself, they were determined not to stir up a powerful opposition. Their conservatism was reflected in the limited significance of the handful of trade agreements negotiated before World War II.[14]

In 1939 war broke out in Europe, and by 1941 the United States was fully involved. For the time being, projects such as the trade agreements program almost disappeared from the foreign policy agenda. But not everybody had forgotten the lessons of the classical economists a generation earlier or the trauma created by the Great Depression. Throughout the war, a relatively small group of strategically placed academics and bureaucrats devoted to the achievement of an open trading world managed to keep the issue alive. By 1942, the fruit of their efforts could be seen in a significant provision embodied in the Anglo-American Mutual Aid Agreement of that year.[15] Once the war had ended, their project became one component of an American effort to shape a brave new world.

LAUNCHING THE GATT REGIME

The pocketbook hypothesis is even less adequate for explaining U.S. trade policies in the six or eight years following World War II than in the depression era. Those six or eight years were a period in which leaders from business, labor, agriculture, and government shared many common views regarding the shaping of a new international economic order, and in which the usual struggle over such issues was muted and restrained. The common wartime experiences of these leaders, coming directly on the heels of nearly a decade of depression, helped to create a sense of shared purpose. Basking in an atmosphere of seeming economic invulnerability, they were extraordinarily receptive for the time being to policies whose rewards would appear only over the longer term, such as the development of a relatively open system of international economic relations. By the same token, they were less than usually responsive to proposals for adopting measures like import restrictions, aimed at producing short-term advantages for the interests they represented.

To be sure, the degree of consensus reached among the various interest groups during the immediate postwar years can easily be exaggerated. Struggles within the executive branch and with Congress over international trade issues could still be sharp and bloody, producing defeats for one faction or another. Free traders, for example, found themselves obliged to accept an agricultural regime in the United States that included the extensive use of import restrictions and export subsidies.

Still, until the election of President Eisenhower in 1952, the degree of consensus on foreign economic policy issues among U.S. leaders was remarkable. Before that era came to a close, the U.S. government had promoted the creation of the International Monetary Fund and the World Bank, had launched the General Agreement on Tariffs and Trade, had completed the European Recovery Program (or Marshall Plan), and had framed the Point Four program for the support of developing countries.

Among the projects that officials in the executive branch had hoped to complete in that early tide of postwar initiatives was an International Trade Organization (ITO), an institution with a broad mandate over the development and functioning of an effective international trade regime. In pursuit of that objective, the U.S. government convened an elaborate conference attended by 57 governments at Havana in 1947. In meetings extending over a five-month period the conference ground out a charter composed of 106 articles and 16 annexes. The draft charter gives the impression of a project of profound importance, embracing rules regarding foreign trade policy, foreign investment policy, international cartels, and international commodity agreements.[16]

Despite the fundamental nature of the government's initiative, the executive branch felt no need to engage in very extensive consultation with Congress or the private sector during the process of formulating the U.S. position on the ITO. The habits of wartime as well as the sense of shared agreement may have accounted for the sense of self-assurance in the executive branch that so ambitious a project would prove acceptable to the American public. In any case, no institutional structure existed, either in Congress or the private sector, through which the executive branch could conduct serious sustained consultations over so wide a range of subjects. In any event, in the end, the text of the charter was based largely on the enthusiasm and creativity of a relatively limited group of officials within the executive branch.

With hindsight, it seems evident that the ITO charter was doomed from birth, not so much because of the executive branch's failure to touch base with all of the affected interests as because of the inclusion of provisions inimical to basic U.S. values. For example, the charter legitimated international commodity agreements, even though such agreements sometimes tolerated an active transactional role for governments in the control of markets. In addition, the agreement acknowledged the right of governments to impose restrictions on the direct investments of foreign firms. In the eyes of U.S. business in the 1940s, these were fighting propositions, a fact that became apparent as the congressional hearings dragged out over many months. After two years of delay, the administration became involved in more pressing matters, including the prosecution of the Korean War, and withdrew the ITO charter proposal, thereby putting an end to the ambitious project. The decision was reported in a press release issued by the State Department. The withdrawal, however, was credited to a determined group of protectionists in Congress, headed by Republican Senator Eugene D. Millikin of Colorado. As he observed with delight, "The State Department may have written the obituary but I was in charge of the funeral."

One important legacy of the charter remained, however. This was the General Agreement on Tariffs and Trade, originally considered a stop-gap executive agreement providing the basis for trade negotiations during an interim period before the charter was ratified. As far as Congress was concerned, the GATT presented no particular threat to its freedom. It was an agreement entered into by another branch of government, and its existence placed no restraint on congressional behavior. Besides, the chapter on commercial policy of the ITO charter on which the GATT was based included familiar provisions that had been developed in earlier bilateral agreements. The U.S. negotiators, moreover, had struggled to avoid any blatant conflict with existing U.S. law in drafting the agreement. The GATT, for example, carved out exceptions that would legitimate restrictions and subsidies in agricultural products, thus allowing the U.S. government to continue its existing restrictive trade practices in accordance with U.S. law. Indeed, under the GATT's protocol of provisional application, all national legislation already on the books was excepted from the GATT's provisions. As long as Congress did not pass new laws with terms violating the GATT, the president could base his participation and adherence solely on his existing powers without the approval of Congress.

Confronted with a *fait accompli*, the Congress for some years thereafter chose ostentatiously to ignore the GATT's existence, repeatedly enacting laws in violation of the agreement's terms and nudging the executive toward actions that were contrary to the spirit and letter of the agreement. Individual congressmen often invoked one provision or another of the GATT, it is true, if it seemed to support some objective that the congressmen were trying to achieve. There were a few rare occasions when the Congress actually modified its actions to avoid conflict with a GATT provision. And the 1988 omnibus trade legislation even went so far as to authorize the president not to retaliate against a country that the United States judged guilty of unfair trading practices if retaliation would be in violation of the GATT. But the characteristic position of the Congress was that the GATT's existence had no bearing on what the Congress chose to do.

The postwar foreign trade policies of the United States, therefore, were hampered from birth by questions about their legitimacy. As the rest of the world saw it, the various strands of U.S. trade policy appeared to be emerging from several directions at once—from the executive, from Congress, and eventually from the courts.

THE EVOLUTION OF U.S. TRADE POLICY

Economic Developments

To understand the complex character of U.S. trade policy in the four decades following World War II, one has to take into account both its diverse sources and the enormous changes taking place in the economic position of the United States.

A development that was critical for the direction of U.S. trade policy during the period in question was the relative decline in the country's economic position in general and its exports in particular. So much has been written on those developments that they require only a cursory comment here. The data in Table 3–3 reflect the main trends in exports since 1950, demonstrating that between the war's end and the mid-1970s the decline in the relative export position of the United States was quite substantial. Thereafter, contrary to a widespread impression among policymakers and the public, the U.S. export position remained quite stable. During the 1980s, however, a giant surge in U.S. imports created unprecedented deficits in the nation's merchandise trade balance.

Throughout most of the postwar period, the countries most suc-

Table 3–3   **Exports and Gross Domestic Products of Various Countries and Regions in Percent of Totals for Non-Communist World**

Exports	1955	1965	1975	1980	1985
Non-Communist world	100.0	100.0	100.0	100.0	100.0
Developed market economies	71.3	77.2	72.8	68.6	65.6
United States	23.7	21.6	17.6	15.6	15.4
Europe	41.0	47.0	45.6	43.7	38.9
Japan	2.3	5.1	7.1	7.1	9.1
Others	4.2	3.4	2.4	2.2	2.2
Developing countries and territories	28.7	22.8	27.2	31.2	23.9
OPEC countries	9.0	8.0	15.8	18.8	10.1
Others	19.7	14.8	11.6	12.6	13.9
Gross Domestic Product	**1955**	**1965**	**1975**	**1980**	**1985[a]**
Non-Communist world	100.0	100.0	100.0	100.0	100.0
Developed market economies	n.a.[b]	78.4	76.2	73.3	75.7
United States	n.a.	39.3	29.2	25.4	33.3
Europe	n.a.	29.3	32.5	33.5	26.5
Japan	n.a.	5.2	9.5	10.2	10.9
Others	n.a.	4.6	5.1	4.1	5.0
Developing countries and territories	n.a.	21.3	23.3	26.1	25.8
OPEC countries	n.a.	2.0	4.7	5.9	7.5
Others	n.a.	19.3	18.6	20.2	18.3

[a] Complete figures not available. 1984 data used.
[b] n.a. = not available.
SOURCES: *Handbook of International Trade and Development Statistics* (New York: United Nations, 1986 Supplement); United Nations, *Conference on Trade and Development,* Geneva, various issues; *International Financial Statistics* (Washington, DC: International Monetary Fund), various issues.

cessful in expanding their relative export positions included Japan and a handful of unusual developing countries. The details of their emergence as exporters are familiar enough. In addition to Japan, Korea, Taiwan, Hong Kong, and Singapore—the Four Tigers of southeast Asia—achieved a spectacular expansion in exports of manufactured goods. Almost as impressive were the increased efforts of India, Brazil, and Mexico. And until 1980, a group of oil-exporting countries, benefiting from a sharp rise in the price of oil, also raised their relative export position. As the exports of these countries increased, so too did their imports of foodstuffs, industrial materials, and capital equipment, a development that turned them into important markets for the more advanced industrialized economies.

Nevertheless, on both sides of the Atlantic, public opinion took up the theme that the industrialized nations were being pushed into a corner by the new exporters with the use of devices that were "unfair." Among Europeans, the defensive reaction was heightened by a widespread feeling that European industry was not capable of adjusting to the new sources of competition by moving into high-technology industries such as supercomputers or biotechnology; that adjustment, it was widely assumed, would be blocked by competition from the United States and Japan. Many Europeans also regarded the relative positions of the United States and Japan as "unfair"—in the case of the United States because of support to high-technology industry provided by military programs, and in the case of Japan because of various more obscure forms of support to industry allegedly provided by official government sources.[17]

It was in the United States, however, that the "unfair" issue acquired its widest currency, embellished by repeated assertions from numerous quarters that U.S. trade policy should aim at reestablishing a "level playing field." The metaphor itself was revealing, picturing trade as a zero-sum contest rather than an activity allowing for the possibility of joint gains.

A number of different factors figured in the widespread U.S. view that it was the victim of unfair practices. One was the assumption by many Americans that other countries, after subscribing to the provisions of the GATT, were refusing to honor their commitments. Another element in the picture was the widespread public impression that, whether or not other governments were violating the GATT, they were using national resources more effectively than the United States, employing subsidies and other devices to penetrate selected markets; the playing field accordingly was no longer level.

Gradually, the overall decline in the trade position of the United States began to impinge directly on the economic fortunes of certain key industries, notably including semi-conductors, automobiles, oil, copper, and aluminum. In automobiles, for instance, the production of U.S. industry dropped from 48 percent of worldwide production in 1960 to 19 percent in 1982.[18] In semi-conductors, the change has been even more rapid, though not yet as precipitous: in 1981, the United States controlled slightly over 60 percent of world production; by 1985, its share had fallen to just 50 percent.[19] In agriculture, too, the United States was beginning to slip from its preeminent position and U.S. farmers in the early 1980s began to feel the debilitating effects of lower world prices.[20]

The staggering import balances in the country's merchandise trade that appeared in the 1980s added to the impression of an economy in retreat. Import balances in merchandise were rare for the U.S. economy before 1976; therafter, they became chronic. By 1986, they had reached the altogether unprecedented figure of $144 billion. Economists in the United States and elsewhere sought earnestly to explain to any policymaker who would listen that the deficit in the U.S. foreign trade balance was a function of a distorted exchange rate, and that the observed patterns were an inescapable consequence of the equally unprecedented fiscal deficits generated concurrently by the U.S. government.[21] But their explanations did not appear to have much effect on prevailing opinion in Congress or the public at large.[22]

Changing Politics

During the four decades after World War II, the political structure of the United States was also undergoing a series of fundamental changes that bore directly on the country's foreign trade policies. And with growing frequency, foreign competition was held responsible for the difficulties that some sectors of the domestic economy were experiencing.

One telling consequence of the changes was a reversal in the formal positions of the two political parties on trade policy, a reversal already becoming apparent to observers as early as the 1960s.[23] The Republicans had entered the postwar period with a hoary tradition, going back more than a century in support of protectionism; but four decades later, the party formally supported free trade. The Democrats had been the country's traditional low-tariff party; but by the 1980s, they were unmistakably the main supporters of the protectionist cause.

During the actual process of crossover in the positions of the two parties, their respective positions on the subject of trade were not easily distinguished. For the time being, party labels were poor predictors of congressional voting patterns, and party differences seemed more the product of tactics than ideology.[24] Besides, as we shall point out below, the various trade bills themselves became increasingly ambivalent in content, representing a fragile compromise that satisfied few.[25]

The basic shift that pushed the Republican party off its traditional protectionist position after World War II was a broadening in the horizons of U.S. bankers and industrialists that moved them from the national perspective of Alexander Hamilton to the world perspective of Walter Wriston.[26] That broadening had been a long time in the making. Some faint stirrings could be detected in the late nineteenth century, when Republicans spoke of the country's "manifest destiny" as a world leader.[27] The stirrings were reinforced in the 1920s, as the New York financial community found itself propelled into the role of international banker on a major scale.

By the end of World War II, the Republican party could no longer downplay the fact that the interests of large U.S. manufacturing firms and U.S. banks had become global in reach. True, some branches of U.S. industry suffered from the competition of foreigners. But for the first decade or two after the war, the industries most exposed to such competition were typically composed of small- and medium-sized companies using relatively labor-intensive methods, such as firms producing shoes and toys. What appeared to influence Republican policy at the time was the fact that the country's largest firms were rapidly expanding their stake in foreign markets, partly through a vast increase in exports from the United States and partly through the establishment of overseas factories, mines, and oil fields.

The data in Table 3–4 illustrate the rapid growth in the relative importance of exports for the U.S. economy during the postwar period. The fact that large U.S. firms were the dominant actors in that trend can be gleaned from other data. For instance, over 60 percent of U.S. merchandise exports in 1982 could be traced to a group of 1,215 firms whose relatively large size was reflected in the fact that the average sales of the group were over $800 million per firm.[28]

The stake of large U.S. firms in U.S. exports, taken by itself, provided no sure indication that the Republican party would move to support a policy of freer trade. The new export emphasis did, however, represent a structural economic change of some importance, whose recognition made it clear that pocketbook politics was not

Table 3-4 **Production and Exports of U.S. Sectors, 1950-1984**

Year	Agricultural Sector			Manufactures and Minerals Sectors		
	Production $ billions	Exports $ billions	Exports as % of production	Production $ billions	Exports $ billions	Exports as % of production
1965	21.9	6.3	28.8	342.9	20.2	5.9
1970	26.3	7.4	28.1	467.8	35.1	7.5
1975	50.3	22.2	44.1	714.7	84.8	11.9
1980	65.5	42.2	64.1	1173.9	182.1	15.5
1985	75.5	29.6	39.2	1630.2	184.8	11.3

SOURCE: *Economic Report of the President* (Washington, D.C.: United States Government Printing Office, 1987), compiled from various tables.

altogether defunct. The Republican shift from protectionism was made easier by the fact that during these postwar decades, businessmen and affluent young voters in large numbers were rediscovering the virtues of the untrammeled market.[29] For voters such as these, a party position in favor of freer trade could be a significant political asset.

The Democrats were feeling the effects of a different set of influences, pushing them in the opposite direction on issues of trade policy. For one thing, the old South was rapidly disappearing, together with its one-party system, its dependence on agricultural exports, and its hostility to the northern industrialists. In the new South, a wide array of industries had largely displaced agriculture, including a heavy representation of labor-intensive sectors, such as shoe and clothing manufacturers, especially sensitive to the competition of imports. This transformation of traditional southern interests destroyed a key element in the coalition supporting free trade within the Democratic party.

Meanwhile, the internal divisions that until about 1960 had kept national labor organizations divided or neutral on the trade issue were rapidly dissolving, giving way to a new labor consensus against increased imports. The shift was a direct consequence of the multinationalization of large U.S. enterprises and the increase in U.S. imports. From the viewpoint of U.S. managers and U.S. stockholders, the multinationalization of industry might represent a broadening of opportunities and a promise of higher incomes; but to workers on the factory floor, it was commonly seen as a threat to job security and wage bargaining power. Many U.S. economists, when confronted with this concern, earnestly insisted that the labor unions were failing to identify their pocketbook interests correctly. The economists contended that the increase in U.S. trade and investment was creating a rising economic tide that lifted practically all incomes, including those of labor. But U.S. labor leaders took a contrary position, as did their political allies in the Democratic party.

One reason for the conversion of many U.S. labor leaders to an overt protectionist position during the 1970s and 1980s was a pervasive sense among them that as erstwhile supporters of free trade in the decades immediately following World War II, they had been betrayed by their business allies and isolated from the rank and file of their own union membership. During those early decades, union leaders had supported the idea of open international markets in the face of widespread rank-and-file skepticism.

In a spirit reminiscent of AFL President Samuel Gompers in the 1920s, union activists in the 1940s had supported the cause of free trade. Walter P. Reuther of the United Automobile Workers and David J. McDonald of the United Steel Workers, for example, were both enthusiasts for open markets and democratic governments and could be counted on to fight off protectionist sentiment. In return, these labor leaders demanded that the government institute a program that in principle would assist workers, enterprises, and localities to adjust to any substantial increase in imports.[30]

First enacted in the Trade Expansion Act of 1962, the trade adjustment provisions were hedged in with such tight criteria that for seven years thereafter, no applicant succeeded in getting help under its provisions. Thereafter, the procedures for implementation were so complex that, according to one study, 71 percent of the beneficiaries were already back at work before receiving their first benefit payments.[31] Besides, practically all of the funds distributed under the program went for a relatively unproductive purpose that left the underlying problem of labor adjustment practically unchallenged. For the most part, the available funds were used to extend by a few more months the period in which laid-off workers were entitled to unemployment benefits. Expenditures on retraining and relocation were almost nonexistent, amounting to only 2 percent of total assistance to workers in the years from 1976 to 1985. Deeply disappointed, organized labor turned its face against the trade adjustment approach and by the 1980s was leading the push for a protectionist policy.

A Record of Innovation

Despite those political shifts and a marked decline in the country's international economic position, the United States has managed to retain leadership in the GATT and to launch a series of major trade initiatives. Although they were strung out over a period of 40 years and originated in both Republican and Democratic administrations, a common set of motivations animated most of the initiatives.

U.S. initiatives in the GATT during these years were driven both by a desire for lower U.S. tariffs and a widespread conviction among the bureaucrats in the U.S. government that in trade policy, as in bicycle riding, there was no standing still. Either governments would engage full cry in further reduction of their trade barriers or special interests in each country would force individual tariff rates upward.[32]

In addition, many U.S. bureaucrats shared some widely held perceptions about the role of pressure groups in the U.S. political system. One was that the representatives of trade associations in Washington did not much care what victories they produced for their industry constituents so long as they could claim victories in some form. Such representatives, according to a view common in government agencies, would be just as content to report heading off another deep cut in a tariff rate as succeeding in raising that tariff rate. One authoritative study of pressure group politics suggested that this was a reasonable working assumption; indeed, according to the study, Washington representatives of trade associations often played a pivotal role in defining the basic goals of their organizations.[33]

A second proposition commonly accepted in the U.S. bureaucracy during most of the postwar period was that many congressmen who felt obliged to support protectionist bills targeted for explicit industries would support measures for general tariff reduction. Many members of Congress were thought to be ideologically disposed toward freer trade yet reluctant to resist pressure from specific interests among their constituents who were looking for protection. Besides, some congressmen came to learn through experience that supporting a special interest could spell political trouble; one such case often begot demands from other interest groups, sometimes placing the obliging congressman in the center of a local storm. The challenge to the executive branch, therefore, was to find ways of presenting the trade issue in a form that allowed congressmen to address the larger policy issue without becoming entrapped in the problems of individual industries.[34]

Armed with considerations such as these, policy entrepreneurs within the executive branch were often prompted to seize the initiative in formulating U.S. trade policies. Because Congress periodically has exhibited a willingness to delegate the political burden of dealing with the costs and benefits of trade policy, it has been possible for a leader inside the bureaucracy to take on the task of securing presidential approval for a new trade program and then shepherding it over the domestic and international hurdles. Characteristically, these policy entrepreneurs have been inners-and-outers, political appointees expecting to hold their jobs for only brief periods of time. Some, such as George W. Ball, under secretary of state in the Kennedy administration, could not be dubbed amateurs; but others, such as William Brock in the Reagan administration, had had very little prior experience in formulating trade policies.

When the Kennedy administration took office in 1962, some of its political appointees were already persuaded that the bureaucrats' assumptions were right, that the administration would have to push for lower trade barriers if it were to prevent a return to protection. Moreover, new factors in U.S. trade relations seemed to increase the urgency of moving further in the direction of trade liberalization. First, the U.S. balance of payments position was exhibiting some strain as the U.S. economy exported capital abroad, provided moderate amounts of foreign aid to selected countries, and assumed substantial military burdens in Europe. Consequently, U.S. official gold holdings had begun to trickle away, slipping from nearly $23 billion in 1957 to a little more than $16 billion in 1962.[35] Nearly simultaneously, U.S. dollar holdings in foreign central banks had started to grow, a development that worried the president and some of his close advisers. By 1963, banks outside of the United States held nearly $26 billion in U.S. dollars, up from $19 billion in 1959.[36] Moreover, the treaty creating the European Economic Community had just come into force, setting in motion a process that would soon eliminate tariffs among European member nations while establishing a common tariff for them against the products of the United States.

Like the initiatives of earlier administrations, the exercise culminating in the Trade Expansion Act of 1962 was launched by the executive branch with only the most perfunctory consultations with Congress and the public. As in the past, the State Department, in the person of Under Secretary Ball, dominated the policy-making process, with a lesser role for a special White House representative assigned to the task. Ball was a big man—big in stature, energy, and vision. Following the pattern of a typical inner-and-outer he had moved back and forth over three decades between practicing law and serving the federal government. A close friend of Jean Monnet, author of the idea of a European Community, he shared Monnet's view of the need for a unified Europe operating in tandem with the United States.

With Ball as the driving force, the Kennedy administration asked Congress for a novel kind of authority that would enable it to negotiate effectively with the European Economic Community with respect to its new external tariff. The authority was designed to relieve U.S. negotiators of the need to examine the economic consequences of reducing the tariff for every individual product subject to negotiation; instead, negotiators would be free to agree on tariff reductions based upon formulas applied across broad categories of products. The necessary authority was provided in the Trade Expansion Act of 1962, which was widely supported by congressmen from both parties. It enabled the United States to lead the GATT membership in a prolonged set of negotiations that produced another deep cut in existing tariffs in 1967.

The year 1974 saw another manifestation of the power of the executive branch to initiate dramatic action in the trade policy field. The Trade Act of 1974 authorized the president to engage in yet another round of negotiations that would reduce tariffs and other barriers to trade. Once again, the ambivalent reactions of Congress to freer trade could be seen in the easy passage of the act.

For some time before the enactment of the 1974 trade act, Congress had been signalling its increasing desire to assert some measure of control over the president's actions in the trade policy field. With each successive trade act, Congress had sought to tie the president's hands a little, using various devices that we shall discuss shortly. Congressional leaders were aware, however, that as long as they remained in favor of the general movement toward freer trade, there was a limit to the restrictions they could place on the executive branch. If the authority of the U.S. negotiators was too sharply limited in advance of an international negotiation, eventual agreement might prove impossible; indeed, other countries might even refuse to open such negotiations, putting the longer objective of free trade in jeopardy.

This time, the executive realized that it would have to recognize the congressional need to deal with the pressures of constituents; it did so in a novel and radical fashion. In effect, the president proposed bringing both Congress and concerned sectors of the public into the earliest stages of policy-making and negotiation over trade matters. Intimations of such a trend were present in some provisions of the 1962 trade act, which had made explicit provision for consultation between the two branches. But the 1974 act carried the process very much further. In effect, the president proposed that the separation of powers, which normally was jealously guarded by the three branches of government, should be drastically reduced—that the planning and execution of the next great round of trade negotiations should come closer to being a joint undertaking of the executive and legislative branches.[37]

Under the arrangement eventually incorporated in the statute, the executive's exclusive prerogative to represent the United States in foreign negotiations was effectively curbed as representatives of Congress and the private sector took ringside seats in the initial planning stages of the trade negotiations. To acquire those ringside seats, however, Congress committed itself in advance to vote on any changes in U.S. legislation required to put the negotiated agreements into effect, without amendment, within 60 days of their submission to Congress; that provision, dubbed the "fast track," in effect curbed the power of Congress to check the executive.

Participating in subsequent GATT negotiations under this remarkable arrangement, the U.S. representatives produced substantial results.[38] By 1979, acting under the authority in the 1974 act to reduce U.S. tariffs, the U.S. negotiators joined with those of other countries to bring down the tariff rates of the United States, Europe, and Japan to record-breaking lows. At the same time, they developed a series of novel codes designed to inhibit the use of various so-called nontariff barriers, including notably the subsidizing of exports, the use of dumping prices by exporters, the protectionist practices of government procurement agencies, the use of customs formalities to impede imports, and so on. U.S. adherence to these codes required explicit congressional approval inasmuch as they called for modifications of U.S. law as well as for future self-discipline on the part of Congress; but debate on the issue was restrained by the procedural agreement to which Congress had acceded in the 1974 act. In 1979,

Congress overwhelmingly ratified the GATT agreements under the procedures that had been established. A novel experiment in the modification of the checks-and-balances structure had apparently paid off.

The overwhelming congressional ratification of the 1979 agreement, at a time when numerous interest groups were demanding special treatment for their various industries, has been studied carefully by a number of scholars. Some ascribe the outcome to the political skill of Robert S. Strauss, chief representative of the executive branch, to whom the president had given plenary authority to negotiate with Congress.[39] Strauss was the consummate insider, a politician's politician who was widely admired for his ability to wrest compromises from even the most stubborn adversaries. A lawyer who had served as chairman of the Democratic National Committee, Strauss had a persuasive style of interpersonal diplomacy that made him uniquely qualified to sell the Carter administration's trade policies to a divided Congress.[40] In our view, Strauss benefited from the radical institutional innovation, the fast track, that forced private interests to join the executive branch in the earliest stages of negotiation, thereby giving the concerned parties a stake in the process itself and preempting congressional opposition at a later stage in the negotiations.

In 1984, the president once again demonstrated the capacity of the executive to initiate international projects; he proposed another major round of trade negotiations to the other GATT members and took the leading role in the passage of the Trade Act of 1984. In some ways, this initiative illustrated more vividly than any since the launching of the GATT in 1948 the freewheeling potentialities of the U.S. executive branch. The subject matter to be covered by the negotiations, as proposed by the United States, was to be far more extensive and diverse than in any prior GATT negotiation, covering foreign direct investment, intellectual property, and trade in services.[41] Although these initiatives ranged broadly over many industries and many interests, there was no evidence that the U.S. executive had engaged in any substantial probing of the numerous trade associations and the numerous congressional committees that would eventually signal their interests in the negotiations. The power of the executive branch to initiate had once again been affirmed; whether it would eventually carry the day in international negotiations and in Congress remained to be seen.

An even more striking evidence of the persistent capacity of the

U.S. executive to initiate was provided by the 1987 agreement between the United States and Canada to submit a proposal for the creation of a free trade area to their respective legislatures. In this instance, the early initiative had come mainly from the Canadian side. The U.S. side had responded to the Canadian proposal under a provision in the Trade Act of 1984 that authorized the U.S. executive to engage in required negotiations under a special fast-track dispensation that would expire in October 1987.

A few days before the expiration of this grace period, the negotiations seemed hopelessly deadlocked. In this instance, however, the Reagan administration's persistent innovator, James A. Baker III, secretary of the treasury, came to the rescue.

Like Strauss, Baker was a lawyer by training and a politician by nature. After swapping his original job as White House chief of staff with then-Secretary of the Treasury Donald T. Regan, Baker assumed nearly full control over the country's economic policies, filling a vacuum created by the departure of David A. Stockman from the Office of Management and Budget and the replacement of the outspoken Martin S. Feldstein as chairman of the President's Council of Economic Advisers by the more quiet and accommodating Beryl W. Sprinkel. From the start, Baker placed himself in the center of the Treasury's activities, maintaining one-on-one relationships with many of his subordinates and ensuring that he had a hand in nearly all of the department's activities.[42] This personal involvement, combined with Baker's special status as a close confidante of the president, quickly made it possible for him to launch various initiatives in foreign economic policy. In this case, he used his special status to propose radical departures in U.S. practices that succeeded in breaking the deadlock; these included a remarkable provision allowing an international commission to serve as an appeals court to review the application of some of the trade laws of the two countries.[43] The free trade proposal reaffirmed the U.S. executive's support for broad schemes to reduce trade barriers, notwithstanding the country's protectionist decisions in individual cases. It reaffirmed the capacity of the innovative individual, when strategically located in the U.S. system, to launch major proposals despite the formal distribution of power within the system.

CHECKS AND BALANCES

The governmental structure of the United states, we have suggested, makes it easy for the executive to perform an initiating role; at the same time, the structure makes it difficult to predict the country's behavior. Especially since the 1970s, private interests and congressional demands have constrained the capacity of the executive branch to implement its trade policies as originally conceived. While these pressures have not gone so far as to challenge the executive's right to launch initiatives, the overall structure of U.S. trade policy-making has undergone significant changes.

Congressional Involvement

Traditionally, of course, individuals and interest groups have brought their demands or complaints into the political system by appealing to their representatives in Congress. Because the U.S. system places so much value on the rights of an aggrieved party, congressmen are expected to serve as watchdogs for their constituents, seeking to protect them from disproportionate harm as a result of national policies. Indeed, from the executive's point of view, the power of Congress to balance the actions of the executive branch in trade matters with subsequent actions of its own had always been seen as a Damoclean sword. The demise of the project for an ITO charter in 1950 was a classic illustration of the business community's use of Congress to apply checks on the executive branch and the extent to which the executive's initiatives are vulnerable to congressional opposition.

Much more striking manifestations of congressional power have been that body's repeated successes in forcing the executive to violate the provisions of the GATT. Occasionally, these successes have taken the form of measures in various pieces of legislation involving specific commodities such as cheese, textiles, and oil that obliged the executive to impose restrictions on trade in these commodities.[44] More often, Congress has exercised its balancing power through repeated amendments to the trade acts, defining U.S. standards and procedures in the application of tariffs and other trade restrictions in terms that were inconsistent with the GATT.

For the most part, Congress was noticeably reluctant to involve itself in the intricacies of U.S. trade policy until the mid-1970s. Part of that reluctance could be attributed to the general liberal bent of most members of Congress and to a desire to avoid the mistakes of the Smoot-Hawley tariff. At the same time, however, Congress was eager to buffer itself from the intense political pressures that foreign trade issues have traditionally incited. Realizing that every trade debate was likely to pit numerous interest groups against one another,

Congress usually sought to avoid choosing the winners and losers, preferring to leave that dangerous exercise to the executive branch.

Because so many members of Congress had little desire to front for the special interest groups among their constituents, they accepted with a certain equanimity the dominance of the aging southern chairmen that presided over the committees responsible for trade legislation—in the House, the Ways and Means Committee, and in the Senate, the Finance Committee. Because the power of these committees was well recognized by the public and by representatives of interest groups in Washington, individual members of Congress could fend off pressures by expressing their sympathy and confessing their impotence.[45]

The extent to which the Congress was willing to leave control over foreign trade issues in the hands of an authoritarian figure was symbolized by the reign of Wilbur Mills, a Democrat from Arkansas who chaired the House Ways and Means Committee in the 1950s and 1960s. Throughout his tenure, Mills dominated legislation in the House of Representatives, carrying on the tradition of the southern congressional bloc. Although a staunch believer in free trade, Mills sometimes threatened the executive with protectionist measures; nearly always, however, he reported out liberal legislation. Because the committee meetings remained closed to outside observers, committee members were free to claim that they had defended a particular interest to the end, only to be defeated by the powerful chairman.[46]

In the 1970s several factors converged to undermine this protective arrangement. First, Mills retired, putting an end to the dominance of the House Ways and Means Committee over foreign trade legislation. Second, the changing character of international trade meant that a much greater number of issues—from government procurement practices to interest rate subsidies—impinged upon trade policy, which added to the members of Congress and the congressional committees involved in the formulation of U.S. trade policy. And third, a wave of newly elected Democrats pushed through a series of measures aimed at decentralizing power in Congress and opening up its procedures to greater public scrutiny. As committee meetings were opened to the press and the public, members of congress could no longer afford to overlook the special interests of their constituents or to disclaim responsibility for unpopular legislation.

All of these developments, whether intentionally or not, worked to strip members of Congress of their insulation from pressure groups. The 1987 trade legislation, for example, involved so many issues and so many committees that the conference committee to resolve differences between the House and Senate bills included about 200 members, nearly two-fifths of the Congress. Many members of Congress who had previously considered foreign trade out of their jurisdiction began to take a lively interest in it, occasionally even using their position on trade issues to gain national prominence. One, Senator Richard A. Gephardt, based a presidential campaign largely on a "tough" trade position. Although most of the legislators remained sensitive to the risks of a general policy of protection, increased public pressures and a more open Congress were compelling them to be responsive to the demands of special interests.

Throughout the late 1970s and 1980s, this resurgence of congressional involvement in trade policy was matched by a new willingness on the part of special interest groups to employ the various provisions enacted by Congress in earlier decades. Traditionally, Congress formulated these provisions as a convenient means of deflecting public pressures. By enacting such provisions or strengthening those already in place, individual members of Congress could vote for liberal trade measures while still providing some comfort to their complaining constituents. In the end, these provisions gave the complainants such easy access to the executive as to justify maintaining a strong lobby in Washington. And with a strong lobby in place, Congress found itself more exposed than ever to the pressures of special interest groups.

The history of the so-called escape clause that would eventually emerge as Section 201 of the Trade Act of 1974 illustrates the process in pristine form. When the U.S. government adhered to the GATT in 1948, no provision existed in U.S. law under which an aggrieved party might petition the U.S. government to withdraw a tariff concession previously negotiated in a trade agreement. Although such a procedure was available to industries that claimed serious injury from imports, it had been created in 1947 by executive order rather than by law. U.S. negotiators, when drafting the relevant provisions of the GATT, had been guided by the text of that executive order.[47] From time to time, one industry or another complained about increasing imports under the new procedure. But the industries typically were not very large—they included producers of garlic, grass seed, safety pins, rosaries, and pregnant mares' urine. Such cases involved no great political stakes and could be weighed on their economic merit.[48]

In 1951, Congress incorporated the text of the escape clause in U.S. legislation, a step that created no conflict with the GATT. In later renewals of the president's negotiating authority, Congress progressively widened the escape clause, softening the standards by which troubled industries might claim the right to tariff relief and straying farther and farther from the narrower provisions of the GATT. As it appears in the GATT, the escape clause applies to those domestic producers who are suffering "serious injury" as a result of unforeseen developments and trade concessions. U.S. statutes, on the other hand, have gradually drifted from these rather stringent provisions, interpreting injury to include underemployment, idling factories, and growing inventories. Moreover, in recent years, "significant" has begun to replace "serious" as the standard by which the U.S. measures injury; in the case of some products, such as motorcycles, even the threat of injury has sufficed to make an industry eligible for escape clause relief.[49]

Until the mid-1980s, the president was able to exercise every scrap of his remaining jurisdiction to hold egregious breaches of the GATT under the escape clause to only a handful of cases. But the 1984 trade act threatened to cut off that line of retreat by providing that Congress could override a presidential decision in escape clause cases through a joint resolution.[50] The amendments to the trade act under consideration in 1987 promised to weaken the president's powers even further.

The antidumping provisions of U.S. law went through a similar evolution, obliging the U.S. government in the end to act under standards that were inconsistent with the GATT. Since 1916, the U.S. statute books have carried provisions authorizing the imposition of countervailing duties against imports dumped on the U.S. market. As with the escape clause, U.S. legislators had been guided by the U.S. antidumping provisions when developing a parallel rule for the GATT. Once again, however, Congress eventually decided to widen the definitions involved.

Under the GATT, dumping is said to occur when the imported product is priced lower than its "fair market value." Recent U.S. Department of Commerce regulations, however, provide that the price of an imported product is not "fair" unless it covers the full cost of production plus an 8 percent profit margin, standards far more rigorous than those associated with the GATT's antidumping provisions.[51] Thus, the U.S. interpretation of the antidumping provision places a powerful tool in the hands of U.S. domestic producers, who can effectively harass U.S. importers with antidumping suits, and it obliges the U.S. executive to adjudicate those suits according to standards that are inconsistent with the GATT.[52]

Moreover, Congress has added a maze of regulations that effectively force the executive branch to resolve antidumping complaints as quickly as possible, on the assumption that the pressure for a speedy resolution will generate more decisions in favor of the complainants. Under the provisions of the 1984 trade act, the International Trade Commission must make a preliminary determination of injury under the escape clause within 45 days of the time the petition is filed. The Commerce Department then has another 115 days to release its preliminary findings and an additional 75 days in which to render a final determination of the case. The end result, it appears, is to compel the already overburdened federal agencies to work faster and faster, leaving them less and less time to examine fully the merits of each case.[53]

U.S. laws against the use of subsidies in international trade have been undergoing similar changes. Under Section 701 of the Trade Act, aggrieved parties have acquired increasing powers to command consideration of a specific case by the U.S. government and to obtain a ruling on its merits. At the same time, the U.S. law on subsidies has moved beyond the GATT by explicitly dubbing various widely used governmental measures as export subsidies. In two particularly contentious cases, the United States retaliated against Canadian exports of tires and fish, claiming that the Canadian producers were the recipients of federal subsidies. In one of these cases, the "subsidy" was government-assisted financing of a factory in economically depressed Nova Scotia; in the other, the subsidy took the form of unemployment benefits paid to fishermen in off-seasons.[54]

Still another provision of the current Trade Act, Section 301, illustrates the extent to which Congress has felt free to breach the GATT's provisions. The ostensible purpose of Section 301 is to open up the economies of other countries, not to close down the U.S. market. To that end, the section invites petitions with regard to "any act, policy, or practice which, while not necessarily in violation of or inconsistent with the international legal rights of the United States, is otherwise deemed to be unfair and inequitable." The act goes on, in disregard of GATT provisions, to authorize any retaliatory action that is "appropriate and feasible." By the mid-1980s, a handful of petitions were being processed, with many others in the wings.

To highlight even further the feebleness of GATT pressures as a restraint on the United States, the president in 1984 announced his intention to launch several Section 301 investigations on his own initiative. Subsequently, he ordered the Office of the Special Trade Representative to investigate a new Brazilian law that had virtually closed the Brazilian market to a wide range of high-technology imports. Soon after, the president initiated similar investigations under Section 301 into South Korea's policies regarding U.S. insurance companies and Japan's barriers to cigarette and tobacco imports.[55]

At times, it is true, the knowledge that the U.S. government will not be restrained by contrary provisions in the GATT has increased the executive's negotiating power with foreign countries. The president, for example, has frequently used the possibility of congressional action as a bugaboo to force the cooperation of the governments adversely affected by executive positions.[56] Because other governments have recognized that the three branches of the U.S. government are autonomous to a considerable degree, that threatening tactic has often been fairly effective.

Over the longer term, however, the executive's use of the bugaboo tactic has had its cost. One of the earliest uses of the tactic, involving Japan in 1957, illustrated some of the dangers associated with it. At the time, the U.S. executive demanded that Japan "voluntarily" curtail its exports of cotton textiles to the United States. This action was equivalent in effect to the U.S. government's imposing a discriminatory import quota on the Japanese product; hence it was in egregious violation of the GATT's intent. Far from forestalling further congressional action, however, the executive's success suggested to special interest groups another approach for restricting U.S. imports, and they were quick to press it on their congressional representatives. Subsequent versions of U.S. trade legislation directed the president to initiate such bilateral negotiations in other cases.

Pathology: The Case of Steel

The extent to which special interest groups have developed a capacity for initiating action on individual products is illustrated graphically by the tactics employed by the U.S. steel industry in seeking import protection. Such efforts by the steel industry have continued almost uninterrupted over the past 25 years as U.S. producers have lost increasing portions of their markets to lower priced imports.

Initially, fears of growing competition and falling profits prompted industry leaders to seek relief on the grounds that foreigners were dumping their products in U.S. markets. Between 1961 and 1967, the industry filed nearly 300 petitions to secure countervailing duties against imports allegedly dumped in the U.S. market, but evidence of dumping was established in only eight of these cases.[57]

By 1968, steel producers were trying another tack. Taking their cue from earlier successes of the cotton textile industry, industry leaders called for high level negotiations to persuade other countries to limit their steel exports "voluntarily." By 1969, the administration had responded to these demands by negotiating a set of agreements with the EEC and Japan, limiting their steel exports to the United States to an annual target of 14 million tons.

When the voluntary restraints expired, however, the protests from the steel industry began anew. In 1971, representatives of the industry met at the White House to impress the urgency of their plight upon the president. Between 1959 and 1968, they informed him, steel imports had risen more than 400 percent, and imports as a percentage of U.S. domestic consumption had grown from 6.1 percent to nearly 17 percent. Once again, the executive branch responded. By May 1972, the State Department had negotiated a new and expanded program of voluntary restraints. This time, the United Kingdom was included in the agreement, various certain specialty steels were assigned their own limits, and aggregate imports were lowered.

When these agreements expired in 1974, the steel industry still had not found the means to survive the onslaught of foreign competition. In 1976, specialty steel producers began to petition again, switching techniques this time to request new relief under the provisions of the escape clause, Section 201 of the 1974 Trade Act. As a result, they managed to secure a three-year quota restraint on specified steel products, which eventually was extended until 1980.[58]

Meanwhile, the industry continued to threaten steel importers with a barrage of antidumping suits, a step that would effectively slow down imports until the suits could be settled. In a forestalling response, the Treasury Department in 1978 enacted a novel import control, the so-called trigger price mechanism, whereby any steel entering the country below a specified price would be subject to a dumping investigation automatically.

Still, the industry lobbied for greater protection. When the quota restraints expired in 1980, the specialty steel producers returned to the executive's doorstep, claiming that they were suffering from the effects of foreign subsidies and demanding retaliation in accord with

Section 301 of the Trade Act. Domestic firms received six awards of escape clause relief in 1981, but still returned in 1982 to file a record-breaking 144 antidumping and countervailing duty petitions.

When this assault produced only meager results, the industry leaders switched their tactics again, making the Congress their principal target. In early 1984, the industry launched a three-part campaign designed to exert pressure on the Congress, the ITC, and the president simultaneously, hoping that all three bodies would prove vulnerable to the pressures of an election year.

This time, the ITC proved more sympathetic to the industry's claims, finding evidence of injury in many steel products. More importantly, an industry-supported bill—the Fair Trade in Steel Act of 1984—gained widespread support in the Congress.

The executive branch, however, balked at the thought of providing steel producers any further relief. Indeed, the U.S. trade representative, William Brock, argued instead that free competition was the only way to ensure the long-term success of the industry. But in the autumn of an election year, the White House decided otherwise. The president's plan called for a continuation of all existing voluntary restraints and pledged to negotiate new controls on imports from certain foreign sources.

In the end, the steel industry won longer lasting relief under a program that combined the White House approach with the more protectionist measures of the Congress. The Trade and Tariff Act of 1984 recommended that foreign penetration of the U.S. market be kept within the range of 17 to 20 percent and provided the executive with the authority to restrict steel imports from nations agreeing to voluntary restraints. In addition, the act warns that if the steel policy "does not produce satisfactory results within a reasonable period of time," Congress "will consider taking such legislative actions concerning steel and iron ore products as may be necessary or appropriate to stabilize conditions in the domestic market for such products."[59] All told, the U.S. steel industry has extracted so many exceptions from the principles of U.S. trade policy that, for practical purposes, the principles have ceased to apply.

Although steel may be an extreme case, it is not unique. By the mid-1980s, a new industry had developed in Washington; it consisted of trade associations and law firms devoted principally to exploiting the provisions of the trade acts and generating other pressures on the executive branch to restrict imports. These developments created the widespread impression that the U.S. government had lost control of its national trade policy, that, in effect, the country's trade positions were being determined primarily by the initiatives of interest groups.

With the passage of the Trade Act of 1984 and with the added revisions under consideration in 1988, a disinterested onlooker was entitled to ask how much evidence existed to support the widespread U.S. perception that the country's policy still stood for nondiscrimination and lowered trade barriers. At that point, the exceptions seem to have gained an importance equal to the avowed principles. Both the 1984 act and the revisions that were under consideration in 1988 grant new powers to the president to negotiate further lowering of trade barriers. Yet in both the 1984 and the 1988 provisions, aggrieved parties are also offered new powers to curb or reverse the president's actions. The ambiguities created by this double-pronged approach were rendered even more acute by the singular legislative history of the 1988 bill. At the time that this book went to the printer, the 1988 bill had just been blocked by a presidential veto, based on a number of different provisions to which the president objected. But the chances that a bill would be enacted containing most of the schizophrenic provisions of the vetoed bill seemed fairly high. Two lines of policy seemed to coexist, moving in opposite directions.

The Strategic Use of Reciprocity

Without relinquishing these two lines of policy, some politicians were beginning to explore still a third approach to a national trade policy. In essence, this approach would extend the strategy already implicit in Section 301 of the current Trade Act, the provision authorizing the president to retaliate against countries engaging in "unfair" trading practices. Under this approach, the U.S. government would systematically threaten to impose discriminatory tariffs on products from selected countries unless they removed some specific restrictions that the United States regarded as injurious. In 1987, for instance, the Reagan administration retaliated against an EEC ban on meat imports from the United States, threatening to impose punitive duties on an entire list of European food products, ranging from canned ham to licorice extract. At the same time, the White House held out the carrot of a negotiated accord eliminating the proposed bans on both sides.[60] Selected threats, it was argued, could produce a freer trade environment than could be created by multilateral trade negotiations or by trade rules of general application.[61]

This formulation has found easy support from various interests, most of whose objectives have not extended to improving the national welfare. Some, to be sure, have sought to expand into foreign markets. Others, however, have been more interested in maintaining trade protection in the United States and have hoped, therefore, that the American threats would be rejected by the targeted country.

By the latter 1980s, the propensity of the U.S. government to use its economic power in the form of explicit threats was appearing not only in the application of Section 301 of the current Trade Act but also in other aspects of its foreign economic policy. Accordingly, one found the U.S. Export-Import Bank (Ex-Im) much less inhibited in making subsidized loans to U.S. producers facing subsidized foreign sellers. At times, Ex-Im engaged in eyeball-to-eyeball competition with foreign governments over individual sales. Until the early 1980s, international agreements were the principal means by which the U.S. government attempted to hold such subsidization in check. Negotiated under the aegis of the OECD, the agreements sought to place a floor on the interest rates at which governments financed their export sales. Some governments, however, notably including those of France and Japan, were blunting the effects of such agreements by making gifts of foreign aid to the importing countries that they could use to reduce their purchasing costs and the amount of their borrowings, a practice known as mixed-credit loans. The U.S. government, far less effectively organized to combine foreign aid with subsidized loans, found itself for a long time unable to match that practice.

In 1985, the president proposed a special "war chest" fund designed to support up to $1 billion in mixed-credit loans,[62] and Congress obliged with a $300 million appropriation.[63] In addition, the Ex-Im launched a campaign aimed at displacing French suppliers from certain markets in developing countries, claiming that the French firms were benefiting unduly from mixed-credit financing.[64] As part of the new package, the Ex-Im promised large loans to India and Brazil, on condition that they sign new multimillion dollar contracts with designated U.S. firms.[65]

An even more striking variant of the new aggressiveness of U.S. policymakers appeared in two cases occurring in 1986. In one, a U.S. supplier of electric generators encountered competition in the United States from a Brazilian exporter allegedly subsidized by the Brazilian government. In an unprecedented move, the Ex-Im provided subsidized financing to the U.S. producer to enable it to compete within the United States.[66]

The same spirit could be seen in the U.S. Department of Agriculture's new policy of giving U.S. exporters free surplus farm products to enhance their export sales to targeted markets. In that case, the offending competitor was the European Economic Community, notorious for its subsidization of grain exports.[67]

Manifestations of the shift in U.S. policy have also appeared in connection with service industries, such as banking, finance, advertising, and construction. In these fields, the bilateral tit-for-tat approach has not been precedent breaking, having existed for a long time in the assignment of air routes and in various other service areas. The Federal Reserve Bank of New York broke new ground, however, when it extended its list of primary U.S. government bond dealers to include several Japanese firms, accompanying its announcement with the statement that it expected reciprocal concessions from the Japanese government for U.S. firms—and, almost immediately therafter, getting such concessions.[68]

Subsequently, a congressional conference committee voted to prohibit Japanese construction companies from participating in U.S. public works project, a thinly veiled retaliation against Japan's refusal to allow U.S. companies to play any role in the construction of a new airport at Osaka.[69]

In effect, the U.S. government has been rapidly adding another emphasis to its complex mix of international trade policies, an emphasis on bilateralism together with calculated threats to discriminate. Whether such a policy can be expected to produce the desired results of freer trade is an issue of the first importance, one to which we shall return later.

4

The Politics
of Foreign Exchange

BETWEEN MARCH 1985 AND DECEMBER 1987, while tens of billions
of dollars poured back and forth across the U.S. border every day,
the U.S. dollar fell in value by about 35 percent when measured
against the other principal currencies of the world.[1] During those 34
months fortunes were made and lost on changes in the U.S. dollar
rate. The public press attributed a considerable part of that movement in the dollar to the policies and pronouncements of the Reagan
administration. Yet the political response of groups in the United
States affected by the changes was subdued and unfocused, profoundly different from the response that a trade restriction such as a
ten percent tax on imported crude oil might have evoked.

THE POLICY INSTRUMENTS

Whereas trade issues in the United States provoke classic struggles
among interest groups, policies directed at the country's foreign exchange flows have characteristically been settled by tight-lipped bureaucrats and taciturn bankers, rarely generating public scrutiny or
political struggle. To be sure, some U.S. policies that sharply affect
the country's money flows have been the subject of heated debate;
U.S. fiscal policies, for instance, have always been a battleground
for special interest groups. But until the 1980s, the impact of such
policies on the country's foreign money flows was always a periph-

eral issue in these battles, generally regarded as a problem best left to the experts. The reasons for this striking indifference need to be understood, because they help define the future capacity of the United States to engage in international cooperation.

The history of U.S. policies with respect to foreign exchange suggests a number of reasons why these policies thus far have been formulated by processes so startlingly different from those in the area of foreign trade. One is the fact that until the 1980s, very few members of the American public saw any connection between their personal well-being and the flow of money across the U.S. borders; hence the urge to influence such flows was muted. Another reason was that even when such groups were concerned about the size and direction of such flows, as many became in the 1980s, they had considerable difficulty in deciding where their interests lay. Accordingly, special interest groups have been slow to form, and legislators have been slow to take positions on the issues.

In the absence of political pressures, it has been left to the bureaucrats to frame such policies as have existed. The central agency in the policy area—the semi-autonomous Federal Reserve Board—has traditionally held the executive branch at a distance and has exercised its power to alter the country's money supply without input from Congress, the courts, or special interest groups. Another agency with direct responsibility for money flow issues is the Treasury Department, which derives its powers mainly from the operation of currency stabilization funds and its capacity to borrow from foreign governments. Quite apart from their uncertain effects on interest groups, these Treasury operations have been cloaked in a secrecy that Congress has been reluctant to penetrate.

Despite the insulation of these agencies in the exercise of foreign exchange policies, such policies have not been noticeably more coherent or consistent than those in the areas of trade, aid, and investment. To explain this apparent anomaly, we return to some familiar themes: the characteristic reluctance of the executive branch to exercise an active role in the management of the economy and the traditional U.S. aversion to the centralization of power. The careful insulation of monetary policy has meant that the various policies affecting foreign exchange flows are not easily coordinated.

In other countries, some coordination among policies relating to money flows is not out of the question. In the United Kingdom, for instance, the existence of a parliamentary government has somewhat reduced the likelihood that fiscal policies and monetary policies would work at cross purposes; in Germany, the dominance of three or four giant banks and the national tolerance for corporatist processes of consultation has had a similar effect; in Japan, a habit of decision making requiring policymakers to deal with all dissenting elements has also permitted some integration of these different fields. In the United States, the autonomous behavior of the various agencies in a position to affect money flows has remained an abiding characteristic of the system.

THE BRETTON WOODS REGIME

Despite that characteristic, the creation of the Bretton Woods regime under U.S. leadership in 1944 is generally seen as a major innovation, reflecting boldness and vision. The generalization is justified in many respects. In one respect, however, the Bretton Woods innovations were extraordinarily conservative: They permitted the U.S. government to continue in its accustomed ways, without substantially altering its autonomy over monetary matters and without requiring it to depart from its accustomed passivity with regard to foreign exchange.

Until the 1970s, then, the U.S. economy played the role of a passive giant, dominating international money flows but lacking the drive or capacity for consciously directing the flows. Thereafter, however, as the international position of the dollar underwent major changes, the interest of the U.S. government in influencing such flows greatly increased. As usual, the institutions and values of the United States have been much slower in changing.

Setting the Stage

Until 1936, the role of the U.S. government in international monetary affairs had been one of almost total disengagement from the crises of European currencies. In the last decade or two before 1936, Europe had gone through a succession of monetary convulsions. Germany had experienced a searing episode of hyperinflation and economic collapse, an experience that would deeply influence the country's policies for more than half a century after. British policymakers had been forced to accept the shattering realization that the country no longer was capable of maintaining the world's key international currency. France had managed miraculously to develop by far the strongest currency in Europe, humbling the British monetary authorities and casting off the country's dependence on London's capital markets.

Throughout most of this process, the U.S. government had managed to distance itself from the fray. At the time, the governor from the Federal Reserve Bank of New York was a person of outstanding power and prestige, Benjamin Strong. His capacity for innovation and his leadership qualities were so widely recognized that he might well have assumed a major international role, if he had so chosen. But in fact he spent little time or effort on international issues. There were occasional consultations with European counterparts and even on rare occasions some limited attempts at monetary coordination. But overwhelmingly, U.S. monetary policy was based on domestic factors and took little account of international repercussions. Some foreign observers—especially those in Great Britain—saw the U.S. disengagement during the 1920s as self-seeking and malicious, a national policy aimed at undermining the role of sterling to replace it with the dollar.[2] Much more plausible however, is the view that U.S. policies were being determined by indifference, an indifference fostered by its earlier national history and its current domestic goals.

George Washington's admonition against "entangling alliances" with the sovereign powers of Europe was a message to which most Americans were altogether receptive; and it guided U.S. foreign policy for the first century of the country's existence. But, by the closing decade of the nineteenth century, U.S. interests in foreign markets were becoming fairly extensive and interaction with the Europeans more frequent. By that time, U.S. leaders were talking of the "manifest destiny" of the U.S. economy, were demanding not to be shut out of China, and were playing at the colonial game with a trumped-up war against Spain that netted Cuba and the Philippines for the Americans.

Nevertheless, the heart of the country was not yet in the game of international politics, a fact soon underlined by its rejection of the League of Nations. The disposition of the U.S. government was to remain aloof from European economic and monetary concerns after World War I. It was a disposition strongly fortified by the way the U.S. government was organized to deal with monetary matters.

To begin with, until late in the nineteenth century banking credit in the United States was primarily regulated by individual states, without oversight or coordination at the national level; insofar as national policy had any bearing on international monetary affairs, it largely was limited to the question of the type of metallic backing required for money issued by the U.S. government. Accordingly, until the creation of the Federal Reserve system in 1913 with its power over credit formation, the idea of a national policy regarding international monetary relations could not have been entertained seriously; for many decades after the establishment of the system, that state of mind persisted.[3]

Once the Federal Reserve machinery was in place, its governing board was predictably and characteristically set up to act autonomously, detached from the policies of the government's executive branch.[4] The 14-year term of the Board's governors, along with the requirements to include representation on the Board from all corners of the country, was intended to fortify the governors' capacity for independence. The fact that ownership of the system's 12 regional banks rested nominally with the commercial banks of their respective regions was expected to add to the independence of the system from the political structure in Washington.

Until World War I, to be sure, the central banks of most countries in Europe were also private institutions; superficially, therefore, the Federal Reserve pattern at the time of its founding was not strikingly different from that of European central banks. But the implications of private ownership in the United States were substantially different from those in most foreign countries. Although governors of the central banks in other industrial democracies were occasionally found following independent monetary policies in defiance of politicians in temporary control of the government, none emphasized their autonomous rights as strongly and persistently as those making up U.S. Federal Reserve Board.[5]

The American presumption that governments should exercise a limited role in international economic affairs, when coupled with the country's historic aloofness from European politics, was sufficient to block the U.S. government from participating with the leading European countries in their various efforts to expand international economic relations after World War I.[6] Nevertheless, events during and after the first world war were pushing Wall Street increasingly into the role of international banker. During the war, London had been unable to perform its usual role as the world's principal capital market. With the British capital markets operating under wartime restraints, almost the only countries capable of providing a key currency and mobilizing foreign capital were the United States and Switzerland.

To understand why, recall some of the characteristics that served to endow the British pound with its key currency and capital market attributes. One factor was an early start, which was responsible for the creation of institutional structures and the presence of managerial skills in London that for a time were unique. The U.S. economy could not, of course, duplicate that advantage. But when the special circumstances of the war took the United Kingdom out of the running, the adolescent U.S. banking community began to develop new international skills as investment and commercial bankers.

It takes more than institutional skills, however, to create an international money center. What was needed in addition was an expectation in the minds of prospective foreign participants that the value of the currency in which the money center dealt would remain relatively stable and that access to the country's capital markets would be unimpaired. Apart from maintaining a fixed relationship of the dollar to gold, the U.S. government could be counted on to exercise a passive and nonselective role with regard to foreign borrowers and lenders.[7]

On rare occasions, the U.S. government would show small signs of exercising some controls. In 1922, for instance, the State Department requested that it be informed "in due time" of the "essential facts and subsequent developments" of all foreign loans. In practice this request was not enforced, and the government maintained its position of benign indifference.[8] By the 1920s, it was already obvious that the U.S. government, unlike France or Germany or even Great Britain, was not likely to interfere with the choice of borrowers and lenders by its banking community. If the government did decide to regulate capital flows across its borders, the regulations would be general in application. While foreigners might be hurt by U.S. actions that affected U.S. credit and interest rates, the hurt would probably be the consequence of official indifference to the foreign implications of these actions rather than of targeted discrimination.

Accordingly, as European capital markets languished in the 1920s, U.S. capital markets boomed, supported by the heavy participation of foreigners as borrowers and lenders. By the mid-1920s, the United States had emerged as the principal source of new international capital flows.[9] In the latter 1920s the Federal Reserve Board adopted a tight-money policy that proved disastrous to foreigners. True to expectations, however, it was policy taken with an eye to the domestic economy and without apparent regard for international consequences.[10]

Scholars are still debating whether the leading industrial countries could have done much through cooperative measures to mitigate the disastrous economic contraction from 1929 to 1933. In the event, no serious efforts at coordination were attempted during these critical years. Each country was maintaining policies that made borrowing by foreigners extremely difficult: the United Kingdom, primarily in order to protect the shaky value of the pound; the United States, primarily to protect the uncertain solvency of its banks; and France, primarily because it had always limited access by foreigners to capital markets. The consequences were a shrivelling in the supply of funds available to borrowers, defaults on the part of debtors, bankruptcies on the part of lenders, suspension of the convertibility of major currencies, and competitive devaluations.

In retrospect, given the critical conditions of the period, the amount of time it took for the three countries to agree on some limited measure of exchange rate coordination seems remarkable; an agreement did not emerge until 1936. In the meantime, each major country pursued policies reflecting its distinctive history. The United Kingdom, having been forced to suspend the convertibility of sterling in 1931, sought to gather up the remnants of the sterling area into a bloc of countries that would discriminate in trade and payments against the rest of the world under British leadership. The government of France, having savored the independence and power associated with a strong currency in the 1920s, and having managed to retain plentiful quantities of gold throughout most of the depression, clung to its old parity as long as it could, even though the decision meant slowing up the recovery of the French economy. It was not until 1936, after several years of economic stagnation and heavy gold losses, that France decided to devalue the franc. And the U.S. government, fully occupied for the time being with pressing domestic concerns such as restoring the vigor of the economy and the strength of the banking system, pushed away the overtures of other governments for a collective international approach.

When a tripartite monetary agreement was finally reached in 1936, much of the impetus for agreement could be ascribed to the emergence of a common threat, Hitler's Third Reich. Even then, the U.S. and British governments were insistent on avoiding the form of an international commitment, so that the agreement was issued as "three simultaneous statements of willingness to engage in consultations among Treasuries and central banks."[11]

Eventually, the general commitment among the three countries was built into an actual practice of day-to-day consultation over the stabilization of their exchange rates. Even in this context, however, the persistent differences that distinguished the economic behavior of the three countries became evident. The Americans quickly settled on a policy that returned U.S. exchange rate policy to a passive role, in which the bureaucracy had no need to exercise day-to-day discretion. The dollar was pegged to gold at a price of $35 an ounce, and the other countries in the arrangement were left to align their currencies to the dollar. The French bureaucracy, having returned exchange rate policy to the kit of instruments available for use in the management of the economy, used its new tool vigorously in the form of a series of substantial devaluations. The British presided over the management of the pound with policies aimed at holding together what was left of sterling's international position.[12] Some years later, when the Bretton Woods agreements were negotiated, these same characteristic preferences would reemerge.

The System in Operation

The U.S. government's decision to assume leadership of the international financial system by promoting the Bretton Woods regime did not mean that it was prepared to modify its own practices and institutions in the field of monetary policy. U.S. negotiators pushed for international arrangements that would leave untouched the autonomy of the United States in monetary matters. Moreover, they exhibited a persistent reluctance to have governments exercise an active role in the market unless the role was of a mechanistic kind, requiring a minimum of choice and discretion on the part of the bureaucracy. Operating within these constraints, the U.S. government nonetheless took a central position in the new system. It made large dollar loans and dollar gifts, first to the Europeans and then to the developing countries; it contributed heavily to the resources of the IMF and various regional banks; and it allowed the dollar to be used as the reserve currency for the world.

Even though the new Bretton Woods institutions were established along lines requiring little change in the institutions or habits of the U.S. government, U.S. policymakers had to play a strong innovative role in bringing them into existence. Most of the innovations could be traced to the work of a small number of key officials, drawn mainly from the Treasury Department and operating under the leadership of Under Secretary Harry Dexter White.[13]

An amibitious and aggressive man, White had travelled from an obscure academic post to the top echelons of government service in only a few short years. He was devoted to the idea of creating an open, expansive world economy that would be consistent with the social and economic goals of the New Deal,[14] but he was not prepared to surrender the right of the United States to act autonomously in monetary matters.

With substantial assistance from the British delegation—particularly from Lord Keynes himself—the U.S. negotiators at Bretton Woods succeeded in producing an agreement for postwar collaboration that encompassed many of White's ideas. The system emerging from the Bretton Woods negotiations rested on the creation of several rather radical international institutions. Each of these was equipped with powers to borrow and to lend in a form and on a scale not previously encountered in international bodies. The discretionary powers granted to the organizations in the processing and conditioning of their respective loans were without precedent. Even the governing provisions were novel: The voting formulas of the governing boards of each institution were based on a system of weights intended to give the participants a voice commensurate with their contributions.

Despite their innovative role, the U.S. team seemed acutely aware of the dangers in agreeing to an arrangement that might threaten U.S. autonomy in monetary matters or demand any significant alteration in the traditional structure of checks and balances operating inside the U.S. system. Thus, the original voting formulas were carefully designed to ensure that the U.S. government could exercise a veto over any significant policy adopted by the governors of the Bretton Woods institutions. And the original capital contributions and subsequent capital replenishments were not exempted from the usual congressional process of authorization and appropriation.

Moreover, U.S. negotiators at the time had no reason to expect that the extensive powers vested in the International Monetary Fund and the World Bank would ever be exercised against a reluctant United States. Those organizations, as they saw it, were intended to help the economies of other countries develop along lines consistent with U.S. policies. Even before the Bretton Woods institutions were created, American policymakers had accepted the fact that Europe would need large infusions of capital for reconstruction, a task to which the World Bank was expected to contribute. These policymakers also were realists enough to realize that for at least a limited period after the war's end the United States could not avoid widespread discrimination against the dollar by countries in balance-of-payments difficulties, a step that the IMF was empowered to authorize. For all the rest, the powers of the World Bank and the IMF seemed directed at holding borrowers, not lenders, in line.

Although U.S. representatives expected the provisions of the IMF to have little effect on the U.S. government's way of doing business, it was evident from the first that many other countries were likely to be deeply affected by the new regime. The IMF's articles anticipated that governments would fix the value of their national currency to gold, with large changes in value requiring the approval of other member countries; they laid down the principle that countries would not restrict payments for goods and services except when in balance-of-payments difficulties; and they made provision for countries in such difficulties to have access to medium-term loans out of a pool of currencies provided by the IMF's member countries. Although in theory these provisions applied to all countries including the United States, it seemed nearly inconceivable at the time that the U.S. government might have to seek IMF approval in the future for a major devaluation of the dollar, or that it might be called upon to justify restrictions on payments for the purchase of foreign goods or services.

To be sure, during the 1950s, the Bank for International Settlements was holding its periodic meetings in Basel, providing a meeting ground in which the heads of the world's leading central banks could discretely commiserate over the shortcomings of their respective governments. U.S. government representatives were also prominent participants in periodic monetary discussions conducted under the aegis of the Paris-based Organization for European Economic Cooperation, the Marshall Plan's lead organization. The institution was converted into the Organization for Economic Cooperation and Development in 1961, and U.S. representatives continued to participate. However, they came from the U.S. executive branch—principally the Treasury, the State Department, and the White House staff—and were in no position to speak either for the Federal Reserve Board or for Congress, where the principal decisions relating to monetary and fiscal conditions in the United States were made. The role of U.S. representatives in international meetings, therefore, was largely to explain, to observe, and to report, but not to commit the United States to any new lines of policy.

In substance, the Bretton Woods accord created a system in which the supply of international money depended heavily on U.S. actions in the monetary and fiscal fields. U.S. policymakers continued to frame these actions with only the barest regard for their international consequences as was the case before World War II. As other governments dismantled the foreign exchange licensing systems they had maintained in the immediate postwar years, and as international trade and international capital movements grew in volume, the exposure of other countries to changes in U.S. monetary conditions increased.

Some implications of that exposure began to be apparent during the latter 1950s, when the world's perceptions of the U.S. dollar's strength took an abrupt turn. During most of the 1950s, the U.S. economy had been selling more goods and services to foreigners than it was buying. But a steady flow of private capital to foreign countries, augmented by loans and gifts to foreign governments and by military expenditures in Europe, was beginning to weaken the U.S. balance of payments.

Abruptly, the world's perception of the dollar shifted from that of a scarce currency to one in too easy supply. In the 1960s, as Table 4-1 indicates, the position of the U.S. dollar weakened further, the result of the government's efforts to finance the Vietnam war and the Great Society programs by deficit spending and public borrowing. These dollars, which were produced without much regard for the dollar's role as an international currency, were being acquired by foreigners in increasing amounts.

With the shift in the prospects of the dollar, the monetary history of the 1920s virtually repeated itself. In that era, Great Britain had struggled to maintain the price of sterling at $4.86. Eventually, the French government refused to hold any added amounts of the sterling that its central bank was acquiring and demanded, instead, that the Bank of England redeem some of the French government's sterling holdings for gold. In the 1960s, as dollars piled up in the Bank of France, the French government again instituted a policy of redeeming some of its foreign exchange holdings for gold. The rationale for France's demands in the 1960s was almost identical to its rationale in the 1920s: Governments whose currencies were accepted by the world as international money—sterling in the 1920s, dollars in the 1960s—were not entitled to abuse their privileged position by generating unlimited quantities of the currencies, especially when their nationals used such added money to buy up assets in other countries.

Table 4-1   **Performance Measures of U.S. Balance of Payments, 1955-1969 (in billions of U.S. dollars)**

Year	Current Account Balance	Basic Balance[a]	Merchandise Balance	Official Reserve Assets
1955	+4.2	—	+2.9	22.8
1956	+6.5	—	+4.8	23.7
1957	+7.8	—	+6.3	24.8
1958	+5.0	—	+3.5	22.5
1959	+2.5	—	+1.1	21.5
1960	+5.8	+2.8	+4.9	19.4
1961	+6.3	+3.2	+5.6	18.8
1962	+5.2	+1.7	+4.6	17.2
1963	+6.2	+1.6	+5.2	16.8
1964	+7.8	+2.0	+6.8	16.7
1965	+6.0	−0.1	+4.9	15.4
1966	+4.8	+0.7	+3.8	14.8
1967	+4.7	−0.6	+3.8	15.7
1968	+1.4	+0.4	+0.6	17.0
1969	+1.9	−0.1	+0.6	14.5

[a] Current account balance plus net outflows of long-term capital.
SOURCE: *Economic Report of the President, 1973* (Washington, DC: United States Government Printing Office).

As the menacing thunderheads piled up during the 1960s, U.S. monetary and fiscal policies appeared on the surface to be quite unaffected by the international dimension. Here and there, one saw signs of some concern in the public press and in congressional hearings. But for the most part, U.S. public opinion and U.S. official policy seemed almost indifferent to the approach of an international crisis.

Within the highest levels of the executive branch, however, U.S. officials observed the international monetary developments with the deepest concern, sometimes ruefully acknowledging the validity of the French government's position. As usual, there was no lack of ideas for responding to the situation. One of them called on the administration to introduce some mild constraints on the flow of direct investment to foreign countries. When it was eventually adopted, that maneuver appeared to have little actual effect on the flow of direct investment out of the U.S. Another idea was to devalue the dollar, a proposal that met with the strongest opposition from government officials who feared the implications of devaluation for both the political and economic strength of the United States. Instead, these officials favored decoupling the U.S. dollar from its remaining ties to gold and introducing a new key international currency. The implementation of this idea exemplifies several characteristic aspects of the foreign economic policy-making process in the United States.

The Special Drawing Right

The implications of creating a new international instrument to take over some of the dollar's key currency functions ran very deep. Apart from its effects on the U.S. balance of payments, such an instrument could alter the competitive position of the U.S. financial community, reducing its advantages as the principal source of U.S. dollars. Moreover, the United States might no longer be able to finance its deficits by expanding the supply of dollars; instead, it might have to cover future deficits by drawing on its reserves or by borrowing from abroad.

Despite the basic importance of the problem and the need to find a correct solution, the public at large and the relevant congressional committees were very slow in showing interest. Among academic economists, on the other hand, the issues were already very much alive by the late 1950s. By that time, some economists had begun to realize that the dollar's role as a key currency entailed costs as well as benefits for the U.S. economy. Although the benefits were obvious, the costs needed spelling out.

For one thing, a country with a key currency risked world censure if it used some of the tools of monetary policy that were ordinarily available to other governments. Those tools included, for instance, changing the value of the currency and limiting the access of foreigners to the country's capital markets. Although U.S. monetary policy took little explicit account of the U.S. dollar's international function, U.S. officials in the executive branch understood very well that any use of certain monetary tools by the United States would have profound implications for the world monetary system.

Besides, many U.S. economists had come to believe that no national currency, including the U.S. dollar, could play the role of key currency for very long without being displaced. Any currency that played such a role, they assumed, would have to be maintained by its government at some fixed value in relation to gold. On that assumption, they concluded that the national authorities responsible for maintaining the currency's value would eventually confront a dilemma—the so-called Triffin dilemma, named after the economist credited with having formulated it.[15]

According to Triffin, if a key currency is to function as international money during a period when international transactions are expanding, the working balances in foreign hands have to grow as well. But such balances can grow only if the country issuing the currency has a persistent deficit on current account, continuously exports capital for investment, or both. Hence Triffin's dilemma: As those conditions are actually realized, the reserve position of the leading country must deteriorate, forcing foreigners eventually to mistrust the value of the currency they have been holding as working balances. That mistrust will lead foreigners to draw down their working balances in the key currency, a tendency that will drain gold and foreign exchange from the key currency country, further undermining the currency's value.

In 1963, worries such as these led President Kennedy to announce to the IMF Board of Governors that the U.S. government stood ready to support any measures necessary to increase international liquidity. For the next five years, various working groups within the international financial community debated the need for and the possible shapes of a new reserve asset. During the debate, the historical conditioning that influenced the attitudes of the various governments was strikingly in evidence. The Germans, as usual, were acutely uneasy over the creation of a new source of money, unless at the same time they could exercise the tightest possible control over the supply. The French were torn: On the one hand, they were reluctant to see gold lose its position as the world's preferred medium of exchange; on the other, they were pleased at the prospect of an instrument that might one day displace the dollar as the leading international currency. The British, repeating Keynes's choice at Bretton Woods, were ready to accept the promise of added balance-of-payment support implied by the U.S. proposal, especially if the new instrument was administered under tight controls in which the United Kingdom could play a dominant role. And the developing countries insisted that any new instrument should be issued first in the form of grants to them alone, rather than as allocations to all members of the IMF.

The debate was inconclusive until a small group of officials in the U.S. government decided to throw their weight behind a specific set of proposals. These officials included Secretary of Treasury Henry ("Joe") Fowler, an outsider who refused to be captured by the traditional caution of his agency, as well as a presidential assistant, Francis M. Bator, who bore impeccable credentials as a skilled economist.

Both Fowler and Bator were among the U.S. leaders who were particularly sensitive to the potential consequences of unilateral actions by the United States for its allies and thus tended to favor multilateral negotiations. Both were firm adherents of the Triffin school, convinced that as long as the U.S. dollar played the role of key currency, the U.S. balance of payments was bound to suffer. Since the early 1960s, both men had been speaking out in favor of a major international liquidity reform.[16]

Once invested in his office as secretary of the treasury in 1965, Fowler used his position to spearhead an international move that would both separate the world's principal currencies from their link to gold and create a new international currency through the IMF. The early stages of the negotiations took place among the so-called Group of Ten, a core of mature industrialized countries representing the world's principal currencies. Accepting the idea of a new currency in principle, the group insisted that they alone be the guardians of any such currency. By 1966, however, Pierre-Paul Schweitzer, managing director of the IMF, had garnered support for a worldwide arrangement that would operate through the IMF and include all IMF members.

As usual, it took a crisis to launch the scheme. In 1968, new signs of weakness in the dollar led speculators to increase their sales of dollars and to buy gold in the open market. To counter these moves, the U.S. government managed to extract an equivocal commitment from six other members of the Group of Ten (France being conspicuously absent) not to tender their official holdings of dollars to the United States for gold and not to trade in gold in the private market: The effect was to weaken the link between gold and national currencies drastically.

Shortly thereafter, the IMF began implementing Fowler's proposal for a new currency, the so-called Special Drawing Rights, or SDRs. These SDRs, it was thought, might eventually shoulder some of the key currency functions then being performed by the dollar. The official proposals for the creation of a new international currency, strikingly reminiscent of Keynes's proposal at Bretton Woods, called for the IMF to create the new instrument out of thin air, with a value derived as a weighted average of the principal currencies of the Fund. Each IMF member would be entitled to draw upon the new instrument up to specified amounts, such amounts being determined by the member's quota in the Fund.

A new instrument of this sort could have major advantages for the United States. In the short run, it could provide the U.S. government with a new source of foreign exchange and so relieve the pressure on the dollar; in the long run, it might save the U.S. dollar from the threatening horns of Triffin's dilemma. To be sure, the new instrument might also imperil the earnings of U.S. financial intermediaries by creating a rival to the U.S. dollar in international markets, but in the late 1960s, the financial community had not yet mobilized in opposition. Meanwhile, the U.S. executive had the unquestioned right to propose such an initiative for international discussion.

In the short run, the initiative was a striking success. Once again, however, there was a demonstration of the fact that U.S. representatives might readily launch new initiatives for international considerations, but it was much more difficult for the U.S. government to follow a steady course in the pursuit of those initiatives. With the departure of President Johnson and the inauguration of President Nixon in 1969, the top-level policy agenda was turned primarily to domestic politics and security issues, leaving international economic initiatives to simmer on the back burner. Throughout its tenure, the Nixon administration was content to leave international economic issues in the hands of other governments, playing an active role only when domestic concerns assumed crisis proportions.

By 1971, such a crisis had arisen. With swelling balance-of-payments deficits and rampant domestic inflation, it became obvious that the U.S. economy was in disequilibrium. In an abrupt step, the president unilaterally suspended the convertibility of the dollar and took various other emergency measures, which we shall explore shortly. Faced with rapidly fluctuating exchange rates and an enigmatic U.S. administration, the IMF's other members grew increasingly uncertain about the dollar's capacity to serve as the world's key currency. In that context, the countries agreed to inject a new shot of life into the SDR proposal, expecting to transform SDRs eventually into the primary reserve asset of a reformed monetary system. During the period from 1972 to 1978, the IMF took steps to ensure the SDR's position as a reserve asset. These measures included using the SDR as a unit of account in the Fund's own transactions; raising the interest rate paid on SDRs; agreeing to allocate $4 billion worth of SDRs in each of the three years, 1979, 1980, and 1981; and raising the total allocation of SDRs from 9.3 billion to 21.3 billion units, the equivalent of $15 billion U.S. dollars.[17]

Despite these expanded allocations, the SDR has played only a minor role as an international currency. The possibility of expanding its role has been placed on the international agenda from time to time, notably when U.S. officials or academics have sensed disadvantages in the dollar's continued role as key currency. In 1978, for instance, a swift fall in the value of the dollar briefly revived discussions of an expanded role for the SDR.[18] At that time, U.S. officials worried about the risk that foreigners might try to reduce their dollar working balances, pushing the dollar down even further and accelerating the inflationary trend already evident in the country.

Meanwhile, the conflicting interests of U.S. bankers and other financial intermediaries have been sitting unresolved in the background. Most would see themselves losing if the paramount position of the U.S. dollar were challenged, a fact that has probably inhibited U.S. officials from pushing harder on the SDR. In the absence of acute crisis, the SDR issue is likely to rest in limbo, awaiting the day when new crisis with respect to the dollar prompts some entrepreneurial U.S. official to place the issue on the president's desk once more.

ENDING THE BRETTON WOODS REGIME

In 1971, the U.S. government unilaterally abandoned its commitment to redeem U.S. dollars for gold, leaving it to the open market to determine the value of the dollar in relation to other currencies. That action effectively ended a central feature of the Bretton Woods system, namely, the commitment of governments to maintain a fixed exchange rate in relation to gold. Governments could continue to link their national currencies to that of another country in some fixed relationship if they chose. Indeed many smaller countries have followed that practice. To maintain such a linkage, the countries concerned must acquire and hold the linked currency in the amounts needed to maintain the fixed relationship, even though the currency itself is no longer tied to gold.

The decision of the president to break the dollar's link to gold was not quite a bolt from the blue; a number of academic economists had been urging that action for some years before. Some were supporting the step as a second-best U.S. policy, having reluctantly con-cluded that the U.S. government could not maintain its commitment to gold convertibility. Others were urging the step as a first-best eco-nomic policy, contending that an exchange rate freely determined in the market would generate a superior economic performance for the economy. Eventually, well before the president took the momentous step, even a few important bankers had been converted to the new orthodoxy.[19]

Nevertheless, from the president's point of view the decision to suspend convertibility was a tactical decision, a response to crisis rather than a consequence of deliberations over a long-term strategy. Speaking in military analogies, the Cuban missile crisis would be more apposite than the Strategic Defense Initiative.

The president's decision to suspend convertibility has been the subject of some unusually extensive research, which has produced revealing glimpses of the principal actors and the processes of deci-sion-making.[20] The president's approach, it is clear, was unencum-bered by any strong convictions regarding the preferred shape of international monetary relations; indeed, the president had no real interest in the subject except as it related directly to his domestic political position. Before taking a position on the convertibility is-sue, the president had been exposed to a variety of briefings on the state of the dollar and its prospects, ranging from the view that it would all come right of its own accord, to the one that the dollar was on a slippery slide. Of the various rival views, he seemed per-suaded that America's monetary troubles were due in considerable part to unfair treatment at the hands of the European Community's members and Japan. Therefore, one of the principal objectives guid-ing his strategy was to alter that treatment.

With such a mindset, it was not surprising that the president should have ignored his cabinet-level Council on International Eco-nomic Policy and delegated the principal policy-making role in the crisis to his new secretary of the treasury, John Connally. Connally's performance thereafter was one that would have been hard to picture in the government of any other advanced industrialized country, such as the United Kingdom, France, Germany, or Japan.

Connally, a successful businessman and politician and a former governor of Texas, was a tyro in monetary affairs. Asked by a skepti-cal observer about his qualifications to serve as secretary of the trea-sury, he once replied, "I can add."

From a technical point of view, Connally was perhaps least qualified among the high-level officials in the administration concerned with foreign economic policy-making. Within the administration, he was admired as a quick learner and a tough negotiator, but his abilities as treasury secretary, as one associate noted, "did not come from profound knowledge, great study, or strong convictions."[21] Moreover, unlike Fowler and Bator, Connally had little interest in the international ramifications of U.S. actions. Such matters as the international consequences of floating exchange rates, for instance, simply did not concern him.

Instead, like the president, he seemed to believe firmly that the troubles facing the United States were the result of other countries' unfair practices, including Europe's restrictive policies on the imports of agricultural products and Japan's restrictive approach to foreign direct investment.[22] He seemed temperamentally resistant to trying to work with other countries. At the same time, lacking any close ties to the international financial community in New York, Connally had no strong attachment to the idea that the dollar must retain its position as the key international currency nor any strong rapport with the central bankers and financial leaders of foreign countries.

As U.S. reserves continued to leak away through the first half of 1971, Connally prepared a package of unilateral measures aimed at improving the U.S. balance of payments. Other leading figures in the government had an opportunity to criticize Connally's proposals, an opportunity that some of them exercised in meetings with the president, albeit with considerable restraint. The president, reflecting once again the power of the office to take major initiatives on such matters, chose to override those objections.

On August 15, 1971, the U.S. government announced that it was closing the gold window, imposing a 10 percent "additional tax" on imports, and taking various measures to stimulate U.S. production and hold down U.S. inflation, including a 90-day freeze on wages and prices. By closing the gold window, the U.S. government put the world on notice that the value of the dollar would be determined in the foreign exchange markets of the world, which presumably would push down the value of the dollar in relation to the yen and the deutschemark. Inasmuch as these measures were intended partly as tactical opening salvos in a struggle to alter the behavior of other governments, it was not clear how long the U.S. government would keep them in force. In any event, scarcely any complaints were heard from U.S. interest groups.

Other countries reacted in a variety of ways to the U.S. initiative, usually along lines predictable from history. France, for instance, was willing to accept a change in the relation of the dollar to the franc but adamant in refusing to achieve that result by increasing the franc's value in relation to gold. The French were insistent that any change in the dollar's value should come about through devaluation of the dollar, a step that they perceived as much more humbling for the United States than breaking the dollar's link to gold. Meanwhile, France was prepared to cope with the chaos a floating dollar would create by introducing a complex regulatory regime, one that would have the Europeans maintaining a set of fixed rates for trade among themselves and a floating rate for capital transactions.[23] That approach, if it worked, would limit the handicap that European exporters otherwise might suffer from the appreciation of their currencies in relation to the dollar. But Germany predictably resisted so *dirigiste* a proposal, and Europe for a time was deadlocked.

Japan, meanwhile, attempted to pretend for a few weeks that the dollar was not depreciating on world markets while it sought through frenetic internal consultations to decide how to respond. As the internal debates were going on, the Bank of Japan was obliged to buy billions of unwanted U.S. dollars in an effort to keep the yen–dollar rate from falling. After a few weeks, the Bank of Japan reluctantly allowed the yen–dollar rate to fall below its legal ceiling, although it continued to purchase dollars in an effort to dampen this fall.[24]

In the months that followed, while Connally showed little interest in reaching an agreement with the Europeans and the Japanese, other U.S. officials—notably including the chairman of the Federal Reserve Bank, Arthur Burns—felt no restraint about making contacts with their foreign counterparts.[25] In effect, the diplomacy of U.S. economic policy was being conducted as usual by a number of different principals. By mid-1971, partly as a result of these backstairs contacts, U.S. officials were openly negotiating with the Europeans on a new set of exchange rates that would encompass a significant devaluation of the dollar as well as a substantial appreciation of the deutschemark in relation to other currencies. By that time, too, Japan had agreed to new restrictions on its textile exports, and Europe to new restrictions on its steel exports. One might have concluded that the Bretton Woods system, though badly mauled, was still intact.

Although agreement was soon reached on a new set of exchange rates, there was less to the agreement than met the eye. The United

States devalued the U.S. dollar by announcing a new value of $38 per ounce of gold to replace the former $35 figure, but it did not agree to open the gold window. Nor was the U.S. government prepared to intervene in the foreign exchange market in order to maintain a set of exchange rates consistent with its new parity; that task was left to the central banks of other countries. In short, the new U.S. agreement did not represent a long-term commitment to a new policy; its principal effect was to return the U.S. government to its preferred position as a passive participant, leaving the task of exchange rate stabilization to other governments.

Characteristically, within five months after Connally had completed the December 1971 agreement, he stepped down from his office as treasury secretary, relinquishing it to a new officeholder and a new policy. The new incumbent was George Shultz, a professional economist who was influenced by profoundly different values from Connally. Like many other economists, he had come to the view that the market should be allowed to determine the value of the dollar, and he was eager to have other governments acquiesce in such a regime.

The available record does not tell us exactly how Shultz obtained the president's consent to launch still another initiative on exchange rates. But this was a period in the Nixon administration when a trusted cabinet officer could sometimes secure the approval of the president without necessarily capturing his ear. The question of the dollar exchange rate was no longer one of high political importance, either at home or abroad, and was no longer capable of commanding much sustained attention from President Nixon. Besides, by 1973, the Watergate affair was beginning to build. Experienced and self-assured, promoting a policy that had achieved considerable orthodoxy among economists and bankers, Shultz apparently had no difficulty in gaining approval for the launching of one more initiative.

As an initial step toward allowing the market to determine the dollar's value, Shultz in February 1973 proposed to some of the Group of Ten countries that they accept a second devaluation of the dollar or move to an open international float. After extended negotiations, the other nations agreed to a further devaluation.

The agreement proved short-lived, however. In only 18 days, the market was pushing the dollar below its new value. At that stage, the U.S. government refused to intervene further. True to a long-standing U.S. preference for nonintervention and passivity, Shultz argued that the U.S. government could no longer afford halfway measures

and that a floating exchange regime was superior to periodic interventions in the international financial market. In early March, the
U.S. government and 13 other countries signed a communique whose
language offered clear hints that the commitment of governments to
fixed exchange rates had ended. A few weeks later, 14 states met in
Paris and ratified what West German Finance Minister Helmut
Schmidt called "the end of Bretton Woods."[26]

AFTER THE BRETTON WOODS REGIME

Exchange Rate Relationships

With the end of a regime of fixed exchange rates, the environment
relating to international monetary issues changed dramatically. Some
changes, such as the appearance of a chronic instability in exchange
rates, were directly associated with the end of the fixed rate regime.
Others, including the sharp increases in the price of oil in 1973–1974
and 1978–1979, were independent elements among the forces producing monetary change.

Some of the environmental changes were altogether compatible
with the preferences of U.S. policymakers. For one thing, once fixed
exchange rates were abandoned, governments no longer were obliged
to accept responsibility for intervening in the market to maintain a
given price for their currencies. As a result, the U.S. government was
back to a system in which it could choose to exercise a passive role.
To be sure, for national economies in which international trade and
capital movements played a very large role, the prospect of marked
instability in the exchange rate was profoundly disconcerting. Most
governments were unwilling to leave their exchange rates to the
vagaries of the open market and sought to institute some measure of
stability in their exchange rate relationships. In 1985, for instance,
32 nations still anchored their exchange rates to the U.S. dollar; 18
others linked their rates to the pound, the franc, or other national
currencies; and 43 tied themselves to the value of the IMF's SDRs
or to some other composite basket of major currencies.[27]

Still, after 1971, the dollar underwent substantial changes from
time to time in relation to other important currencies, including the
yen, the deutschemark, the French franc, and the British pound. The
French, always eager to free themselves from the influences of the
U.S. dollar, began casting about for new ways of insulating their

economy. The Germans, always concerned with the threat of inflation created by unstable currency relationships, shared some of the
French concerns.

As early as the 1960s, the Europeans had been experimenting with
various arrangements aimed at protecting themselves from the dollar's threatened instability, developing agreements that were reminiscent in many ways of those first developed under the stimulus of
the Marshall Plan. Of these arrangements, the European Monetary
System, which was established in 1979, is the latest, most elaborate,
and most durable.

Like its predecessors, the European Monetary System contained
provisions linking the values of the main European currencies more
closely to one another than to the dollar. It included arrangements
among the member countries for exchanging lines of credit in order
to increase their ability to maintain the promised links. And it incorporated procedures for consultation over national policies and for
the coordination of policies necessary to support the objective of
increased exchange rate stability. As usual, the British showed some
hesitation in accepting a total embrace from their European neighbors; the U.K. authorities agreed to participate in exchanging lines
of credit but refused to commit themselves to hold the pound's value
within limits.

Meanwhile, although the U.S. dollar was floating, it remained the
world's leading international currency. Despite occasional revivals of
the discussion to enlarge the role of SDRs, the worries of the U.S.
financial community over the loss of its private seignorial rights and
the worries of Germany over the inflationary implications of a new
money source were enough to put a damper on such possibilities.
Even in 1972, over half of the foreign exchange reserves of the
world's governments were denominated in dollars.[28]

Accordingly, when the principal oil exporters began to pile up foreign exchange reserves in 1973, they found themselves obliged, *faute
de mieux*, to invest most of those reserves in dollar instruments. Notwithstanding the appearance of deficits in the current accounts of
the United States, it was not until 1977 that the dollar began to show
much weakness relative to other currencies. That weakness lasted
only a few years, to be followed by a period of extraordinary
strength from 1980 to 1984, then by marked weakness again. As this
book went to press, the end of the period of weakness was not in
sight.

Among the experts, the profound significance for the U.S. economy of living with a floating dollar was obvious from the first. For a wider circle of policymakers, however, and for the public at large that realization would come much more slowly. It was not until the latter half of the 1980s that the public media began to link domestic monetary and fiscal events with the dollar's gyrations. During the intervening years, to be sure, the Federal Reserve Board could occasionally be observed leaning into the wind, that is, taking measures aimed in part at mitigating exchange rate movements. But by and large, to the extent that U.S. policies were responsible for the creation of the exchange rate movements, they were policies taken primarily with domestic objectives in mind—such as stimulation of domestic activity or avoidance of inflationary pressures in the economy.

There were small flurries in the decade between the first oil crisis and 1984 that illustrated again the capacity of a small cadre of highly placed officials in the U.S. government, once having captured the attention of the president, to launch a new international initiative. The roster of high-level economic policymakers in the Carter administration included men particularly well suited to such initiatives. In that administration, the links between economic policymakers in the State and Treasury Departments were by chance remarkably felicitous; Under Secretary of State for Economic Affairs Richard N. Cooper and Under Secretary for Monetary Affairs at the Treasury Department Anthony M. Solomon were longtime friends who, a decade earlier, had worked together harmoniously on international economic policies at high levels in the State Department. In addition, the under secretary of state's contacts with President Carter dated back to the era when Carter, while governor of Georgia, had been a member of the Tripartite Commission, a prestigious group of private citizens from Japan, Europe, and North America concerned with international economic issues. The strategic positions and prior connections of these two officials did not exempt them from having to steer their proposals through the usual network of interagency committees; but their starting advantages weighed heavily in ensuring a favorable outcome.

Not surprisingly, then, the Carter presidency claimed responsibility for launching two rather daring economic initiatives which, if implemented, would have signalled significant departures from the habitual policies of the United States.

The first of the initiatives had its origins in the so-called economic summit at London in 1977, when Carter advocated to representatives of the other six attending countries an integrated strategy aimed at producing widespread economic expansion. The U.S. team urged Germany and Japan in particular to boost their national growth rates in the hope that such growth would spill over into other economies via the international monetary system.[29] Initially, Germany and Japan balked, and the initiative failed. In 1978, however, the U.S. plan reappeared at the Bonn Summit and was transformed into an unprecedented accord between the major industrial powers.[30] Under the agreement, the United States, in exchange for German and Japanese expansion, promised to reduce its oil imports and to hold down domestic inflation. In reality, none of the heads of government present at the meeting had the unqualified power to deliver on the commitments; no U.S. president, for instance, could deliver on a promise to reduce oil imports. But as an indication of intent to coordinate disparate national policies, the agreement broke new ground.

Even before the Bonn agreement was reached, the U.S. government and three of four other governments had started to collaborate closely in their interventions in foreign exchange markets. Following closely on the Bonn meetings, the key economic officials in the Carter administration proposed a joint effort with Japan, Germany, and Switzerland to slow the continuing decline in the value of the dollar, an effort that would include a forced hike in U.S. interest rates. After some hesitation, Carter accepted his economists' plan.[31]

Any large-scale program of intervention was out of character for the U.S. government, however, and this one proved predictably short-lived. U.S. resources available for exchange rate intervention were quite small. And although the U.S. president could demand that others alter their monetary and fiscal policies, his ability to meet similar demands from them was greatly limited. As usual, the Federal Reserve Board was determining the country's monetary policies, while its fiscal policies were the outcome of protracted struggles between the president and Congress over taxes and expenditures. In any case, with the inauguration of President Reagan in 1981, there was an abrupt suspension of cooperative monetary measures with other countries and of governmental interventions in the markets for foreign exchange. Thereupon, for a two- or three-year period, the U.S. government turned back to a slightly exaggerated version of business as usual.

The determination of the U.S. government to suspend its cooperative programs with the leading countries did nothing, of course, to change the underlying facts. The U.S. exchange rate was rapidly becoming a major factor in the performance of the U.S. economy. The exchange rate was affected not only by the policies of the U.S. government but also by those of other governments. Any administration that felt accountable for the performance of the national economy could not fail to concern itself with movements in the value of the dollar. The increasing futility of trying to deal with that problem by unilateral measures was being demonstrated by a general weakening in the power of governments to control international money flows.

The Weakening of Jurisdiction

With radical improvements in international communication, the channels for moving money across international borders were proliferating, and the flow of money through such channels was growing at phenomenal rates. These greatly enlarged flows meant, of course, that any government whose policies were inadvertently inflating or deflating its national economy could usually count on having some of these effects dissipated through the international money flows they generated. Thus, the fiscal deficits of the United States in the 1980s, by raising U.S. interest rates, sucked in Japanese funds; and the availability of these funds helped hold down these rates. At the same time, any government deliberately attempting to inflate or deflate its economy would find the effects of its measures more rapidly diffused by leaks across its borders into other economies. Moreover, all governments would be vulnerable to the autonomous measures of other economies.

Adding to the difficulties of national policymakers, vastly augmented money flows were occurring between affiliated units—between parent banks and their branches, between the affiliates or manufacturing enterprises, between members of banking and service syndicates, and so on. When money flows were internalized in this way, the capacity of government regulators to control them was greatly complicated; only deeply intrusive measures could be expected to work. Those who managed such internalized money flows—for example, treasurers of a multinational enterprise—usually had much more flexibility in moving money than did independent parties. Besides, governments were usually hesitant to impose regulations on enterprises headquartered in their home territory that might handicap them in their competition with firms from other countries.

As a result, the measures taken by the U.S. government to prevent the outflow of dollars usually proved too feeble to be effective. In some cases, special interests could eventually exert pressures for modifying the program where it pinched. In other cases, affected parties could avoid the effects of the program altogether by drawing on alternative channels for acquiring dollars. For instance, efforts to avoid U.S. regulations contributed in considerable part to the development of the various new money markets in Europe, notably the Eurodollar, Euromark, and Euroyen markets.

The Eurodollar first arose as a direct consequence of cold-war tensions. In the aftermath of the Hungarian uprising of 1956, Soviet authorities feared that their U.S. currency holdings might be blocked by the U.S. authorities. To protect their funds, the Soviet agencies transferred their dollar bank deposits to a London merchant bank, accepting an obligation from the London bank to redeem their funds in dollars at a later date. This transfer created a new money instrument—Eurodollars—dollars that could be lent and repaid outside the U.S. banking system and beyond the easy reach of U.S. monetary authorities.[32]

The supply of Eurodollars grew quickly, augmented by depositors who were trying to avoid still another restriction that U.S. authorities were attempting to impose, namely, a ceiling on the interest rates that banks located in the United States could pay on time deposits. That ceiling had been imposed by the Federal Reserve Board under its Regulation Q, because of fear that the banks might otherwise compete recklessly for deposits and thereby jeopardize their solvency. If the restraints had been applied to the foreign branches of U.S. banks, however, the banks would have been handicapped in their competition abroad. Accordingly, the foreign branches and subsidiaries of the U.S. banks were left free to accept dollar deposits without restriction, thereby encouraging the creation of another source of Eurodollars.

Still a third restraint contributing to the acceptance of dollar deposits by banks outside the United States were the reserve requirements imposed by the Federal Reserve Board. Whereas banks in the United States had to maintain reserve accounts with the Federal Reserve banks, representing some stated fraction of their deposits accepted in the United States, no such provision applied to deposits of U.S. dollars that branches of these same banks accepted in foreign locations.

Once the Eurodollar market came into existence, it proved to have a variety of other virtues for savers and lenders. For instance, some depositors concluded that dollars deposited in Swiss banks were less likely to be known to their home governments than dollars deposited in U.S. banks, and interest earned on such deposits was less likely to be subjected to national taxation. Eventually, success generated success; the market for short-term dollar loans and deposits became so large and so liquid that it rivaled any competitive facility available in the United States. For large investors, especially those whose deposits were so large that they could get little protection from the U.S. bank deposit insurance system, the Eurodollar's high liquidity and marginally higher yields have proved to be irresistible attractions.

The situation posed by the growth of the Eurodollar market has no real precedent in the history of international money. Its operations have been intimately linked to the U.S. economy in numerous ways, yet have remained beyond the direct control of U.S. financial authorities. The existence of the Eurodollar market has been critical in ensuring the continuance of the U.S. dollar as the world's key currency. Its capacity for mobilizing dollars and making loans has substantially affected the liquidity and solvency of the U.S. banking system and the supply of U.S. credit. For there is nothing to prevent a U.S. investor, including a U.S. bank, from investing in Eurodollar instruments rather than in dollar instruments at home; and nothing to prevent a U.S. parent bank from borrowing from its London branch, a right commonly exercised whenever the Federal Reserve Board has sought to tighten up on the volume of credit that banks located in the United States could extend to their customers.[33] In short, the existence of these Eurocurrency facilities has substantially weakened the capacity of the national authorities responsible for monetary policy to influence the credit conditions in their home economies.[34]

Another symptom of the erosion in the capacity of national authorities to control their respective capital markets has been the growth of the so-called Eurobond market. This is a market whose offerings are composed of medium-term and long-term bond issues denominated in a given national currency but offered for sale outside of the country in whose currency the issue is denominated. As Table 4–2 shows, such offerings have been growing steadily. Moreover, they have begun to include offerings demonstrated in two basket currencies, the European Currency Unit (ECU) and the SDR.

The attractions of bond issuers to these Eurobond markets have varied according to the nature of the regulations and the degree of liquidity in their home markets. Issuers of dollar bonds have been

Table 4-2 **Growth of the Eurocurrency and International Bond Markets, 1970-1986 (in billions of U.S. dollars)**

Year	Eurocurrency[a]	Eurobonds[b]	Foreign bonds[c]
1970	110	3	3
1971	145	4	4
1972	200	7	4
1973	305	5	5
1974	375	5	7
1975	460	11	12
1976	565	15	19
1977	695	20	17
1978	950	16	22
1979	1235	18	20
1980	1525	21	19
1981	1954	28	22
1982	2168	51	25
1983	2278	47	27
1984	2386	80	28
1985	2846	137	31
1986	3579	189	39

[a] Based on foreign currency liabilities of banks in principal centers outside of the United States; adapted from Morgan Guaranty, *World Financial Markets*, various issues.
[b] Offerings by foreigners in currencies other than that of the market in which offered; adapted from Bank for International Settlements, *Annual Report,* various issues; Morgan Guaranty, *World Financial Markets,* various issues.
[c] Offerings by foreigners in currency of market in which offered; adapted from Bank for International Settlements, *Annual Report,* various issues; Morgan Guaranty, *World Financial Markets,* various issues.

attracted by the opportunity to avoid the regulations of the Securities and Exchange Commission associated with a flotation in U.S. markets. Issuers of yen bonds have been looking for an escape from the restraints of the Japanese Ministry of Finance on bonds floated in Tokyo.[35] Some monetary authorities, although unwilling to allow their nationals to make public offerings in Eurodollar markets in their own national currencies, have nevertheless permitted them access to funds raised in those markets by others, thus encouraging arcane arrangements entailing swaps of currencies between borrowers of different currencies.

U.S. authorities concerned with banking and credit, including the Federal Reserve Board and the Comptroller of the Currency, have been reluctant to move ahead of other countries in placing restraints on U.S.-based financial intermediaries operating abroad. Although organized interest groups in the United States have had very little to say about the big decisions in foreign exchange policy, representatives of U.S. banks and other financial intermediaries instantly become evident whenever any proposed regulation threatens to hamper them in their competition with foreigners. Accordingly, U.S. authorities have been hesitant to extend their restraints on credit and their surveillance of bank lending portfolios to the foreign branches of U.S. banks, and even more hesitant to attempt controlling Eurodollar transactions through restraints imposed at the U.S. borders.[36] Given prevailing U.S. values, the sentiment against imposing restrictions has been very strong. Moreover, the authorities have been realistic enough to recognize that, where the control of money flows is concerned, the risk of evasion is very high.

As facilities for raising capital in foreign markets have expanded over the decades, transactions in foreign exchange have grown as well. Indeed, the growth in such transactions has been so rapid as to dwarf the expansion of the Eurocurrency markets. Whereas in 1975, the world's foreign exchange markets were thought to be handling about $10 or $15 billion in transactions daily, the analogous figure in 1986 has ballooned to about $200 billion, some 25 times the world's average daily trade in goods.[37] With money pouring across their borders at such unprecedented rates, the capacity of national monetary authorities to influence their national money supplies, to affect their national exchange rates, or even to supervise their banking systems has been reduced to new low levels.

In fact, signs of a decline in the supervisory capacity of national authorities were already beginning to appear during the 1970s. Among the most disconcerting was the appearance of sudden crises in a number of large banks.

In 1974, the Herstatt Bank collapsed in Germany, and another bank, the Franklin National, was imperiled in New York, both in connection with large-scale transactions in foreign exchange.[38] The new era of uninhibited foreign exchange markets, it was beginning to be evident, entailed certain risks. But the picture still could be diagnosed at that stage as a case of growing pains, requiring only a little more restraint on the part of the international banks and a little more diligence on the part of bank supervising authorities.

By 1981, however, it was becoming evident to knowledgeable observers that the problems created by the new opportunities in international markets were running much deeper than anticipated, largely because some developing countries were piling up enormous quantities of debt. The history of the debt problem has been recounted in numerous studies.[39] With the growth in the dollar reserves of the oil-exporting countries during the 1970s, a relatively small number of large banks, organized to do business in both the Eurodollar market and in national financial centers, had begun to acquire deposits of dollars that would eventually reach some hundreds of billions of dollars. Those deposits set off a competition to find borrowers on a scale never before seen.

Until the 1970s, the developing countries were not a particularly promising market for private lenders of foreign currency. Previously, inflows of foreign capital to those countries primarily had taken the form of loans from governmental institutions such as the World Bank and the U.S. Export-Import Bank, augmented to a limited degree by the investments that large manufacturing and raw material enterprises were making directly in their foreign subsidiaries and branches. To the extent that banks were involved in loans to developing countries, the involvement mainly took the form of suppliers' credits, and even such credits were quite limited.[40]

The 1960s, however, had been a period of sustained and solid growth for many developing countries, accompanied by an expansion in their foreign trade and investment. Coupled with this growth was a relative decline in foreign aid as aid-giving agencies began to concentrate their support on countries with the lowest per capita incomes. As a consequence, some developing countries turned to the private market for development capital and trade-related financing. This transition was made easier by the booming Eurocurrency markets and by the desire of a growing number of banks to move into international finance. With the dollar deposits of the oil exporters piling up in the big international banks and with Eurodollar loans lying outside the surveillance of national supervisory authorities, a new era of private lending was taking shape.[41] Soon the uninhibited lending would generate a crisis that threatened the solvency of some banks and saddled some developing countries with unsustainable debt burdens.

COPING WITH THE NEW ENVIRONMENT

After the mid-1970s, the policies of the U.S. government toward exchange rate issues were being driven by the increasing monetary and financial ties of the U.S. economy to the rest of the world. In earlier decades, it is true, U.S. government officials were often as concerned with the effective functioning of the international monetary system as they were in the 1970s and 1980s. Their concern, however, had been of a kind reminiscent of the shepherd overseeing his flock. When the U.S. government did engage in international consultations on money matters, it was usually to demand that other governments alter one policy or another in order to ease the economic burden of the United States. Signs that this asymmetrical attitude would eventually have to change could be detected in the mid-1970s, following the destruction of the regime of fixed exchange rates in 1971 and the first oil shock of 1973–1974.

The response of the U.S. government toward its increased exposure had taken various concrete forms. Beginning in 1975, for instance, the U.S. government actively participated in a number of international agreements aimed at improving the surveillance of governments over multinational banks[42] and strengthening the banks' capital structures.[43]

When the first Reagan administration took office, its response to the exposed U.S. position took a somewhat different turn, emphasizing unilateral measures of liberalization rather than measures of international cooperation. In that spirit, banks located in the United States were permitted to accept Eurodollar deposits from foreigners, free from the reserve requirements and interest rate limitations imposed on U.S. dollar deposits.[44] In the same spirit, the Tax Reform Act of 1984 repealed a withholding tax formerly levied against all interest earned by foreign investors in U.S. securities.[45]

Moreover, as long as the developing countries continued to service their mounting debt, the preference of the new administration was to ignore the growing threat, a position consistent with its general desire to reduce governmental interventions. For instance, the U.S. government refused for a time to support a proposal for the enlargement of the resources of the IMF but supported various changes in the IMF's internal rules that would impose stronger conditions on new loans.[46] At the same time, as part of the same bent, the U.S. government was insisting that countries in balance-of-payments difficulties deal with the IMF and the creditor banks to whom the debts were owed, rather than look for new sources of bilateral aid.

Nevertheless, the U.S. authorities were not immune to the pressures that eventually arose from the growing debt crisis. Mexico's debt problems, for instance, were bound to command the close attention of the administration and to push it toward new cooperative measures.

In the summer of 1982, Mexico suddenly faced an acute balance-of-payment crisis, the second in a two-year period; with some $80 billion of foreign debt outstanding, and with capital flowing from the country, the country's foreign exchange reserves would shortly disappear. This was an emergency with grave implications for the U.S. banking system and the Mexican economy. With the emergency, the characteristic U.S. capacity for instant initiatives became evident again. Prominent in the exercise that followed was the chairman of the Federal Reserve Board, Paul A. Volcker, as well as the president of the Federal Reserve Bank of New York, Anthony M. Solomon, who in earlier years had been a leading member of similar emergency teams in the Kennedy, Johnson, and Carter administrations. Within a few days, a $3 billion package of U.S. aid had been assembled, drawing on resources requiring no added congressional authorization; $1 billion was lent as credits for agricultural products, another $1 billion as an advance payment for purchases of Mexican oil for the U.S. federal oil stockpile, and some $700 million as part of a swap loan between the central banks of the two countries.[47] In addition, the Bank for International Settlements was enlisted to plug the dike with added short-term credits of $1.8 billion.

In fact, under the pressure of the debt emergencies, U.S. authorities were joining in a number of international procedures that were becoming highly institutionalized. Those procedures, far from reducing the role of government and limiting the discretion of the bureaucrats, were elevating the governmental role to new levels of importance.

Countries in balance-of-payment difficulties by reason of their heavy external debt, whether the debt was owed to public or private lenders, were expected to develop a program of austerity and retrenchment with the IMF that promised to restore them to external equilibrium.[48] Thereafter, in an institutionalized procedure taking place in Paris, each debtor country would meet with representatives of the various governments to which it was indebted in a gathering that came to be known as the Paris Club. Taking into account the IMF plan, these representatives would then agree to stretch out the maturity dates of the loans they had previously made.[49] With loans from official lenders settled for the time being, representatives of the debtor government would move over to London to face their private bank creditors for a similar—and much more complex—exercise in rescheduling their private debts. The novelty of this arrangement, involving close cooperation between governments and with the private sector, was quite striking. The fact that the U.S. government was willing and able to participate in the arrangement suggested that the normal U.S. preferences for limiting public power and restraining the discretion of bureaucrats did not constitute an absolute bar to international collaboration.

In early 1985, the team at the U.S. Treasury Department was displaced, giving way to a new secretary and under secretary. The new secretary, James A. Baker III, had been President Reagan's chief of staff in the White House, a position that he filled with marked distinction. Baker acquired his job as secretary of the Treasury as a result of a bizarre swap arrangement with the incumbent, Donald Regan. At the time of the swap, it was widely assumed that Regan was aspiring to a Rasputin-like role in the White House, while Baker appeared to have both the status and the motive to play a strong innovative role and was thus more disposed to tackle substantive problems of foreign economic policy.

Once again, the world was treated to the familiar phenomenon of a shift in U.S. policy linked to changes in the preferences of key bureaucrats. By September 1985, the new Treasury team had devised and steered through the executive branch the so-called Baker plan, a proposal for expanding the role of the international agencies in the management of difficult debt situations. The plan envisaged a combined effort between private banks, multilateral banks, and the debtor nations. It called for the private banks to resume their lending on a modest scale and for the industrialized states to increase their contributions to the World Bank and the IMF, and it proposed that these two institutions then accept a greater role in coordinating medium- and long-term debt strategies.[50]

Two years later, in December 1987, Baker played a key role in a much more innovative move aimed at dealing with Mexico's threatening debt problem. The scheme, which involved using the creditworthiness of U.S. government bonds as a prop for reducing Mexico's debt burden, had been developed primarily by Morgan Guaranty, a large holder of Mexican debt. But it could not have gone forward without Baker's wholehearted support and the president's concurrence.

The scheme was built on the fact that the U.S. Treasury was prepared to issue and Mexico was prepared to buy special 20-year U.S. Treasury bonds that would serve as collateral in the refinancing of the Mexican government's debt to U.S. banks. Because these special bonds were "zero coupon" bonds, they were slated to have a value at maturity equal to five times their original cost, reflecting the normal interest rate for long-term U.S. Treasury bonds. The hope was that the U.S. banks would turn in their old Mexican debt at a huge discount, and would accept new Mexican debt at par collateralized by the U.S. Treasury bonds.

As it turned out, the scheme failed to produce the hoped-for results.[51] The scheme's sponsors had anticipated that Mexico might shrink its debt by $10 billion simply by encumbering $2 billion of its reserves. In the end Mexico only succeeded in shrinking its debt by about $1 billion, as Mexico's creditors refused to accept substantial discounts on the Mexican paper in their portfolios. On the other hand, the capacity of the U.S. government for innovation and improvisation had once more been demonstrated.

The efforts of the Baker team to deal with the vulnerabilities of the U.S. economy were not confined to the problem of developing country debt. Shortly after Baker took office, he produced another initiative, strikingly like the so-called locomotive proposal floated in the Carter administration nearly a decade earlier. Over a two-year period from 1985 to 1987, Baker returned repeatedly to the proposal that Germany and Japan should stimulate their economies as a means of increasing the demand for U.S. goods and reducing the U.S. trade deficit. In the end, that initiative also produced some visible results.

At first, the responses of the two governments most immediately affected were characteristic and predictable. German officials protested over the inflationary implications of the policy, while Japanese officials equivocated in public and debated in private. At the same time, echoing the point that American economists had been trying to teach American politicians, both governments insisted that the surest way to reduce the U.S. trade deficit was to reduce the U.S. fiscal deficit. When in 1987, Congress and the president showed signs of a determination to squeeze back the U.S. fiscal deficits, the German and Japanese governments took some moderate measures to stimulate their economies.

The Baker initiatives served to confirm the existence of many of the tendencies demonstrated by previous history.

As long as initiatives required only executive action, the chances of their being launched were quite good. But any proposals requiring congressional approval for implementation would activate the ponderous U.S. system of checks and balances. In that context, a struggle would be inevitable. The exact forces arrayed in the struggle would vary, depending on the form of the proposal under consideration.

On the whole, even when the executive was authorized to move ahead on his own authority, the government continued to be drawn to policies that assigned the bureaucracy a limited and passive role. Usually, it took some palpable emergency to create the basis for a more activist set of policies. Nevertheless, when such emergencies have arisen, policy entrepreneurs enjoying the confidence of the president have managed to push more activist policies onto the executive's agenda.

A HINT OF CHANGE

All told, the executive branch has had greater room for maneuvering in matters relating to foreign exchange flows than in matters involving international trade. To be sure, where questions of tax revenues or tax expenditures have been involved, the power of the executive has been much more constrained than in monetary affairs. And whenever the executive has contemplated measures that might handicap U.S. banks in international competition, the political capacity of the banks to resist has been apparent. Despite these constraints, the president has been left with plenty of power for creative international cooperation, provided he has the wisdom and the energy to exploit his opportunities.

The relative autonomy of the executive branch in international collaboration on monetary matters is an anomaly in the U.S. system, one that begs for an explanation.[52] An obvious one is that the foreign sector of the U.S. economy did not take on a critical role until the 1970s. Moreover, as long as the U.S. dollar was fixed in value, the link between international collaboration and domestic consequences was attenuated and indirect. When floating rates made the link more obvious, no institutions were in place that could mobilize the special interests to take one side or another on the issues. Given the complexity of the issues involved, those institutions have been slow in forming.

Today, however, with so much at stake among traders and investors in every movement of the exchange rate, it seems only a matter of time before the special interest groups emerge. Indeed, some unprecedented provisions of the omnibus trade bill debated in 1988 suggest that such groups are already forming. One provision of the bill would oblige the president to hold multilateral talks with other major nations to improve the coordination of economic policies as well as the existing mechanisms for stabilizing exchange rates. Another provision would direct the president to hold talks on exchange rates with any country that runs trade surpluses with the United States and that the president believes is "manipulating" its exchange rates, a barb clearly aimed at Korea and Taiwan. The era of autonomy for the executive on exchange rate policy seems to be drawing to a close.

5

The Politics
of Multinational Enterprises

THE HISTORY OF international economic relations is punctuated with bitter clashes over the operations of multinational enterprises, from Mexico's seizure of its foreign oil companies in 1938 to the U.S. government's veto in 1987 of Fujitsu's bid for control of Fairchild Semiconductor. By and large, however, the 1980s was a relatively peaceful period for such enterprises. Most governments, preoccupied with increasing their exports or managing their debts, were more disposed to welcome the subsidiaries of foreign enterprises than to repel them. Yet the fundamental forces responsible for friction between governments over the operation of such enterprises had not gone away. On the contrary, as multinational networks continued to expand over the globe, the potential for conflict in the unresolved issues of overlapping national jurisdictions and uncertain national control continued to grow.

Although no U.S. administration has developed a policy on multinational enterprises as such, practically all U.S. administrations have wished to avoid unnecessary restraints on the development and operation of multinational enterprises. Apart from that general inclination, however, successive U.S. administrations have tended to deal with the problems associated with multinational enterprises as functional issues, such as problems in the taxation of foreign income, application of the antitrust laws, control of security, protection of consumers, safety of depositors, and so on.

In terms of a general approach to the multinational aspect of the enterprises concerned, these functional approaches have had almost nothing in common. In application, they have exhibited the characteristics usually associated with other foreign economic policies of the United States. Initiatives have appeared sporadically in each administration, fueled by the energies of a few policymakers in the executive branch; thereafter, the diffusion of authority, coupled with the operation of checks and balances, has produced a wavering and inconsistent performance over time.

In the 1980s, a spectacular increase occurred in direct investments by foreign enterprises in the United States, led by Japanese automobile and electronics firms. Toward the close of the decade, U.S. subsidiaries of foreign enterprises had come to account for about 3 percent of the U.S. labor force. That shift in the wind brought on a wave of concerned reactions from politicians and political scientists, reactions strikingly reminiscent of European reactions to the "invasion" of Europe by American business two decades earlier. But these reactions, like those of the Europeans, were largely unhelpful in identifying the basic problems associated with the operations of multinational enterprises and contributed nothing to their solution.

To date, the U.S. government has not developed a coherent position regarding the fundamental problems generated by the operations of multinational enterprises. The issues continue to mount in diversity and intensity, decade by decade. The responses continue to be slow and uncertain.

THE ISSUES

In the course of the last century, world business has come to be dominated by multinational enterprises.[1] National enterprises have gone international, creating networks of affiliated firms located in different countries that are linked together by a common parent, draw on a common pool of resources, and respond in some measure to a common strategy. These networks have come to include practically all the familiar names associated with international markets, such as IBM and Citicorp, Philips Electric and St. Gobain, Nestlé and Ciba, General Motors and Olivetti.

The reasons for the creation of these multinational enterprises are well enough known, having been scrutinized assiduously by a generation of scholars.[2] The efforts of businessmen to achieve appropriate scale, to reduce avoidable risks, and to exploit more profitably some unique technological and managerial skills all figure in the creation of these networks. They have been, in brief, an important manifestation of the opportunities created by modern technology and an important source of added technological change.

Although these networks have become familiar and ubiquitous, they also are anomalous in many critical respects. Each unit in any network has been created under the laws of the country in which it operates, thereby acquiring the legal right to buy and sell, lend and borrow, sue and be sued. Yet, the strategies of each unit in a multinational framework are a function of the strategies of the network as a whole. Accordingly, each unit is exposed simultaneously to the commands of foreign parents and the pressures of the government that authorized its existence.

Other problems have arisen, more limited in character but no less difficult. In greater or lesser degree, each unit's record of profits is a function of the combined profits of all the others, influenced by a shared technology, by a shared reputation, by shared costs, and sometimes even by shared marketing. In this tangle of interrelationships, how is one to define the profit of any unit for purposes of taxing its income without raising major issues of double taxation and tax avoidance? Similar problems occur regarding the control of capital flows, antitrust problems, the control of sensitive technology, and questions of corporate disclosure—in short, with regard to any issue of public policy involving substantial interaction among the units of a given multinational network.

From the public point of view, the results of such interaction may be threatening or benign. In either case, governments are bound to develop acute anxiety from time to time over their ability to monitor and control, as did the U.S. government when faced with Fujitsu's prospective acquisition of Fairchild. Over time, such tensions have come and gone; they have fallen away whenever governments were hungry for technology or capital from foreign sources, and they have risen to a brief crescendo when governments have felt naked to foreign intrusions of their sovereignty.

The difficulties of finding a common international basis for handling issues relating to the multinational enterprise have been exacerbated by the fact that such arrangements involve issues perceived by most governments as primarily domestic in character. In fields such as antitrust, corporate disclosure, consumer protection, and labor practices, national policies have usually been framed without much regard for their international implications and implemented through institutions operating inside the country rather than at its borders.

As a result, differences among governments in the norms by which they administer their programs of regulation have often proved a powerful obstacle to international agreement. U.S. norms, in particular, have posed problems because they tend to differ so markedly from those of other countries.

THE U.S. RESPONSE

The extent to which any national government attempts to steer the behavior of its multinational enterprises is likely to be influenced by the larger relationships existing between business and the state in that country. In the case of the United States, as we have repeatedly observed, public opinion attaches considerable importance to maintaining the line of demarcation between the public and private sectors. Although the U.S. military establishment tends to give special attention to a few key producers, such as Boeing and General Dynamics, none can claim any special status against competition. The U.S. government maintains no cluster of state-owned public utilities delivering essential services, no national champions designated to carry the flag in international competition. No business organization at the national level is capable of representing the country's business community to the federal government. By the same token, there is no agency in the government that looks upon the performance of business, whether at home or abroad, from a systemic vantage point.

Various U.S. government decisions, it is true, have greatly influenced the conduct of U.S. business abroad. That influence, however, has resulted from the actions of a number of agencies whose responsibilities were only peripherally related to the international business community. For the most part, these agencies arose to meet needs in very diverse policy areas, from unfair business practices to consumer safety. Once created, each agency acquired its own distinctive mandates and missions and its own constituencies in Congress and the electorate. The historical record, therefore, is episodic. It includes long stretches in which the U.S. government seemed indifferent or oblivious to the operations of multinational enterprises abroad, punctuated occasionally by the regulatory initiatives of U.S. agencies turning their sights to developments abroad.

Antitrust Policies

Perhaps the earliest U.S. policy bearing on multinational enterprises emerged out of the country's adoption of antitrust policy, a step taken in popular reaction to a great wave of monopoly building by U.S. business. In 1882, John D. Rockefeller had created the Standard Oil Company, a trust designed to monopolize the country's oil trade. By the turn of the century, over 300 trusts had been created, each designed to protect major producers in a given industry from the cold winds of competition.

The Sherman Antitrust Act, enacted in 1890, declared that "every contract, combination . . . or conspiracy in restraint of trade or commerce among the several states or with foreign nations . . . is illegal." The act's objectives were reenforced by the subsequent enactment of the Clayton Act in 1914, which specifically prohibited enterprises subject to U.S. jurisdiction from any acquisitions the effect of which "may be substantially to lessen competition or to tend to create a monopoly."

Under the U.S. system of checks and balances, it took more than the congressional enactment of antitrust legislation to launch a program so patently threatening to business organizations. Still required was an administration prepared to enforce the legislation and a court prepared to uphold it, and these indispensable elements were slow in appearing. By World War I, a few antitrust suits had been tried and won, including the landmark case against the Standard Oil Trust that led to its dissolution in 1911. But by and large, prosecutors in the executive branch were slow to exercise their powers under the new statutes, and the courts were slow to uphold them. In practice, therefore, the antitrust statutes had little real effect during the first few decades after enactment of the Sherman Act.[3] The force of the statutes was diluted further by the successful efforts of U.S. exporters to carve out a limited exemption for themselves. With passage of the Webb–Pomerene Act in 1918, U.S. firms were allowed to enter into restrictive agreements to promote their exports, provided the agreements were administered through associations registered with the Federal Trade Commission and provided that domestic competition was left unaffected.[4]

In the first stage of enforcement, the application of the antitrust laws to multinational enterprises was slight. It was not until 1909 that the courts even considered the international activity of U.S. firms as potentially subject to U.S. law.[5] Even then, the Supreme Court declined the opportunity to extend its jurisdiction and, instead, asserted that "the general and universal rule is that the character of an act as lawful or unlawful must be determined wholly by the law of the country where the act is done."[6]

In the 1930s, the antitrust laws took on a new significance, both domestically and internationally. The depression had elevated the public's resentment against big business, a resentment expressing itself partly in an urge for regulation and partly in the desire for increased competition. Both themes could be detected in the landmark reports and hearings of the Temporary National Economic Committee, a committee of Congress charged with studying the concentration of economic power of U.S. industry and its effects on competition. The work of the committee gave wide publicity to the participation of U.S. firms in various international cartels.[7]

Through these channels and others, the U.S. public began to learn that U.S. firms had been participating quietly in a burgeoning number of European "producer agreements" whose participants were engaged in an effort to divide and control global markets. Illustrative of such agreements, General Electric in 1924 had initiated a worldwide cartel of incandescent lamp producers. In 1928, a series of restrictive agreements had linked the economic fortunes of Standard Oil, the Anglo-Persian Oil Company, and Shell. And in 1928, Dupont and the British Imperial Chemicals Industries had created an elaborate division and sharing of world chemical markets.[8]

The disposition of the U.S. public to bridle at the operations of international cartels in the 1930s was increased by the fact that the European participants were often seen as agents of their governments. German firms, in particular, came to be regarded as agents of a hostile power as the Nazi movement gained control over the German government. Various congressional committees explored this possibility, throwing new light on long-standing agreements that previously were regarded as innocuous or even constructive. For instance, an agreement between I. G. Farben and the Standard Oil Company of New Jersey, once welcomed by the U.S. press as a harbinger of industrial peace, was seen in retrospect as a Nazi ruse for restricting the development of the synthetic rubber industry in the United States.

Under the characteristic pattern of U.S. policy making, the situation was ripe for the appearance of a policy entrepreneur, eager to innovate and capable of securing the attention and support of the president. In this instance, the role was filled by Thurman W. Arnold, who in 1938 was appointed to the position of assistant attorney general in charge of the Justice Department's antitrust program. Arnold was deeply devoted to the antitrust objective and was slated to raise a generation of lawyers and economists in the U.S. government sharing his commitment.[9] Between 1939 and 1945, he launched 52 antitrust proceedings against international cartels.[10] As Arnold's protégés moved up through the ranks, hostility towards international cartels became entrenched within the U.S. executive branch.

By the end of World War II, preventing restrictive business practices in international trade had become an established goal in U.S. government agencies. Accordingly, when the European Recovery Program took shape in 1948, the United States signed a series of bilateral agreements with member states that, among other things, pledged cooperation in the elimination of restrictive business practices.[11] Similar clauses appeared in the more traditional bilateral treaties of friendship, commerce, and navigation between the United States and other countries.[12]

During this period, the U.S. courts redefined the jurisdictional application of the antitrust statutes in ways that were of great significance to multinational enterprises. In 1945, Justice Learned Hand departed from the precedent of the 1909 *Banana* case to proclaim that, "Any state may impose liabilities, even upon persons not within its allegiance, for conduct outside its borders that has consequences within its borders that the state reprehends."[13] This so-called effects doctrine has been consistently interpreted by the U.S. legal community as giving U.S. courts the power to apply U.S. laws to foreign nationals for behavior outside the United States provided that the behavior had adverse effects within the territory of the United States, even if such behavior was legal in the territory where it was conducted.[14]

Nevertheless, neither the active program within the U.S. government against international cartels nor the web of international agreements on the subject had much staying power. Too much depended on the sustained capacity of the U.S. government to persuade other governments to go along with a policy in which they had little interest. That capacity depended, among other things, on the continued interest and concern of a staff devoted to the goal.

Within a few years after the end of World War II, neither condition was being satisfied. By the mid-1960s, antitrust suits involving foreigners in foreign jurisdictions had become infrequent. And efforts by the U.S. government to gain the cooperation of other governments in the suppression of international monopolies of restrictive business practices had grown rare.

Part of the reduced emphasis on restrictive business practices in international markets can be laid to the altered character of international markets in the 1950s and 1960s. In most of the industries previously identified prominently with restrictive business practices, such as steel, oil, chemicals, and electric machinery, the trend was toward greatly increased international competition, with new producers from Asia and Latin America pushing aggressively into the markets of the established U.S. firms.[15] But much of the change can be ascribed to the shift to a Republican administration in 1953, following 20 years of Democratic rule; programs such as antitrust enforcement, although written in law, were especially vulnerable to the ideological tilt of each administration and to the entrepreneurial proclivities of the officers in the Justice Department and the Federal Trade Commission charged with administering the programs involved.

However, the coup de grace to the policy against restrictive business practices in international trade came from another direction, namely, from a growing realization of the difficulties of unilateral action. Those difficulties showed up especially in the process of attempting to collect the necessary evidence and apply the appropriate remedies.

In their early efforts to apply U.S law, the U.S. enforcement agencies and the U.S. courts had occasionally commanded firms in Canada, Britain, the Netherlands, and other countries to produce evidence or to desist from engaging in practices thought to be materially harmful to U.S. trade. Commands of this sort generated a predictable response; they were so threatening to the concept of national sovereignty that governments in target jurisdictions were bound to resist. Indeed, a number of governments enacted statutes prohibiting enterprises in their jurisdictions from responding to subpoenas and other demands from foreign governments.[16]

Without any international mechanism in place to deal with such issues, the only way to reduce tensions arising from attempts by U.S. antitrust authorities to reach foreign jurisdictions was to ensure that they occurred as infrequently as possible. Through a series of agreements reached in the OECD, the United States and other governments undertook in effect to proceed with the utmost restraint in antitrust matters affecting foreign jurisdictions. Accordingly, the record of antitrust prosecutions since 1960 is almost devoid of cases involving international trade.[17]

Although governments rarely are prepared to confront the problems created by restrictive business practices in realistic terms, the issue is not disappearing from the international agenda. Indeed, in 1980, a UN conference brought antitrust issues back to an international forum by unanimously adopting a "Set of Principles and Rules for the Control of Restrictive Business Practices." The text itself was so lacking in substantive and legal bite that it had little potential for actually influencing any of its signatories.[18] But its adoption indicated that concern for the issue had not wholly evaporated, especially on the part of developing countries.

In the foreseeable future, the issue of restrictive business practices is unlikely to take on the importance it had in the period between the two world wars, but a new wave of cross-national linkages between firms threatens to bring it back into some prominence. The new links, which include cross-licensing, joint ventures, and consortia among erstwhile competitors, have characteristically involved major firms operating with complex technologies, including aircraft, electronics, and computer companies.[19] As a rule, the primary purpose of these arrangements has not been to reduce international competition but to couple the complementary capabilities of two capable firms: American Telephone's switching technology, for instance, with Olivetti's access to European markets; Boeing's skills in aircraft design with Mitsubishi's financial resources; Motorola's logic chips with Toshiba's memory-chip technology; and so on. Nevertheless, the likelihood that some of these arrangements will eventually reduce competition in ways that are harmful is not insignificant. When that happens, it remains to be seen whether the governments concerned will reconcile the differences in values and institutions that have prevented them from cooperating on such problems in the past.

Restraining Capital Exports

From time to time, bureaucrats in the executive branch have tried to tighten control over U.S. multinationals in order to achieve some overarching U.S. objective. When that has occurred, it has been instructive to observe how rapidly the attempted programs have been modified or abandoned, as the underlying values of private property and governmental noninterference have reasserted themselves. In one such episode during the 1960s, multinational enterprises became the target of a restrictive program aimed at improving U.S. balance of payments; the effort proved predictably short-lived.

Worries over the U.S. balance-of-payments situation had mounted gradually during the early 1960s. By 1963, with increasing concern over the loss of foreign exchange reserves, the U.S. government had practically reversed an earlier policy of encouraging the exportation of U.S. capital. In that year, the U.S. government enacted a so-called interest equalization tax. Its purpose was to tax some of the foreign issuers selling securities in the United States, thereby reducing the attractiveness to them of the relatively low interest rates prevailing in U.S. capital markets. Although such a measure was quite at odds with the country's role as manager of the world's key currency during those years, it managed to remain on the books in some form for 11 years thereafter.

Because the interest equalization tax was applicable mainly to securities offered by foreigners, it drew little protest from U.S. interests. But by 1965, U.S. policymakers concluded that the operations of U.S.-based multinational enterprises were responsible for increasingly important capital flows and that a program was needed to curb them. Accordingly, the U.S. government announced a so-called voluntary program, exhorting all large U.S. corporations to hold down their outflows of capital and to limit their build-up of assets in foreign countries.[20] Concurrently, U.S. firms were also urged to step up receipts from exports, dividends, and interest from abroad. The "voluntary" character of the program represented the administration's effort to forestall the protests of businessmen over any regulation that might inhibit their freedom to move money across borders or undermine their ability to compete abroad with unregulated foreign firms.

Almost from the first, the program was doomed. Following many revisions over the succeeding two or three years, its voluntary character was acknowledged to be a failure, and, in 1968, the administration tightened the existing guidelines and imposed mandatory restrictions on direct investments abroad.

However, the mandatory restrictions fared no better than the voluntary ones. Regulations were drawn up and administered in characteristic U.S. style; they were explicit and detailed, leaving as little discretion as possible in bureaucratic hands. The regulations distinguished among three groups of countries, imposing limits of different severity on each of the three, and they laid down detailed provisions for all manner of technical issues, including the treatment of depreciation reserves and local borrowing.

Subsequently, what bureaucracies in other countries would have dealt with through administrative discretion, the U.S. bureaucracy handled by amending the regulations. A constant stream of ameliorating amendments were issued—to deal with unforeseen consequences, to handle anomalous cases, to exempt trivial transactions, and so on. Eventually, the program was so weighted down with escape clauses that its restrictive aspects were negligible. In 1974, despite the fact that the balance-of-payments problem was still thought to be acute, the program was terminated.[21]

Security Export Restrictions

Although the U.S. public has been strongly disposed to limit the discretionary power of the bureaucracy and to contain its role in the marketplace, it has been somewhat more tolerant of the government's interventions when they were justified in the name of national security. In such cases, the U.S. public has shown very little disposition to challenge the action. Occasionally, as in the case of South Africa in the 1980s, U.S. public sentiment has favored export restrictions despite an official reluctance to impose them.

Intractable problems have arisen, however, when U.S. administrations have sought to make export restrictions more effective by imposing restraints on the subsidiaries of U.S. enterprises located in foreign countries. At that point, security export controls have become one facet of a more general problem: that of jurisdictional conflict over the operations of multinational enterprises.

From the onset of the Cold War shortly after the end of World War II, the U.S. government has imposed restraints on the export of goods, technology, and capital to the Soviet Union as well as to other countries identified as allies of the USSR. The restrictions have varied according to the level of tension existing between the United States and the Soviet bloc. They were, for instance, extremely tight in the era following the end of World War II, covering the last years of the Stalin regime and the Korean War; they were measurably relaxed in the period of détente, beginning in 1972, and continuing for three or four years thereafter; and they were returned to a high level of restrictiveness in the last years of the Carter administration.[22]

In this instance, U.S. policymakers had no illusions that unilateral

U.S. action could produce the results they were hoping to achieve. From the first, therefore, they tried to persuade Japan and the principal European allies of the United States to join in a common restrictive scheme. The upshot of these efforts was a two-tiered set of restrictions: one level of restrictions imposed unilaterally by the U.S. authorities; another lower level imposed by a group of countries under the aegis of an international committee.

The differences in the two levels of restriction were explained in part by differences in the relative importance of trade with the communist countries. Because economic relations with the Soviet bloc were never of much importance to the U.S. economy, commercial considerations at first were not a major element in the shaping of U.S. trade policy with respect to the bloc. Instead, the internal U.S. debate over the desirability and feasibility of economic restrictions focused mainly on the war-making capabilities of the Soviet Union. The Europeans and Japanese, however, took the view that economic factors had to be given greater weight in their situations.

A two-tiered system was bound in the end to create difficulties for the United States. U.S. enterprises made periodic protests over the extent to which the U.S. system of export controls handicapped them in their competition with the Europeans and the Japanese. Despite widespread doubts as to the effect of the restrictions on Soviet technical capabilities, however, the executive branch continued assiduously in its attempts to control the flows of exports to communist countries.[23]

In these efforts, multinational enterprises presented an especially difficult problem. As we suggested earlier, the international networks created by multinational enterprises constitute one of the principal channels through which products and their related technology move abroad. As firms have established subsidiaries abroad, it has often been their foreign subsidiaries rather than the U.S. parents that provided technology to the Soviet Union and its allies. Unlike most other governments, the United States occasionally has attempted to require the foreign subsidiaries of U.S. enterprises to abide by the same standards as those imposed upon firms located in the United States.

Attempts by U.S. officials to extend their extraterritorial reach, however, met with vigorous protests from foreign governments. A typical confrontation occurred in 1965, when the U.S. government sought to extend its embargo on the export of sophisticated technological products to the People's Republic of China. The government of France had entered into a bilateral agreement with China, by which the French subsidiary of the U.S.-based Fruehauf Corporation was to export tractor-trailer parts to that country. Working through the U.S. parent, U.S. authorities tried to block the sale. In response, the French courts appointed an administrator to take control of the company and allow fulfillment of the Chinese order.

Another well-publicized effort with a somewhat more ambiguous outcome was the attempt of the U.S. government in 1982 to prevent several European-based subsidiaries of General Electric and Dresser Industries from providing key components for compressors to be installed in the Soviet Union on a pipeline built to deliver gas to Germany. The gas deal, a long-term undertaking on a grand scale, worried U.S. policymakers, who were fearful of Germany's future vulnerability to Soviet economic blackmail. In this instance, the Europeans were adamant. Italy announced that any firms in its jurisdiction would honor their existing contracts, and the French and British governments actually forbade the companies on their soil to obey the U.S. mandate. Five months after the U.S. government announced its new restrictive policies, the regulations were withdrawn.[24]

An added straw was placed on the camel's back in 1986, when the U.S. Defense Department sought to prevent the sale of a computer in Germany by one German national to another. IBM's German subsidiary was one of these German nationals; the other was a Hamburg-based shipping company in which a Soviet company had a 51 percent interest.[25] In the end, the Soviet company was served with compatible equipment from another U.S. source, leaving the German officials furious and the basic issue unresolved.

Altogether U.S. efforts to control trade and investment in the name of security appear to have been costly when measured either by business opportunities foregone or by political capital expended. What such restrictions have contributed to U.S. security is uncertain; the security effects are so subtle and run in so many different directions as to defy objective measurement. But the issue is bound to persist in the years ahead, gaining added emphasis as the U.S. economy continues to exhibit its interdependence with other economies.

A hint of the importance that the security issue is likely to have in the future is the emphasis placed on that subject in various provisions of the 1988 omnibus trade bill. One provision of a "liberalizing" character would reduce the handicap of the U.S. business in international trade by attempting to clip the wings of the Pentagon in its perennial efforts to stretch security export controls as wide as possible. Another provision, however, would empower the president in some cases to punish firms abroad that export products to destinations on the U.S. proscribed list, even if the enterprise is not breaching the laws of the country from which it is exporting. And still another provision would authorize the president to block foreigners' acquisitions of firms in the United States if he thinks that national security requires it.[26] It was unclear as this book went to print whether these provisions of the bill would ever become law. But their capacity to survive the legislative obstacle course to so advanced a stage presaged heated internal and international debates in the future.

Tax Policy

Not all of the efforts at international cooperation launched by U.S. officials have had equivocal outcomes. In at least one area, that of tax policy, governments have managed to develop some reasonably effective arrangements for dealing with problems associated with multinational enterprises. Their relative success can be attributed to two factors. First, the multinational enterprises themselves have been supportive on the whole of some measures of international cooperation, fearful that they might otherwise be subject to double taxation. Second, the agreements could be grafted into the systems of tax collection in the countries concerned without greatly affecting their existing practices and institutions.

The tax policies of practically all governments with respect to multinational enterprises are based on a common assumption: A net profit can be calculated for each taxing jurisdiction that bears some reasonable relationship to reality and is not determined by wholly arbitrary allocations. To obtain a new profit figure for each jurisdiction, however, the multinational enterprise must be in a position to assign every sale and every purchase of its network to a given territory. In practical terms, of course, the affiliates making up enterprises like IBM or General Electric are so intimately interlinked that any such assignment is bound to involve arbitrary allocations on a large scale. How is one to assign the research expenditures of the network as a whole to each subsidiary? And how is one to say if the sale of a mainframe computer by one multinational to another took place in São Paulo, New York, or Paris?

Most taxing jurisdictions have preferred to ignore the fact that these allocations cannot escape being arbitrary. The U.S. system, for instance, begins with the presumption that realisitic allocations are feasible and doggedly challenges the tax returns of any multinational enterprise with which it happens to disagree. Once determined, however, the income of subsidiaries abroad is only taxable when it actually has been received by a U.S. taxpayer, whether in the form of dividends, royalties, or interest. At that stage, the obligation of the U.S. parent to pay is reduced by the amount already paid in income taxes by the subsidiary in the country where it operates.[27]

Since 1963, tax relations among member states of the OECD have been governed by a model convention that lays out guidelines for the creation of bilateral tax treaties. The model itself is not a formal legal document, but its provisions have been accepted and adopted by nearly all member states and even by some nonmembers.[28] As usual, the U.S. government has refused to alter its own tax approach when that approach deviated from the OECD model. The U.S. model published in 1977, for instance, identified the home territory of an enterprise by its place of incorporation, whereas the OECD followed the practice of many European countries in identifying the home territory as the place of management.[29] For the most part, however, the models followed by the United States and other OECD states are similar enough to make negotiations between them relatively simple. Moreover, building on their common approach, the United States and the other OECD nations have signed bilteral treaties of taxation with a number of other states, overcoming the political and economic differences that have so often hindered other types of international negotiation.[30]

The acceptance of common principles notwithstanding, the practice of partitioning profits among the various affiliates of a multinational enterprise has left many questions unanswered in individual cases. Illustrative of such a case was the aborted effort of the U.S. executive to enter into a tax treaty with the government of Pakistan. The treaty sought to deal with the Pakistani government's practice of granting temporary tax exemptions to the subsidiaries of foreign enterprises operating in its jurisdiction. Under U.S. law, when such a subsidiary remitted profits to its U.S. parent, the parent could not claim a credit for the foreign taxes that would have been paid in the absence of the exemption, a fact that served to defeat the purpose of Pakistan's tax exemption. One object of the bilateral treaty was to reestablish a credit for the U.S. parent in the payment of its U.S. taxes, as though the subsidiary had actually paid Pakistani taxes. But the effort of the U.S. executive to secure the adoption of that provision was unavailing; the U.S. Senate, exercising its traditional checking powers, refused to go along.

The various initiatives of the U.S. government in dealing with the foreign taxation of U.S.-based multinational enterprises have never questioned the idea that a strong rational basis exists for partitioning the profits of such enterprises among the various national jurisdictions in which they operate. Yet the unreality of that assumption has been too evident in some cases to be altogether overlooked. For a number of years, in fact, certain states in the United States have taken the position that for some firms the partitioning of profits among jurisdictions was an arbitrary exercise, and have demanded that the partitioning be done according to rules specified by the tax authorities. Such state formulas, for instance, have begun with the consolidated global profit of the parent and its subsidiaries and then have used a number of yardsticks for determining what proportion of the global profit should be assumed to have arisen in the taxing jurisdiction of the state. The allocating measures have characteristically been three: the ratio of employees in the state to global employment; the ratio of assets in the state to global assets; and the ratio of sales in the state to global sales. The share of global income allocated to the state has then been based upon the mean of these three measures. The application of these formulas by California and other states drew howls of protest from a number of governments, including Britain and Japan, as some of their subsidiaries in the United States were subjected to the new state formulas.[31]

From the viewpoint of multinational enterprises, of course, the use of such criteria has been threatening in several respects. First, it has exposed the enterprises to the risk that some taxing jurisdictions would use one approach and some another, leading to the double taxation of a part of their profits. Second, it has deprived multinational enterprises of the flexibility they retained as long as they could use internal rules of thumb to allocate their sales and expenses to various jurisdictions. And third, by forcing U.S. affiliates to provide highly detailed information about their parents' global affiliates, it has imposed major administrative burdens on the multinational enterprises.[32]

Most states, disconcerted by the protests of the multinationals, returned to the practice of assuming that the U.S. income of the multinational network could be separated out from the global income of the network. But one or two dragged their feet, thereby highlighting the extent to which the diffusion of power in the United

States can restrain the U.S. government in its conduct of international economic relations.

Despite issues such as the unitary tax problem, U.S. cooperation with other countries in the taxation of multinational enterprises must be counted a success. What has accounted for that success more than anything else has been the recognition by multinational enterprises that the agreements involved have served their interests rather than damaging them. Clinching acceptance of the agreements was the absence of any significant group that saw its interests imperiled.

POLITICS AND THE MULTINATIONAL ENTERPRISE

In the end, the most formidable obstacles to international cooperation on multinational enterprises may prove to be political rather than economic: an unwillingness on the part of governments to dilute their control over what they may regard as a potent instrument of the state, and a suspicion that other states may be using their multinational enterprises for just such purposes. In the extensive commentaries on the operations of multinational enterprises around the world, that possibility has emerged repeatedly, with U.S.-owned enterprises often cast in the role of agents of the U.S. government. In the recent expressions of concern of some Americans over the growing role of Japanese-owned firms in the U.S. economy, worries of that sort have also had a prominent place.

There can be no blinking the fact that governments have occasionally sought to use the foreign subsidiaries of their home enterprises to promote their national interests. When such efforts have surfaced, the foreign governments affected have usually been quick to cry foul. Of all such efforts, those of the U.S. government have been the most transparent, in accordance with the characteristic American style of governance; U.S. measures under its antitrust laws and its security export control regulations, for instance, have been widely publicized. Other countries, it can be assumed, have made similar efforts from time to time, although more quietly and discretely. On the basis of such evidence as exists, our strong impression is that governments have not succeeded very often in making effective use of the foreign subsidiaries of their home enterprises for national purposes. But it is the potentiality of such maneuvers rather than the actual effects that appear to constitute the real political problem.

In the case of the United States, part of the reason why multinational enterprises have not proved to be a very valuable national agent for the U.S. government has been that deeply embedded values have made it difficult for the government to develop close working relations with its multinational firms over any sustained period. The country's pervasive emphasis on the rights of individuals and enterprises to resist the command of governments as well as its consistent disposition to hold bureaucrats in check have effectively limited the scope of such working relationships. For the most part, the U.S. government's role in relation to its multinational enterprises has been limited to protecting the interests of U.S. citizens abroad, a role that it is commonly thought to pursue less assiduously than other governments.

Nevertheless, the U.S. government—like any other goverment—has sometimes engaged in a working relationship abroad with one of its multinational enterprises that could be construed as interfering in the internal affairs of other countries. United Fruit's role in the overthrow of the Guatemalan government in 1954 and the part played by ITT in the army takeover in Chile in 1973 were egregious illustrations of such a relationship, enough to create the impression that multinational enterprises based in the United States operate hand in glove with the U.S. government. A critical question facing policymakers therefore, is how much the U.S. government would be giving up in political terms if its authority over U.S.-based multinational enterprises were diluted by international agreements seeking to define their rights and responsibilities.

Because the question of the relationships between business and government in foreign affairs has been so contentious, no large generalization on the subject is immune from challenge.[33] Nevertheless, the relationship between the U.S. government and the U.S.-based international oil companies over the decades offers some telling indication of the limits of multinational enterprises as adjuncts for the execution of U.S. policies. The oil industry, of course, is the extreme case. Governments have rarely lost sight of the vital importance of oil, and the oil firms have rarely overlooked the political vulnerability of their foreign holdings. If a close partnership between business and government were feasible in any industry, it would surely appear in oil.

Yet the deeply embedded characteristics of the U.S. system to which we have repeatedly referred have greatly limited the value of that relationship for furthering the country's policies abroad. To be sure, during the rare episodes in which threats to the U.S. oil supply have assumed a distinctly military cast, the president has been free to make any demands on the oil firms and on the regulatory agencies he thought necessary. Once such crises have passed, however, the government's approach to the oil industry has been conducted at arm's length, subject to the usual checks and balances that shape U.S. economic policy. Individual agencies concerned with their respective objectives, whether antitrust policy, foreign aid, pollution control, or taxation, have dealt with the industry, including its critics and supporters, almost like any other.[34]

The Pre-cartel Era

An early illustration of the U.S. government's readiness to apply its various programs to the oil industry without much regard for the industry's strategic role was provided by the break-up of the Standard Oil Trust in 1911.[35] The institutions responsible for the action were the Department of Justice and the courts, operating under a law of general application, the Sherman Antitrust Act. Neither of these institutions was empowered or expected to weigh the foreign policy consequences of its actions. Indeed, despite the U.S. oil industry's commanding position in world petroleum trade at the time, the international ramifications of the government's suit barely figured in the case. Yet the ultimate effect was to alter the oil industry's foreign position by multiplying the number of U.S. firms engaged in U.S. exports and exploitation of overseas oil resources.

With the end of World War I, the fear arose in some U.S. official circles that the country might soon be running out of oil. In an uncharacteristic reaction, the government undertook to support the U.S. oil companies' efforts to gain concessions in the oil-rich areas around the Persian Gulf, areas under the control of Great Britain and France. The story of these efforts has been told in considerable detail and in several different versions.[36] What is clear beyond question is that a program that started as a government-sponsored effort to increase the supply of oil soon strayed from that objective and emerged a decade later as a company-sponsored effort to limit oil supplies.

The change in direction and the shift in control were probably connected to a change in the American political scene; the program was launched in a Democratic administration and pursued in a Republican one. But the shift was made easier by the fact that communications between the government and the companies in the intervening years were fragmentary and sporadic. During the decade after the start of the program, government fears of shortage had given away to company fears of glut. Accordingly, the government's efforts to find a *modus vivendi* for the U.S. companies with their British and the French rivals only laid the foundations for an international oil cartel, which took shape in 1928 in a series of private agreements between the four or five companies then dominating the world oil trade.

Eventually, in order to make the cartel's operations more effective, U.S. production was brought under control through the intervention of state regulatory authorities, among them the Texas Railroad Commission. That step could not have been achieved without the active support of the domestic oil producers who, in the depths of a depression, were pleased to support any measures that would avoid a glut of oil. The U.S. government remained largely a passive partner in the affair, uninvolved in the policies or operations of the cartel. It was not until the latter 1930s, under the stimulus of congressional investigations, that the government again exhibited an active interest in the international operations of the vital industry.

Preparing for War

The events leading up to the creation of the international oil cartel do lend some support to the "capture theory" of the U.S. governmental process—the theory that U.S. special interests often determine the purpose and direction of government regulations. They are also consistent with the picture of a government whose approach to problems involving the international business activities of U.S. firms is poorly coordinated as a rule, with a short span of attention for any given issue.

Occasionally the U.S. government has exhibited a capacity for some consistency in its relations with the international oil companies. During the 1930s, for instance, the government engaged in a sustained effort to check Japan's various military ventures in Asia. That U.S. interest stemmed in part from the passionate desire of old-line State Department bureaucrats to protect U.S. treaty rights in China, an objective for which they had labored since the last decade of the nineteenth century. A second objective, which only emerged as the dominant purpose very late in the 1930s, was to keep Japan from building up the potential to make war against the United States and its allies. In that exceptional situation, the U.S. government was prepared to make direct demands on its oil companies in the national interest, and the oil companies were prepared to respond to those demands.[37]

Foreign policy objectives also were a determining factor in how the U.S. government handled the expropriation of U.S. oil companies by Mexico in 1938, a move that followed closely upon the less extensive Bolivian nationalization of oil in 1937.[38] Though the affected oil companies urged the State Department to become involved, the U.S. government's principal concern at the time was to keep German and Japanese interests out of the western hemisphere; accordingly, it made only limited efforts to press the companies' claims.[39] As World War II closed in, the U.S. government quietly settled the oil companies' claims on terms favorable to Mexico.

Whereas the events of the 1930s suggest that larger foreign policy objectives were likely to take precedence over the more parochial interests of the oil companies when the two seemed in conflict, events of the 1940s present a picture that is both more complex and more familiar. As in the case of trade policy, warring factions seemed engaged in a continuous process of advances and counterattacks, employing the various checks and balances built into the U.S. policy-making system. Once again, one can detect the extent to which a well-placed official in the executive branch could seize the initiative, avoiding the opposition for a time in the promotion of large new ideas. Once again, one can glimpse the strength of the U.S. government's aversion to a direct transactional role in international markets. Both of these patterns are illustrated in the initial launching and eventual fate of a wartime proposal that would have made the U.S. government a partner with the Standard Oil Company of California (Socal) and the Texas Company (Texaco) in the production and transportation of Saudi Arabian oil.

That the proposal could have been entertained seriously inside the U.S. government over a period of months was due to the qualities of an unusual secretary of the interior, Harold L. Ickes, a man closely associated with President Roosevelt over a number of years. A hothouse wartime atmosphere had briefly increased the country's tolerance for assigning the U.S. government an aggressive economic role. Ickes, worried about the prospects of an adequate long-term supply of oil to the United States, proposed in 1943 the establishment of a Petroleum Reserve Corporation to purchase the Saudi and Bahraini oil concessions from Socal and Texaco.

Soon, the familiar process of checks and balances came to bear on the proposal. Although every government official except the secretary of state supported the purchase of the Middle Eastern concessions, representatives from the oil industry predictably resisted the arrangement. Oil executives were able to voice their opposition to Congress, which responded by creating a special Petroleum Committee in the spring of 1944. On the Hill, corporate pressure was aided by the usual deep-seated distaste for governmental intervention in the private sphere. By 1944, the objections of the oil industry had killed the project.[40]

The Postwar Adjustments

A similar fate befell the proposed Anglo-American Petroleum Agreement. This agreement was a brainchild of officials in the State Department, who saw it as a means of arranging U.S. and British petroleum interests in the Middle East so as to provide a secure and equitable supply for the companies headquartered in the two countries and of continuing some of the market controls that the international cartel had applied. A preliminary agreement was concluded by Britain and the United States in 1944. Almost immediately, its proponents ran into opposition from various members of Congress who argued that the government-sponsored agreement would preclude independent U.S. oil companies from gaining their rightful share of the market. Unwilling to risk a confrontation, particularly with Tom Connally of Texas, chairman of the Senate Foreign Relations Committee, the bureaucrats invited six industry "advisors" to help them renegotiate the agreement with the British government in order to meet some of the objections.

However, even these efforts proved ineffective. By the time the treaty reached the floor of Congress in 1947, a basic division between the international oil companies and the domestic oil companies, which had surfaced repeatedly at critical junctures in the past, was once more in evidence. The domestic producers feared that such an agreement would transfer regulation of the industry to federal agencies and that the transfer would weaken their power while building up that of the international companies. At the same time, the glut at the war's end anticipated by the oil industry failed to materialize, reducing the industry's interest in finding an effective successor to the prewar international oil cartel. Shorn of industry backing, the coalition of Ickes, the State Department, and the international oil companies crumbled.[41]

Anyone seeking to generalize about the nature of U.S. official support for the international oil companies in the first decade after World War II will find some evidence for almost any proposition, ranging from the argument that the U.S. government was hostile to the companies to the contention that it was strongly supportive. In actual fact, no coherent government policy emerged, and a number of different agencies pursued their own distinctive programs without any effort at coordination, applying measures ranging from the hurtful to the helpful.

The disparate and unfocused nature of U.S. policies toward the international operations of the oil companies was especially evident in the early 1950s. In a lingering echo of Thurman Arnold's crusade against international cartels, the Federal Trade Commission in 1952 produced its celebrated report on the international oil cartel.[42] The Justice Department made immediate use of the report, recommending that the facts go to a grand jury for a possible criminal indictment against the U.S.-based oil companies.[43] Almost at the same time, the U.S. Mutual Security Agency, which was financing oil supplies from the Middle East purchased under the European Recovery Program, decided to stop financing such purchases on the grounds that they were overpriced. A short time later, the Justice Department filed suit against the five U.S.-based multinationals operating in the Middle East, charging that their high prices were created by restrictive business practices. The debate that ensued was fierce, dividing the antagonists in terms of both interests and ideologies. The antitrusters drew their support from the usual U.S. distaste for monopoly power. The oil companies maintained that their elevated prices and collusive agreements were essential to protect the resources of the free world from communist takeovers.

By late 1952, passions began to cool, and sights were turned on the imminent Republican transition. A few weeks before leaving office, President Truman announced his decision to drop criminal charges against the oil companies but to continue a civil suit for the recapture of excessive profits. For the moment, at least, security concerns appeared to have tempered the drive against monopolistic control.

New Threats to Stability

In hindsight, it appears that the administration's change of heart was conditioned by a dramatic episode, in which oil once again figured in U.S. strategic interests.

Between 1951 and 1954, a rebellious prime minister in Iran had gained control of the government, nationalized the British-owned oil properties in the country, and then was himself ousted by the Shah.[44] The resulting turmoil threatened two vital U.S. interests. The oil companies and other commercial interests feared that even a tacit acceptance of the Iranian nationalization would undermine other contractual obligations between U.S. firms and foreign states in the Middle East and elsewhere. In addition, the U.S. military, still reeling from the onset of the Korean War, worried about the possibility of new oil shortages and about the Soviet Union's exploiting any political unrest in Iran. If U.S. firms could take a direct hand in managing the oil industry in Iran, it was thought, the noncommunist world's oil supplies would be assured and Iran would be restored to economic and political stability.

Working in an atmosphere of crisis created by the seizure of the British oil properties, U.S. government officials early in 1951 hastily put together a Foreign Petroleum Emergency Committee, composed primarily of corporate oil executives and intended to reorder the existing pattern of petroleum supplies to compensate for the gap created by the Iranian nationalization.[45] At first, officials at the Justice Department and the Federal Trade Commission objected to the arrangement as a blatant violation of antitrust regulation. In the end, however, even these officials were persuaded to accept the argument that the security of petroleum and the stability of Iran had to prevail over the enforcement of the antitrust laws.[46]

As the Iranian situation evolved, it became obvious that Iran would not reverse its earlier nationalization of the British oil company. Accordingly, U.S. negotiators began to work with elements within Iran to carve out new arrangements. What emerged in the end was the so-called consortium concession under which an 8 percent share in Iranian oil was allotted to each of the five major American petroleum companies operating in the Middle East, with a remaining 60 percent shared among a British, a Dutch, and a French firm. Subsequently, the U.S. government persuaded the five American companies to relinquish a portion of their new interests to a group of eight independent companies, all of them eager to gain access to the relatively cheap oil supplies of the Persian gulf.[47]

Of course, the political power of the so-called independent oil companies in the United States was nothing new; it had been evident on numerous occasions in earlier years. Because the independents produced oil in many states, they were able to put together a fairly large coalition of congressional supporters. Perhaps the clearest manifestation of the power wielded by the independents was the policy adopted in 1954 of restricting oil imports from the Middle East through a system of quotas. Instituted originally as a so-called voluntary program, the quota system was based on the contention that U.S. security interests were best served by restricting the country's dependence on overseas supply, a position that some observers derided as a policy to "drain America first." President Eisenhower himself favored an alternative policy by which low-cost foreign oil would be purchased and stockpiled.[48] Nevertheless, he bowed to the recommendation of his Advisory Committee on Energy Supplies and Resources Policy, aware that the quota system had widespread support in Congress.[49] Predictably, the voluntary system gradually lost its bite, and in 1959 an official import quota system was imposed.

The mandatory program was a victory for protectionist forces within the country, especially for the domestic oil and coal industry. The victims of the program, of course, were the majors, who would have been the beneficiaries of expanded Middle Eastern oil imports. Adding insult to injury, the U.S. government not only limited the volume of crude oil imports but obliged the multinationals to share with other U.S. refiners the extra profits on imports resulting from the protection.[50]

Over the years the mandatory system became a weight around the necks of successive administrations. Consumer groups resented the higher prices they were forced to pay at the pumps, and the State Department constantly reiterated its fear that the U.S. import quotas would force the exporting countries to form a cartel.[51] Most importantly, the program also came under attack by the larger U.S. oil firms, who saw themselves losing out in the complicated series of allotments and exemptions. During the Johnson administration in the latter 1960s, the program contained so many loopholes that it became nearly impossible to administer. Moreover, gasoline prices reached new highs, while domestic production continued to decline.[52] By the early 1970s, it became clear that the mandatory import program had broken down, to be displaced by new measures addressed to a very different set of problems.

More Middle East Uncertainties

Despite an occasional experiment using multinational enterprises as agents for the execution of national policies, the U.S. government has been generally unwilling—or unable—to use the multinational oil companies in that role. That characteristic of U.S. behavior is illustrated strikingly by the interactions between the U.S. government and its international oil companies during two major oil crises: the French-British-Israeli invasion of Egypt in 1956, aimed at depriving the Egyptians of their control over the Suez Canal; and the oil crisis in the fall of 1973, a byproduct of the so-called Yom Kippur war between Egypt and Israel. In both situations, the logistical performance of the oil companies was critical in terms of U.S. national interests; yet, in both instances, official U.S. guidance to the companies was remarkably limited, indeed almost altogether absent.

Egypt nationalized the Suez Canal in July 1956, thereby creating a major threat to the uninterrupted supply of oil to Western Europe. Immediately thereafter, the U.S. government established a Middle East Emergency Committee, a structure within which 15 major U.S. oil companies with operations in the Middle East could coordinate their shipping activities, operating under the mantle of an antitrust exemption. That step might have been construed as the beginning of a U.S. effort to shape the actions of the U.S. oil companies; but, as usual, such efforts were limited in scope and feeble in effect. Despite the antitrust exemption, the companies demurred from planning for future contingencies under the aegis of the government-sponsored committee. Instead, each built up its supplies in Western Europe independently in reaction to the threat.

In October 1956, Britain, France, and Israel launched a joint attack on Egypt, a move to which the U.S. government took the strongest exception. In response to the attack, the defending Egyptians blocked the Suez Canal and blew up some critical pipelines between the Persian Gulf and the Mediterranean, thereby choking off oil supplies to Western Europe. The U.S. government was intensely hostile to the British-French-Israeli initiative, resentful that its allies had not consulted with the United States before launching the attack. To express its displeasure, the United States withdrew the oil companies' exemption from antitrust laws.

Once the invasion had been ended, however, the U.S. government reverted to its more traditional stance as an ally of Western Europe and turned its attention to the urgent task of maintaining an uninterrupted supply of petroleum to the area. With the Suez Canal effectively blocked, some other means had to be found for supplying the continent with its daily needs of about a half million barrels of petroleum products.[53]

Once again, U.S. oil companies were the only available conduit, and the State Department, under pressure from its European counterparts, called for increased U.S. production. President Eisenhower then restored the oil companies' antitrust exemption and ordered the reactivation of the industry committee to arrange tanker schedules and plan for orderly allocations of available oil.[54] Despite these gestures, very little coordination was actually achieved, the oil companies preferring to limit their collaboration to some "lukewarm" and "scattered" actions.[55] Indeed, for a two-month period early in 1957, the Texas Railroad Commission, the powerful body regulating production of oil in that state, was allowed to prevent increases in output that might have eased the European shortage.

Throughout the Suez crisis, the U.S. government ostentatiously stayed at arm's length from the actual operation of the scheme for serving Western Europe with oil; government officials left the situation to companies to manage and professed a lack of authority to do more. Only when the actions of the Texas Railroad Commission were directly at variance with the goals of the U.S. government did the president threaten federal action. Even in that episode, however, the president's influence was exerted on the government of the state of Texas, not on the international oil companies.[56]

The 1973 oil crisis was in some respects a rerun of the 1956 affair as far as relations between the U.S. government and the U.S. oil companies were concerned. As a consequence of the 1973 attack upon Israel by Egypt and Syria, Saudi Arabia and other Arab producers embargoed the shipment of oil to the United States and the Netherlands. At the same time, Saudi Arabia instructed the international oil companies operating in its territory to reduce their aggregate production by the amounts represented in the embargoed shipments. That command contributed to a wave of panic buying, along with spectacular increases in oil prices.[57] Once again, vital interests in the United States were at stake; once again, the U.S. government refused to provide any substantial guidance to the international oil companies and refrained from showing displeasure at their ostentatious show of obedience to the Saudi demands.

Another aspect of the crisis was of larger magnitude and longer duration, namely, the allocation pattern that the oil companies followed in distributing supplies during the shortage. Unlike the governments of the United Kingdom, France, and Japan, the U.S. government made no serious effort to influence the distribution. Without explicit coordination, the oil companies reshuffled their supplies in patterns tending to distribute the shortfall quite uniformly among the various major markets.[58]

Before the 1973 crisis highlighted the limited degree of coordination between the U.S. government and its international oil companies, other incidents leading up the 1973 crisis had already suggested the looseness of that relationship. During the latter 1960s and early 1970s, the companies with oil concessions in North Africa and the Persian Gulf were confronting a succession of crises, following repeated demands by individual governments in the oil-exporting countries that the terms of such concessions should be altered in their favor. In the string of negotiations that ensued, each oil-exporting country used the modifications already obtained by another country as the basis for a new escalation of demands.

Although the oil companies made numerous efforts to impress the dangers of this process on the U.S. government, they failed to elicit much more than occasional expressions of sympathy from government officials. Eventually, determined to put a halt to the leapfrogging process, the companies coordinated their negotiating efforts. In order for U.S. firms to use such a tactic, they were required to secure an antitrust waiver from the United States. After some delay, the Department of Justice agreed to issue a carefully qualified waiver just on the eve of a renegotiation with the Shah of Iran.[59]

What followed illustrates the special difficulties faced by the United States in maintaining a consistent course. Twenty-four oil companies joined forces in a well-prepared position aimed at resisting the Shah's demands. Some agencies in the U.S. government presumably hoped that the oil companies would succeed in their efforts to hold the line on their concession contracts. At the same time, others in the U.S. government were eager not to offend the Shah, who was seen as the linchpin in U.S. strategy for containing Soviet influence in the Middle East. Accordingly, in an interview with a visiting under secretary of state in Teheran, the Shah was allowed to come away with the impression that the U.S. government would not take umbrage if he were to impose his demands on the oil companies. Needless to say, that is just what he did. Once again, the separation of the public from the private sector was strikingly evident.

In Summary

A central message conveyed by these various episodes is the significance of the boundary between the private and the public sectors in the conduct of U.S. foreign economic policy. If close and continuous ties had developed between the international oil companies and the U.S. government, the relationship would have created acute discomfiture among many Americans, bringing the system of checks and balances into play.

The distance maintained between the private and the public sector does not stem from the public side alone. The multinational oil companies have shown no strong disposition to bring the U.S. government closely into their plans and operations; on the contrary, the general rule of such companies, consistent with the tradition and preferences of U.S. business, has been to hold the government at a distance, except occasionally as needed. Even when the U.S. government appeared to be needed, the oil industry as a whole has found it hard to agree on exactly what the government was needed for.

On its part, the U.S. government has usually operated in a characteristic pattern. From time to time, it has identified national goals of great urgency that demanded the unqualified support of all sectors of the economy. By and large, however, the government has had difficulty in reconciling its various goals and maintaining a consistent set of priorities. The idea of a symbiotic link between the public and the private sectors gets little support from the history of the U.S. oil industry.

SEARCHING FOR COOPERATIVE PRINCIPLES

In the 1980s, for the first time since World War I, the direct investment of foreigners in U.S. industry and U.S. financial institutions grew to a level that was no longer minuscule. Between 1979 and 1986, foreign direct investment in the United States jumped from a little over $50 billion to more than $200 billion.[60] Suddenly, U.S. policymakers were obliged to take more than a peripheral interest in the activities of multinational firms and to face some of the issues raised by the specter of overlapping and conflicting jurisdictions.

In their search for principles by which to launch international discussions of the questions raised by multinational firms, U.S. policymakers have been constrained by the historical relationship existing between business and the state in the United States. In the past, U.S. policymakers rarely gave much thought to the anomalous aspects of multinational enterprises as institutions. When they did, they settled on formulas that accorded with the general preference of Americans, with the view that enterprises as a rule should be free to respond to market forces and that the U.S. government's position should be neutral as to their choice.[61]

In the past, the desire of the U.S. government to exercise a passive role in the decisions of multinational enterprises has been strongly in evidence, both with respect to domestic controls and in negotiations with foreign governments. U.S. control of multinational enterprises as such has been rare, while international negotiations have been limited to situations in which the multinationals themselves have preferred regulation to anarchy. When negotiations occurred, the U.S. objective usually has been to obtain the widest possible freedom for its enterprises under the laws of other countries.

Illustrative of these tendencies have been the provisions sought by the U.S. government in discussions with member countries of the OECD and in bilateral agreements with other countries. One basic tenet to which the U.S. government has consistently adhered is that the foreign subsidiaries of U.S.-based firms should be entitled to "national treatment" in the countries where they operate, that is, the same treatment accorded to a similar enterprise owned by nationals rather than by foreigners. Going even further, U.S. negotiators have also sought so-called most-favored-nation treatment for U.S. subsidiaries abroad, as well as assurances that foreign governments would adhere to the provisions of any contract negotiated with an enterprise owned by a U.S. national. Finally, U.S. negotiators have tried to safeguard any rights that U.S. nationals might claim under the general principles and practices recognized in international law.[62] In effect, the U.S. government has held out for rights on behalf of subsidiaries operating in foreign countries that exceed the rights available to the nationals of these countries.

At the same time, the U.S. government has refused to relinquish its own right to protect or control the behavior of U.S. subsidiaries located in foreign countries. Furthermore, whenever U.S. interests seemed to require it, various U.S. agencies have been unwilling to acknowledge that the enterprises of other countries were entitled to national treatment. In the case involving the IBM computer sale to a Soviet-controlled company in Germany, for instance, some U.S. officials insisted that the Soviet-controlled enterprise, created under German law, should be treated as if it were located in the Soviet Union. And in the case of Fujitsu, the U.S. government refused to allow the Japanese firm the privilege of acquiring a company created under U.S. law—a company, incidentally, that was already largely owned by foreigners.

Obviously, the U.S. tendency to cut its principles to fit its interests constitutes an invitation to widespread jurisdictional conflicts. As long as foreign-owned enterprises held an insignificant position in the U.S. economy, the U.S. government could afford to deal with issues related to such enterprises on an ad hoc basis. As foreign-owned enterprises acquire an increasing role in the U.S. economy, however, the U.S. government will be obliged to confront the basic questions of jurisdictional conflicts and uncertain control inherent in the multinational structure of enterprise. The preference of governments and enterprises to dodge such issues where they can is likely to give way ultimately to a realization that such issues can only be dealt with effectively by international agreement. But under the U.S. system of governance, it appears unlikely that such agreements will be possible until the enterprises themselves see such agreements as preferable to the existing state of anarchy.

6

The Politics
of U.S. Foreign Aid

SHOULD THE BILATERAL FOREIGN AID programs of the United
States in the 1980s be regarded as an element in U.S. foreign economic policies or as a tool for propping up economies considered
vital to U.S. military security? However one may choose to answer
that question, a review of these programs is invaluable for shedding
light on the role of special interest groups in influencing U.S. foreign
policy.

THE POLITICS OF AID

The U.S. foreign aid program was launched in the same era and
motivated by the same spirit that produced the General Agreement
on Tariffs and Trade (GATT) and the International Trade Organization (ITO). It grew from the minds of a small core of like-minded
bureaucrats conditioned by the Great Depression and World War II,
men and women convinced that the United States had to seize the
initiative in shaping a peaceful postwar order and that the means
most suited to this task were primarily economic. Along with projects to reduce restrictions on the international movement of goods
and services, foreign aid was seen as an indispensable adjunct to economic development, which in turn was expected to contribute to lift-
ing the restrictions on international movements of goods and services.

Over the decades, however, the emphasis on economic development and liberal trading orders in U.S. foreign aid programs gradually declined, to be replaced by a growing concern for the diplomacy of realpolitik. Even with this new focus, foreign aid continued to command the support of the U.S. foreign policy establishment, albeit from different subsets of officials motivated by different international objectives.

The policymakers who have supported foreign aid over the decades, unlike those involved with trade, rarely have had to face the problems created by hostile domestic groups that saw their interests threatened. On the contrary, few groups in the United States have paid much attention to its foreign aid programs; most have been either unconcerned with U.S. foreign aid policies or mildly antagonistic to them. Thus, the challenge to policymakers favoring a continuation of foreign aid programs has been to identify groups with an interest in U.S. foreign aid and bring them together in a coalition sufficiently powerful to keep foreign aid on the country's political agenda.

In the postwar period, four primary motives have compelled groups and individuals to support U.S. foreign aid policies: the security motive, the commercial motive, the ethnic motive, and the humanitarian motive. Not surprisingly, the policies born of such strange bedfellows have often appeared ambiguous and inconsistent.

Of the four, the security motive has been the easiest to identify. Because the appeal to national security has always run deep, foreign aid policies promising to deliver strategic benefits have usually stood a good chance of winning public approval and official authorization. As a result, even when supporters of an aid program have had goals other than security in mind, they have often tried to promote the program under the security umbrella. For instance, although the European Recovery Program was conceived by the various innovators involved in its creation with a number of purposes in mind, it was presented to the public primarily as a defense against communism and, as such, won widespread public approval. Truman's Point Four program for technical aid to underdeveloped nations, first proposed in 1949, did not really pick up momentum until the Korean War and growing Soviet involvement in developing countries created the public opinion that a battle was being waged for the Third World, a battle that the United States had to win. Similarly, the Cuban Revolution of 1959 laid the groundwork for President Kennedy's Alliance for Progress in 1961. The political support for aid to Israel, although pressed hardest by an "Israel lobby" with ethnic and religious ties to Israel, has been based to a considerable extent on Israel's role in U.S. security. By the 1980s, the security motive in U.S. foreign aid policy was unmistakable in the pattern of aid allocation, with the largest percentage of funds flowing to countries perceived as capable of giving the United States some strategic return, such as base rights or access to critical waterways.

Commercial motives also have been a continuing feature of U.S. foreign aid policy, helping to explain the longtime support of foreign aid programs by several key domestic groups. Farmers, for instance, have staunchly advocated the PL-480 (or Food for Peace) program, a means by which U.S. crops have been sold to countries that otherwise would have lacked the foreign exchange to buy them. Exporters of heavy equipment, construction engineering firms, and management consulting firms have had a long-term stake in programs assisting foreign countries in the building of their national infrastructure. Similarly, private firms interested in investing in Third World countries have relied on the assistance and insurance provided by the Overseas Private Investment Corporation (OPIC) and the Export–Import Bank (Ex–Im) and have been ready to support foreign aid policies that promised to improve the conditions for foreign investment in the recipient states.

The humanitarian motive has also been a constant, albeit wavering and inconsistent, element of domestic support for U.S. foreign aid policies. In the immediate postwar period, many U.S. leaders were motivated by a desire to share the benefits of the U.S. economic system with other countries. Even in later years, the charitable motivation was never wholly absent from the hearts and minds of U.S. taxpayers.[1]

More specific manifestations of the humanitarian motive have been evidenced by the many U.S.-based private voluntary organizations and universities making personal and professional commitments to the goal of Third World development. In the years immediately following World War II, voluntary organizations were motivated by the compelling desire of their members to help alleviate the effects of poverty in the developing countries. In addition, university groups were attracted by the challenge of studying and mastering the processes of development. In a decade or two, the research and experience of the voluntary organizations and the universities had added greatly to understanding of the development process. Although the activities of these organizations were partly funded with private capital, as their projects grew more ambitious, they began to rely on government funding; even groups not receiving direct federal support often became linked to large-scale projects that were dependent on federal funds. Humanitarian and educational motivations still could be detected in the 1980s. In the meantime, both the university groups and the voluntary organizations found themselves driven by the need to keep their institutions going.

Less well recognized, perhaps, have been the ethnic concerns that have influenced the shaping of foreign aid policies from time to time, as ethnic and religious groups forced the plight of their overseas kin onto the political agenda. Because these groups have tended to be well organized and deeply devoted to their causes, they have often had a political clout that belied their relatively small size. Aid to Israel is the best-known example of the strength of the ethnic motive, but it can also be seen in U.S. economic support for Poland, Greece, Ireland, and black Africa. While the ethnic motive has rarely been as powerful as the security motive in mobilizing support for foreign aid, the evidence suggests that persistent and focused lobbying by ethnic interest groups has often been sufficient to affect the course of U.S. foreign aid policies.

As we observed earlier, however, public support for foreign aid outside the narrow circle of special interests has rarely been strong. The humanitarian instinct has been visible at times, but since the Vietnam War, it has been increasingly vulnerable to budgetary squeezes. As a result, the officials directing the U.S. aid programs have constantly had to scramble to reassemble a pro-aid coalition strong enough to override the passivity, not to say mild hostility, of the public at large. For the most part, the combination of a few dedicated bureaucrats and several well-organized interest groups has proved successful. The foreign aid coalition that has emerged has managed to continue the U.S. foreign aid programs over the decades, albeit by drastically modifying their content and direction to accord with shifts in political sentiment.

Occasionally, this coalition has benefited from a happy concordance of separate interests. More often, though, there has been no such serendipitous outcome. Rather, the policymakers concerned with foreign aid have constantly had to repackage their programs, stressing the facets most likely to spark the lobbying efforts of concerned groups or gain the ear of a high-ranking politician who might see his own purposes supported by a particular aid program.

The public reaction to the aid-supporting coalitions, although weak, has not been altogether apathetic. From time to time, special interests have arrayed themselves on the other side, eager to curtail or condition the grant of foreign aid. Some of these adversaries have been appeased easily by ensuring that the provision of aid does not damage their special interest. In one case, for instance, the United States gave aid to South Korea but extracted a promise from the South Korean government to restrict its textile exports to the United States to a prescribed limit. In another, aid to Peru and Bolivia was made contingent on their cooperation with U.S. drug enforcement programs.[2] Other groups, however, have posed more difficult problems; some have opposed giving foreign aid to countries that allow abortion, refuse economic reforms, or violate standards of human rights.

Observe, however, that the groups wishing to condition the grant of foreign aid often support the idea of continuing aid programs in general. For many of them, foreign aid has been a lever for influencing the behavior of other governments; in the absence of such programs, that influence could be lost. Accordingly, in sharpest contrast to the foreign trade programs, support for foreign aid itself can usually be mobilized even from among the ranks of those who seem to be in opposition.

THE DEVELOPMENT OF U.S. FOREIGN AID DOCTRINE

The Marshall Plan

In the wake of World War II, the United States was boosted into superpower status and the Truman administration faced the task of rebuilding the war-torn economies of Europe and creating the foundations of a liberal international order. From the start, the officials charged with postwar reconstruction saw themselves facing three major challenges: reestablishing a workable international economic system; reducing the threat of communist expansion; and alleviating the hardships facing the Europeans in the immediate postwar years.

Foreign aid was first proposed as a means of bolstering the floundering Greek and Turkish states against the possibility of a Soviet takeover in the earliest days of the postwar period. At first, Congress balked at the administration's proposal, but it soon relented. Foreign policy was still perceived as the executive's domain, and no interest groups were sufficiently threatened by the proposal to lobby against it. The Truman administration poured $400 million into Turkey and Greece, earmarking most of the funds for the purchase of arms and the provisioning of national troops fighting the communist-backed guerrillas.[3] Within several years the program appeared to have succeeded. Both states were being governed by administrations friendly to the United States, and both economies—although shaky—seemed on the way to recovery.

Over the next few years, U.S. officials drew upon this experience to launch the European Recovery Program, or Marshall Plan, the largest aid program ever conceived. On June 5, 1947, Secretary of State George Marshall presented his historic commencement address at Harvard University. In it, he outlined the plan's goals: to rehabilitate the war-torn economies of Europe and thereby bolster the economic and political strength of the continent. The means to that end would be simple: a massive transfer of U.S. goods and capital to Europe.

In his speech, Marshall emphasized the need for U.S. economic power to provide the basis for European recovery. He asked that the United States take upon itself the burden of doing whatever was necessary to assist in the recovery process.[4] In public forums across the country, administration officials echoed Marshall's plea, gradually supplementing it with warnings of a Soviet threat in Europe. President Truman publicly expressed alarm over the possibility that Europe might stray from the American model of free-market capitalism,[5] and a presidential committee predicted that if the European nations turned toward state-controlled economic policies, the United States would soon have to follow suit.[6]

The response to these pleas was swift and substantial. In 1948, Congress passed the Economic Cooperation Act to implement the European Recovery Program. The act authorized a $17 billion allocation of funds over a four-year period, most of which was to be given as grants to the Europeans to buy U.S. goods. Within four years, the program was completed and declared an unparalleled success. Its stated goals had been achieved at a cost about $4 billion below the projected allocation.[7] Ever since that time, the Marshall Plan has been heralded as an unqualified triumph of U.S. foreign policy.[8] It has come to symbolize U.S. postwar strength and prestige; nearly all succeeding aid programs have been presented to the public as reincarnations of the European Recovery Program.[9]

It is beyond the scope of this book to examine the reasons for the

Marshall Plan's success. What does concern us is why the recovery program was adopted so easily by Congress and supported by the U.S. public. After all, the Marshall Plan demanded a $17 billion outlay of U.S. funds. In a political system relying on the struggle among interests to determine its decisions, why did the U.S. public and the U.S. legislators in Congress agree to spend so much money on the recovery of Europe?

Many observers have claimed that the fear of communism was primarily responsible for catalyzing agreement on the Marshall Plan. Our conclusion, however, is that while anti-communism was indeed a potent factor during the immediate postwar period, it was not the animating spirit behind Marshall Plan aid. Rather, the European Recovery Program was the result of a rare convergence of different interests, all of which appeared to be satisfied by a common instrument.

Early in 1947, the administration had begun to assemble a small group of men under the auspices of the State Department's Policy Planning Staff to hammer out a strategy for bolstering the course of European reconstruction. Led by George F. Kennan, the exercise involved a diverse mix of individuals, including Will Clayton, Charles Bohlen, and Charles P. Kindleberger. All of the men involved were convinced that economic reconstruction was critical to global political stability and that no such reconstruction could occur unless Germany was an integral part of it.[10] Similarly, all were convinced that Europe could only recuperate as a whole and that nothing would be gained by alienating the French or abandoning the British. They reasoned that committing itself to pulling Germany out of economic disarray obligated the United States to extend commensurate aid to the other European nations. Only then would the French relax their demands for full reparations from the German economy. And only then could an economic basis be laid for peaceful stability in Europe.

The final report produced by Kennan and his policy planning staff was a brilliant amalgam of all the worries and hopes that had plagued U.S. policymakers since the war's end. To the president and the public, the Marshall Plan was a shield against communism; to economists, it was the way to avoid an international recession; to the administrators of the occupation zone, it was a chance to rehabilitate Germany without forever alienating the French; and to the concerned bureaucrats, it was a means of reestablishing Europe as a key participant in a new international economic system.

In the months that followed Marshall's speech, the administration launched a remarkable campaign to spread the gospel of the Marshall Plan. In the fall of 1947, just as Truman was calling Congress together to review his request for interim aid for Europe, a presidential committee reported its findings that the European Recovery Program would be good for American business. Former Under Secretary of State Dean Acheson assembled a grass roots Citizens' Committee for the Marshall Plan. The Office of Education put together a comprehensive program called "Zeal for American Democracy," designed to assist U.S. teachers in giving a "patriotic emphasis" to education.[11]

On Capital Hill, as well, proponents of the Marshall Plan quickly learned that while European cooperation was boring to most members of Congress, fighting communism was not. The final assault in Congress took the form of a speech delivered by Truman in 1948, a few weeks before the passage of the required legislation. In it, he argued that the difficulties facing the world were chiefly due to the disruptive actions of the Soviet Union and its efforts to spread communism throughout Europe.[12] Within two days, the House committee debating the bill reported it out to the full House, where it passed by an overwhelming majority.

For our purposes, the main story of the Marshall Plan is the nearly universal consensus that the Truman administration was able to muster on its behalf. This consensus resulted in part from the extraordinary world conditions covering two decades of depression and war that led many of the country's elite to hold certain views in common. The consensus, however, was not wholly spontaneous; rather, it was produced in part by the efforts of several high-ranking officials in the Truman administration who had committed themselves to the Marshall Plan and were determined to sell it to the public.

Point Four

While the Marshall Plan was still under way, the Truman administration launched efforts to duplicate its success. Heady with the victory of European reconstruction, many U.S. officials believed the program could be repeated on a broader scale, with the United States invigorating the lagging economies and strengthening the political structures of other areas of the world.

By all accounts, the Marshall Plan had achieved its strategic goals of strengthening Europe and containing communism at a minimum cost to the United States. The U.S. public, therefore, was prepared to be generous again. Likewise, the officials of the Truman administration were suffused with a certain idealism and a belief in the healing powers of U.S. foreign aid.[13] Truman himself seemed to share these sentiments; much of his correspondence reveals a basic faith in the relationship between economic prosperity and peace and a desire to be remembered as the president who extended Roosevelt's New Deal to the entire world.[14]

Thus, several of the bureaucrats who were present at the creation of the Marshall Plan began to hammer out a new scheme of U.S.-backed economic rehabilitation. This time, the creators envisioned a program carrying the successes of the European plan to the less-developed countries. Once again, the same cluster of objectives was apparent. Strategic considerations were given top billing, while humanitarian objectives and economic development formed a smaller part of the appeal.[15]

Dubbed "Point Four," the new program was first aired by Truman in his 1949 inaugural address, in which he requested a "bold new program for making the benefits of our scientific advances and industrial progress available for the improvement and growth of underdeveloped areas."

In theory, the objectives of Point Four went considerably beyond those sought under the Marshall Plan. Rather than only committing the United States to a one-shot injection of funds for reconstruction, Point Four implied that the U.S. government would involve itself in the much longer and broader processes of Third World development. The authors of Point Four envisioned legislation that would support U.S. technical missions in health, education, industrial development, and other areas associated with the basic transformation of the developing countries.[16]

The process by which the Truman administration promoted the Point Four program, however, differed in some significant respects from its advocacy of the Marshall Plan, reflecting a change in the U.S. political environment. Five years had elapsed since the end of World War II, bringing an inescapable decline in executive authority and an unavoidable weakening of the common views that had been shared by labor leaders, businessmen, politicians, and bureaucrats. Before attempting to win congressional approval for Point Four, therefore, the administration took the nearly unprecedented step of consulting all those who might want a say in the direction of the program and all those whose opposition could mean an end to it.

Numerous members of Congress, private groups, and federal agencies were queried in an effort to ensure that the enabling legislation would be acceptable to the broad spectrum of U.S. public and official opinion.[17]

In the process of consultation, it gradually became clear that Point Four was not just a larger Marshall Plan and that its prospects were considerably dimmer. For one thing, the long-term program implied by Point Four would put the U.S. government in the business of economic intervention abroad, a commitment at odds with the principal admonition of George Washington's farewell address. Moreover, like the proposal for an International Trade Organization, which was debated at the same time, Point Four's agenda suggested building up the economic role of foreign governments in the Third World, an idea offensive to U.S. ideology. The administration's proposal languished in Congress, eventually gaining only a modified approval, and a scaled-down appropriation.[18]

In late 1950, however, the administration's plan for Third World aid was suddenly reinvigorated by the eruption of war in Korea and new fears of communist expansion. Once again, the security motive became preeminent, and, once again, the U.S. foreign aid program became the most convenient means by which to launch a counteroffensive against perceived Soviet aggression. In 1951, Congress passed the Mutual Security Act,[19] a bill explicitly linking U.S. aid policies to U.S. security policies and placing the administration of federal aid activities in a single agency. The act also imposed a new set of political restrictions on nations already receiving U.S. funds. As of January 1952, all European recipients had to agree to fulfill shared military obligations to the fullest extent possible.[20] Aid to non-European states was made contingent on their agreement to "join in promoting international understanding and good will and in maintaining world peace, and to take such action as might be mutually agreed upon to eliminate the causes of international tension."[21]

Not surprisingly, the act was greeted abroad with some resentment. In Europe, its provisions were seen as redundant, since most nations had already signed similar assurances under the newly created North Atlantic Treaty Organization (NATO). In the less-developed regions, certain recipients of technical aid worried that their agreement might imply a rejection of neutrality and a commitment to the U.S. side in an increasingly bipolar world.[22]

The Mutual Security Act remained the principal piece of foreign aid legislation from 1951 to 1961. During that time, it defined an aid program directed primarily toward the threat of communism in the emerging nations of the Third World. What had been only one of the many strands in the Truman administration's conception of aid came to dominate the entire program.

As the Korean War drew to a close, however, public support for U.S. foreign aid began to wane once again. For the remainder of the decade, the security concerns of the war years continued to serve as the official basis for aid legislation, but they were no longer a priority issue and no longer captured public interest. Nevertheless, the foreign aid program itself did not decline; instead, it stumbled along with the support of the diverse groups with a vested interest in it and the indifference of practically everyone else.

The Alliance for Progress

By the mid-1950s the U.S. aid program was becoming the target of a new wave of criticism. The earliest complaints came from Latin American leaders. In 1954, a special session of the Organization of American States (OAS) prepared a report outlining the Latin American position. The Report of the Experts, as it became known, was the first direct plea for U.S. aid from prospective recipients. It proposed new levels of U.S. investment in Latin America, increased U.S. funding for Latin American entrepreneurs, and a special fund to oversee U.S. investment in the region. The Eisenhower administration, however, was not interested in launching a new aid program. Instead, Treasury Secretary George Humphrey, the U.S. representative to the special OAS session, reiterated the administration's position that the best means of aiding Latin America would be through a strong economy in the United States and an international system of free trade.[23]

That same year, a group of distinguished Latin American leaders met in New York to discuss the region's problems and to outline possible solutions. Again, the leaders stressed the need for the United States to play a more assertive role,[24] and again, their pleas were ignored by the Eisenhower administration, which continued to stress trade and private investment as the most appropriate channels for U.S. involvement.[25]

At the same time, there were rumblings within the U.S. development community. An increasing number of academics were becoming convinced that the old tools of development had proven insufficient. Those who saw aid primarily as a means of bolstering U.S.

security interests were beginning to fear that the U.S. approach was no longer adequate for countering a newly aggressive Soviet Union.[26] Added to this was a growing belief that political instability alone could lead to communist revolution and that economic development offered the best chance of avoiding such instability.[27] This thesis was most fully developed by the MIT economists Max F. Millikan and Walt W. Rostow, who asserted that a long-term strategy of economic assistance to the developing countries would simultaneously promote the values of western liberal democracy.[28]

There was, of course, a contradiction inherent in this thesis. Encouraging the forces of change and popular movements in the developing countries risked unleashing the forces that advocated violence and revolution.[29] At the time, however, the contradiction was not evident, or at least not stressed; and the Millikan–Rostow thesis was accepted first by various academics and then by influential policymakers.

By the late 1950s, key legislators in Congress had been persuaded that U.S. foreign aid policies were in need of an update and in July 1956, the Senate established a special committee to review U.S. foreign aid.[30] The committee heard extensive testimony, both from Millikan, Rostow, and their supporters and from others who advocated placing the principal stress on promoting private investment.[31] Although the testimony revealed sharp differences about the best means for fostering U.S.-supported growth abroad, the hearings themselves were evidence of a new congressional willingness to expand the size and regional coverage of U.S. foreign aid.

As usual, it took a perceived security threat to mobilize public support for a new aid initiative. This time it was the Cuban Revolution of 1959 that compelled a change in U.S. attitudes toward aid. With a communist state so close to the U.S. border, a new wave of anti-communism arose, along with a fear that Castro would be able to export his policies throughout Latin America. By the late 1950s, a consensus had emerged that the Soviet Union was launching a new offensive in Latin America, and that long-term assistance was required to help stem the communist threat.

Thus, nearly all of the conditions necessary for the launching of a new U.S. aid program were in place by the time John F. Kennedy entered the White House. As a senator, Kennedy had been deeply impressed with the ideas embodied in the Millikan–Rostow thesis; as president, he was able to galvanize a pro-aid coalition that allowed him to launch a foreign assistance program combining anti-communist objectives with a genuine effort to foster economic and social progress abroad. Kennedy brought into office with him a number of officials similarly committed to the idea that the time was ripe for a new U.S. aid initiative in the Third World. Foremost among them was Douglas C. Dillon, who had previously served as Eisenhower's under secretary of state for economic affairs and had grown increasingly frustrated with the Eisenhower administration's neglect of Latin American affairs. Dillon had advocated an aid initiative emphasizing economic support, and he brought these convictions to his new post.[32]

Kennedy also appointed a special task force to develop a new Latin American program. This panel of experts embodied experience from the New Deal, the Marshall Plan, and academic development projects. All of the panelists shared a common belief that economic development itself had to become the goal of economic aid, and that social reforms and development were the necessary foundations for democratic political stability.

By themselves, the bureaucrats probably would not have been able to sell a new aid initiative to Congress and the U.S. public. Once again, they drew support from some new coalitions in favor of aid and from changing international conditions that again pushed the security motive to the forefront of public debate.

The Alliance for Progress launched by Kennedy in 1961 to initiate a program of long-term aid to Latin America was not a new idea; it clearly echoed some of Rostow's proposals and was consciously patterned after a proposal for an Operation Pan America suggested by a Brazilian leader in 1958.[33] What made the alliance noteworthy was that it drew such widespread support and that it was launched with such general optimism about its success. The U.S. public had once again been mobilized in an anti-communist consensus. In addition, Congress was concerned about redirecting the existing U.S. aid programs, and influential academics and policymakers were anxious to test their new ideas about the relationship between economic development and political stability.

The alliance's popularity was short-lived. Soon after Kennedy's death in 1963, the fragile pro-aid coalition he had fostered was gone. Lyndon Johnson kept the Alliance for Progress on the books but never gave it the personal attention it received from Kennedy; the growing tensions in Vietnam soon overwhelmed all other foreign policy considerations. By the late 1960s, the alliance had been divorced from its political and social components and had lost the constituency that had formerly supported it.

For the next ten years, foreign aid remained a low priority issue. Without a policy entrepreneur to drum up support for a specific campaign, the fragile coalition for foreign aid broke up into its component parts, and the traditional concerns of the U.S. public with regard to the Third World—the protection of U.S. private investment and the defeat of Soviet-backed insurgents—became paramount once again.

New Directions

The U.S. foreign aid programs stumbled along for the remainder of the 1960s, though they suffered from a notable lack of presidential attention as well as from dissolution of the consensus that had initially supported the Alliance for Progress. By 1965, when U.S. bombing of Vietnam began, the security motive was the only consideration of importance in the erstwhile coalition. As the U.S. involvement in Vietnam grew, so did the portion of foreign assistance used for security purposes and diverted to Indochina.

As the war dragged on, the funds spent in Vietnam under the guise of foreign aid became a primary target of popular outrage, and many sectors of the U.S. public became vocal advocates for humanitarian concerns such as world peace and the elimination of hunger.[34] Responding to public pressure, Congress became increasingly insistent about exercising its traditional power to check the executive's actions. Johnson's final economic aid request for $2.5 billion for the fiscal year 1969 was cut by nearly $1 billion in Congress, the largest percentage reduction in the history of U.S. foreign aid.[35]

More generally, the concept of a sustained foreign aid program for military assistance, particularly as a trick to fund the adminatives complained that foreign aid was not doing its job and that the United States was still unable to guarantee the loyalty of its Third World allies. Liberals, on the other hand, saw foreign aid as a mask for military assistance, particularly as a trick to fund the administration's unpopular war in Vietnam. In 1971, the pressure of these forces was so great as to overwhelm the traditional apathy of the U.S. public towards the foreign aid budget, and for the first time in history, Congress defeated the administration's foreign aid bill.

To the bureaucrats in charge of U.S. foreign aid, the events of the late 1960s appeared to have dealt a death blow to foreign aid activities. The only groups that still actively supported them were those that saw foreign aid as a tool for propping up Third World dominoes. As these goals seemed to become dominant, they served to mobilize the once-passive forces of domestic opposition to foreign aid.

Rather than watch all foreign aid efforts disappear, however, those inside and outside of the government with a stake in continuing them in some form undertook a drastic reorientation. Building on the wave of humanitarian concerns that welled up in American politics in the early 1970s, the initiative took the form of legislation establishing a "New Directions" program. In content, New Directions appeared to be animated by the so-called basic needs approach proposed in 1972 by the president of the World Bank, Robert S. McNamara. The policy promised to attack the problems of poverty directly by allocating funds to the most pressing needs of Third World economies: food and nutrition, population control and health, and education and human resources.[36]

The content of this legislation echoed many ideas proposed by both policymakers and academics, who earlier had criticized the Alliance for Progress approach for relying too heavily on the trickle-down effects of economic growth. What is surprising is that the development officials were able to generate a coalition for their program at a time when foreign aid in general was being subjected to hostile public and congressional scrutiny. That success appears to have been due to a coalition spearheaded by key officials in the Agency for International Development (AID) and supported by various public groups such as the Overseas Development Council (ODC). Led by James P. Grant, president of the ODC, a small group of aid officials approached members of the House Foreign Affairs Committee whom they considered most sympathetic to foreign aid. Together, the aid officials and a small coalition of liberal representatives hammered out a new proposal that they presented to Congress as representing "drastic" changes in U.S. foreign aid policy, changes that promised to be "not simply cosmetic, but real."[37]

With so much emphasis on the bill's humanitarian aspects, the strength of the coalition was limited. Yet the required legislation did manage to muster a basic majority, composed of liberals who supported the humanitarian aspects of economic aid and conservatives who saw the new proposal as the only hope for salvaging the security components of foreign assistance. AID's mandate to continue its development efforts in the Third World accordingly received a grudging renewal.

THE EXPANDING ROLE OF CONGRESS

Over the decades, the role of Congress in foreign aid programs has evolved in ways reminiscent of its changing role in foreign trade programs. Although no foreign aid bill has ever been wholly free of provisions favoring the economic interests of particular groups, over the decades congressional enactments have been progressively weighted down with detailed provisions reflecting such interests.

Congress has influenced foreign aid policies principally through its traditional power over the federal purse and its ability to cut back substantially on the executive's requests. In the course of time, the congressional preference for dispensing foreign aid through loans has prevailed over the executive's preference for grants; whereas only 6 percent of U.S. aid was given in loans in the years from 1953 to 1955, the proportion had risen to nearly one-third by 1980.[38]

Guarding U.S. Business Interests

In supporting U.S. business interests, Congress has played its traditional role as the conduit through which special interests could influence the direction of U.S. foreign policy.

Criticism of foreign aid policy by U.S. business has focused on three areas of alleged inadequacy: the protection of U.S.-owned enterprises abroad from the effects of expropriations; the protection of U.S. enterprises from the competition of new producers in the aid-receiving countries; and the promotion of U.S. exports to the aid-receiving countries.

On the expropriation issue, explicit congressional intervention on behalf of U.S. multinational enterprises began in the wake of the Cuban revolution and the subsequent seizure of hundreds of U.S. business ventures located in Cuba. Under pressure from the affected firms, Congress passed the 1962 Hickenlooper amendment, which required the president to suspend U.S. assistance to any country expropriating U.S. foreign investments without making provision for "prompt, adequate and effective compensation."[39]

Not surprisingly, the amendment raised the hackles of the State Department, which saw it as impeding its ability to conduct U.S.

foreign policy. The Kennedy administration lobbied strongly against the amendment but with little success.[40] The executive branch's desire for a cautious and discrete approach to the matter of foreign expropriations was clearly overridden by a congressional concern to ensure that U.S. funds were denied to countries that threatened U.S. business interests located in their territory.

In the end, Congress seems to have used the Hickenlooper amendment more as a bugaboo tactic than an actual check on the executive's power. As with escape clause provisions in U.S. trade legislation, Congress appeared eager to condemn certain actions in principle without tying the executive's hands in the handling of actual cases. During its life, therefore, the Hickenlooper amendment was applied to only one case.[41]

In 1972, Congress passed the Gonzalez amendment, requiring the president to instruct the U.S. executive director to the World Bank to vote against any loan to a foreign government that had expropriated U.S. property without adequate compensation. This time Congress allowed the president to refrain from invoking the statute as long as "good faith" negotiations were in progress. Going even farther towards returning discretion to the executive branch, Congress attached a waiver to the Hickenlooper amendment in 1973, permitting the president to override its provisions if he deemed it in the national interest to do so. With this addition, the Hickenlooper amendment was effectively defused.[42] Nevertheless, the amendment itself had become a powerful issue in the politics of foreign aid. Congress repeatedly threatened to tack new amendments on foreign bills, sending State Department officials scrambling to convince foreign governments to settle their disputes with U.S. firms before the next appropriation bill reached Capitol Hill.[43]

In trying to expand U.S. markets abroad and protect U.S. industry from new foreign competition the record of congressional involvement has been longer and more varied than in the expropriation issue. From the time of the Marshall Plan, Congress has attempted to carve out niches in the U.S. foreign aid program in which the interests of the U.S. business sector could be served at the same time that U.S. foreign policy objectives were pursued. Congress insisted, for instance, that the administrator of the Marshall Plan be a businessman and that he be appointed only with congressional approval. Congress also included several provisions in the Marshall Plan legislation that directly benefited U.S. business interests. One, for example, stipulated that 50 percent of all goods financed under the plan should be transported in U.S. ships; another, that not less than 25 percent of all wheat shipments consist of U.S.-produced flour.[44]

Similar provisions have been scattered throughout U.S. aid programs. Recipients of food under Public Law 480 assistance have been prohibited from exporting food commodities received as aid from the United States on pain of losing such aid;[45] foreign nations have been denied assistance for certain manufacturing enterprises unless they agreed to limit exports to the United States to less than 20 percent of the enterprises' output;[46] beginning in 1964, aid-receiving countries were obliged to ensure that their imports from the United States would increase by virtue of their having received such aid.[47]

The most important basic provision of the aid program in support of U.S. business has been tying U.S. aid to the purchase of U.S. goods. For a time after World War II, U.S. policymakers were hopeful of promoting the principle of giving aid without strings attached, leaving the recipient state free to choose its supplier on the basis of commercial considerations. While some programs—Food for Peace and military sales—were inherently tied to procurement from U.S. producers, in others the link was much less specific. In these cases, the bureaucrats administering the aid programs were reluctant to compel recipient states to restrict use of their funds to the United States, fearing that such provisions would reduce the economic value and the political benefits of the aid.

Efforts to limit the ties between U.S. aid and U.S. products, however, began to draw increasingly bitter criticisms during the 1980s, with representatives of the U.S. business sector repeatedly pointing out that other nations, including France and Japan, have always linked their aid programs to the financing of their own products and services.[48] In response, Congress began to pass legislation designed to tighten the linkages between aid programs and U.S. export sales.

In 1983, for instance, Congress passed the Trade and Development Enhancement Act, directing AID to take funds previously allocated to a commodity import program and use them to provide concessional funding for the purchase of U.S. goods.[49] At the same time, Congress authorized grants to U.S. exporters designed to equalize the difference between U.S. and foreign financing packages offered to Third World clients.[50] In this particular instance, however, the agricultural interests that Congress had tried to protect suffered a long-term, politically-motivated setback. Because Congress was still sensitive about the disastrous subsidy program designed to bolster grain sales to the Soviet Union in the early 1970s, the new legislation explicitly denied any benefits on sales to the Soviets. Offended by this provision, the Soviet government reneged on a prior commitment to purchase 4 million tons of U.S. wheat per year.[51] In the end, a subsidy program meant to increase U.S. exports served, instead, to alienate one of U.S. agriculture's best customers.

Political Interventions

Although most congressional forays into the making of U.S. foreign aid policy have stemmed from the role of Congress as the protector of special interests, Congress has also intervened in the administration's aid programs on foreign policy grounds.

In most instances, these interventions can be understood in a traditional partisan context, with liberal Democrats reacting against the perceived excesses of a conservative Republican administration or security-conscious Republicans trying to put more bite into the Democratic foreign policy agenda. Until the mid-1970s, interventions of this sort were relatively infrequent, and the restraints imposed by Congress on the aid agencies related primarily to communist or communist-supporting states.[52] In the wake of the Arab–Israeli war of 1967, Congress also mandated the suspension of aid to states that had broken off diplomatic relations with the United States following the outbreak of the conflict. Even in these cases, however, Congress followed its usual practice of authorizing the president to continue aid on grounds of national security. A similar congressional prohibition against assistance to a communist country was waived in the case of Yugoslavia, when the executive branch demonstrated that aid to Tito served to promote Yugoslavian independence from the communist bloc.[53]

In the wake of Watergate and Vietnam, Congress showed a desire to play a more active role in foreign policy issues, and its interest in aid policies became particularly strong because U.S. involvement in Vietnam was originally launched under the banner of U.S. aid. Thereafter, Congress was more eager to prohibit aid to specific states or regions, forcing the president to modify his own foreign policies. When, for instance, a majority of the members of Congress disagreed with President Nixon's policies in support of rebel forces in Angola in 1975, Congress enacted a provision cutting off such aid.[54] In 1976, a new amendment made U.S. assistance contingent upon the provision of human rights in the recipient states and enlarged the powers of Congress to review the executive's aid program on a case-by-case basis.[55]

Wielding these new powers, Congress between 1976 and 1977 cut the executive's requests for aid to Argentina, Ethiopia, Uruguay, and Nicaragua.[56] In 1982, the Boland amendment prohibited the president from giving aid to the insurgents fighting the Nicaraguan government, [57] and in 1985 yet another amendment barred U.S. aid to any nation that dealt in nuclear technology without submitting to international safeguards against nuclear proliferation.[58] By the end of the decade, Congress had made it clear that it would no longer give the president free rein in the use of U.S. foreign aid programs to serve political ends. Instead, Congress was emphasizing its power to influence the content of U.S. foreign policies through its control over expenditures.

FOREIGN ASSISTANCE AND REALPOLITIK

The Rise and Decline of Multilateralism

The general direction of U.S. foreign aid programs, as we have already indicated, has been to deemphasize the role of aid as a tool of development, leaving the humanitarian and security objectives as the principal rationalization for such programs. That shift is amply demonstrated by the declining use of multilateral organizations as a conduit for aid.

During the latter 1960s, the United States seemed to be moving toward a greater use of multilateral institutions such as the World Bank and the various regional development banks to dispense foreign aid. Between 1966 and 1970, for instance, the portion of total U.S. aid that was routed through multilateral organizations rose from 3 percent to over 12 percent. By the second half of the 1970s, as Table 6-1 shows, multilateral institutions were receiving over 25 percent of total U.S. aid funds.

One factor in the increased use of multilateral institutions appears to have been the country's revulsion from its entrapment in Vietnam. As we have mentioned, the early 1970s were a time of increased public concern for humanitarian and internationalist causes. With the war in Vietnam still exerting a powerful influence, public opinion turned against direct U.S. intervention in the Third World. In such an environment, multilateral aid seemed to provide the safest means

Table 6-1   **Composition of U.S. Foreign Aid, 1964–1985**
(in millions of U.S. dollars)

Year	Multilateral Aid	Bilateral Aid	Total	Multilateral as Percent of Total
1964	200	3,240	3,440	6.2
1965	160	3,460	3,620	4.4
1966	110	3,550	3,660	3.0
1967	310	3,410	3,720	8.3
1968	250	3,050	3,300	7.6
1969	330	2,830	3,160	10.4
1970	390	2,660	3,050	12.8
1971	430	2,890	3,320	13.0
1972	630	2,720	3,350	18.9
1973	630	2,340	2,970	21.2
1974	880	2,560	3,440	25.6
1975	1,070	2,940	4,010	26.7
1976	1,050	2,840	3,890	27.0
1977	1,260	2,900	4,160	30.3
1978	2,190	3,470	5,660	38.7
1979	619	4,080	4,690	13.0
1980	2,770	4,370	7,140	38.8
1981	1,470	4,320	5,790	25.4
1982	3,340	4,860	8,200	40.1
1983	2,520	5,560	8,080	30.1
1984	2,250	6,460	8,710	25.8
1985	1,220	8,180	9,400	13.0
1986	1,427	12,443	13,915	10.5
1987	1,187	13,341	12,528	9.4

SOURCE: *Development Cooperation* (Paris: Organization for Economic Cooperation and Development, 1964–1986), various issues.

for separating U.S. support for development abroad from its political and military aims.

Another factor in the trend to multilateralism also could be tied indirectly to the Vietnam situation. Multilateral aid usually has had the strong support of a cluster of small nations, led by the Scandinavians, the Canadians, and the Dutch. With little hope or need to use aid as a political weapon, such governments have placed heavy weight on the use of multilateral institutions as a major aid channel. In the 1970s, the U.S. government had little stomach for resisting the pressures stemming from such quarters. Accordingly, U.S. representatives found it easy to acquiesce in increased contributions to the various multilateral aid agencies. Although the United States never contributed as much multilateral aid in relation to its gross national product as did some of its counterparts in the OECD, it continued to send large sums to the various multilateral development agencies throughout the later 1970s and into the early 1980s. Even after the Reagan administration came into office, Congress consistently allocated funds for institutions such as the World Bank and the various regional banks.

For a while, it seemed that multilateral aid might become the dominant form of U.S. aid giving. Such aid even had certain attractions for Congress. For instance, aid routed through multilateral channels could buffer Congress from having to consider the various restrictions that special interest groups were already attaching in numbers to the bilateral aid programs. The groups with narrower targets could still be accommodated under existing bilateral projects.

In the latter half of the 1980s, however, security concerns once again began to overtake humanitarian and development motives. At the same time, mounting worries about holding fiscal deficits in check made the Reagan administration increasingly reluctant to support foreign aid programs in which it had no direct economic or strategic interest. Its unwillingness to contribute to a special $8 billion fund for impoverished African countries supported by practically all other major nations represented a new low in U.S. support for multilateral aid efforts.[59] All told, the percentage of U.S. aid earmarked for multilateral institutions declined precipitously, falling to less than 10 percent by 1987.

Dissolution of the Coalition

By the mid-1980s, it became clear that the coalition which once supported the U.S. foreign aid program had almost completely disintegrated. President Reagan's main emphasis in administering foreign aid, it was obvious, was to support U.S. security interests abroad. Faced with the need to reduce the size of the country's fiscal deficit, the administration sought to concentrate foreign aid even more narrowly on the security objective. Soon, the new administration's preferences manifested themselves in the budgets submitted to and enacted by Congress.

The president continued to cite the communist threat as the factor shaping U.S. aid, but the threat was usually depicted as specific to particular countries rather than a general consequence of poverty and backwardness. Aid programs, therefore, were to be directed to states in which the United States had a clear security interest and were to include a large defense component. In addition, in response to the ideological preferences of the United States, such programs were to assign the U.S. private sector as large a role as possible, even going so far as to facilitate foreign purchases of state-owned enterprises in the Third World.[60] Beyond these preferences, the Reagan administration gave little evidence of having a philosophy of aid giving. Nor did it make any significant effort to package its aid requests within a broader anti-communist appeal, as was done for Kennedy's Alliance for Progress program and Truman's Point Four.

At the same time, the fragile foreign aid consensus was undergoing changes of its own. The enthusiasm that had surrounded the basic human needs approach and sustained the development community during the Carter years was beginning to wane. By the 1980s, foreign aid had become extremely vulnerable to rising pressures for reducing federal expenditures.[61]

Simultaneously, the coalition previously mobilized in support of foreign aid began to show signs of disintegrating. Some of the groups that previously threw their weight behind all U.S. foreign aid as a means of furthering group interests switched their tactics somewhat, concentrating their efforts on protecting only that part of the foreign aid bill directly concerning them.[62]

To be sure, certain segments of the bill adopted by especially influential groups proved relatively immune to budget cutting. The Reagan administration made it clear, for instance, that aid explicitly earmarked for military purposes and directed to strategically located allies was sacrosanct; even aid ostensibly for economic programs was directed disproportionately to the same countries. By 1984, over one-third of all U.S. economic assistance was being spent on just three countries: Israel, Egypt, and Pakistan. Concurrently, all of Africa accounted for only 20 percent of the U.S. economic assistance budget.[63]

In addition, foreign states with strong domestic support within the United States usually managed to survive the budget-cutting process. Support from Jewish groups bolstered Israel's position as a strategically located ally. Greek lobbyists were able to gain acceptance of a formula not only guaranteeing U.S. military aid to Greece but also linking the level of aid to the assistance given to Turkey, Greece's rival. Poland was granted an exemption from U.S. laws that prohibited aid to communist countries. And both Northern Ireland and the Irish Republic, despite their status as developed countries, were recipients of U.S. assistance.[64] Aid based on humanitarian considerations did not disappear completely, of course; but appropriations for such aid tended to stress those causes most likely to appeal to a television-viewing public.

By the latter half of the 1980s, too, the efforts of Congress to influence foreign policy through its power over the purse reached new heights. Congressional committees were summarily eliminating provisions that lacked substantial domestic support and were attaching unprecedented numbers of amendments to aid legislation. Moreover, the legislative processes relating to foreign aid were being used increasingly as launching pads for more general debates about the administration's foreign policy agenda. The inclusion of family planning in AID's health efforts, for instance, launched a protracted debate about the relative morality of overpopulation and birth control, a debate whose implications reached far beyond the aid program on which it focused. President Reagan's 1985 request for assistance to El Salvador catalyzed congressional review of the administration's entire Latin American policy; in the process, it delayed passage of all aid legislation. The search for a domestic drug enforcement policy also affected the aid bills of the 1980s, and U.S. assistance to several nations was made contingent upon their ability to curb drug production within their borders.[65]

By the latter 1980s, the coalition holding together a U.S. foreign aid effort that included substantial developmental and humanitarian objectives was no longer exerting much weight, its ability to function weakened by budget-balancing needs and by the power struggle between Congress and the president. Critics were asserting that the U.S. foreign assistance program had been effectively eliminated, replaced by thinly disguised efforts to bolster U.S. military allies abroad, expand Third World markets for U.S. goods, and further other U.S. objectives not shared by the aid recipients. The economic objectives animating the earliest foreign aid programs had, in the end, proved vulnerable to the other motives that had helped to sustain the fragile aid coalition.

7

Prospects for International Cooperation

BY THE LATTER 1980s, foreign economic policies had taken on an extraordinary importance for the U.S. economy. To a much greater degree than in the past, the wrong policies had the potential of jeopardizing the country's ability to expand its economy and pursue its strategic interests. At the same time, it was becoming apparent that as a means of dealing with many of the country's problems, unilateral measures were often futile or inadequate. On numerous issues, cooperation with other countries seemed indispensable. But what were the prospects for such cooperation?

A CHANGING U.S. ROLE

To begin with, the disposition of U.S. administrations to cooperate with other countries in the handling of common economic problems was qualified in fundamental ways. For a time, the United States had been the leader in such cooperative efforts. Even then, U.S. policy makers did not expect cooperation to require any major modifications of U.S. values and institutions. The national state of mind was that of a benign leader sharing its wisdom and resources with others who would adjust their values and institutions to seize their new opportunities. In short, the U.S. government was not so much cooperating with other governments as it was proselytizing them.

Moreover, while playing its leadership role, the United States was far from consistent in its support for the global institutions it had been so responsible for creating. Although the first preference of Americans was for global institutions and open markets, U.S. leaders were usually found promoting a variety of policies and approaches, incorporating numerous ambiguities and contradictions. For instance, some areas of U.S. economic policy, such as agriculture and ocean shipping, continued under the domination of special interest groups, who managed to produce agreements quite out of keeping with the main stream of U.S. policies. In some cases, these groups supported global organizations, such as the International Maritime Organization and the International Civil Aviation Organization; the policies developed in those organizations were generally protectionist and often discriminatory.

Another striking set of contradictions arose out of U.S. support for the Marshall Plan. For all its benign and constructive intent, the Marshall Plan represented a distinctly different approach from the global vision that had animated Bretton Woods. The Marshall Plan was a program confined to the Europeans rather than global in its reach; besides, it was a program that promoted European discrimination against U.S. goods and against the U.S. dollar. Although these arrangements constituted a flat challenge to the principles and institutional strength of the GATT and the IMF, the U.S. establishment felt very little constraint in pushing simultaneously on both the European and the global fronts with only occasional concern over reconciling the obvious conflicts.

As the years passed, the United States and the leading European countries built on the institutional remnants of the Marshall Plan to create the OECD, the "rich men's club," headquartered in Paris. With U.S. support, that organization sponsored various substantial cooperative undertakings, such as a network of bilateral tax treaties and a set of guidelines for the behavior of multinational enterprises. Even more restricted groups of countries were convened to deal with problems involving international money flows, in meetings that increased in frequency as the years passed. Identified by the number of countries that made up the group—such as G-5 for the United States, the United Kingdom, France, Germany, and Japan, and G-7 when Canada and Italy were added—these restricted groups became the principal decisionmakers on exchange-rate issues.

Not all of these smaller arrangements were devoted to maintaining open international markets. In time, the U.S. government began resorting to bilateral agreements aimed at limiting the effects of the trade-liberalizing measures undertaken in the GATT. An early manifestation of the new trend occurred in 1957, when the U.S. executive pressured Japan to impose "voluntary" restrictions on its cotton textile exports in order to forestall more drastic restrictions being considered by the U.S. Congress. That incident was the forerunner of a new U.S. policy to restrict the import of textiles and clothing through bilateral agreements, a policy that eventually would be adopted by many other countries. In time, such agreements would dominate world trade in those products and provide the prototype for similar agreements on various other products, notably automobiles and steel.

Eventually, the new bilateral emphasis of the United States took tangible shape in various other forms: a free trade agreement with Israel, a preferential agreement on automobiles with Canada, a preferential trade agreement with countries in the Caribbean, and side deals with Japan on government procurement practices and on bilateral trade in semiconductors. In addition, there have been bilateral arrangements with the United Kingdom on the regulation of bank safety and discussions with Mexico on a wide range of economic subjects that once might have been conducted in global institutions—for example, provisions relating to patents, the rights of foreign investors, and the reduction of Mexico's debt burden.

The increased U.S. interest in a bilateral approach to economic issues is attributable in part to the reduced position of the U.S. economy. With that decline, U.S. leaders no longer perceived themselves as keepers of the international laws and builders of international institutions, and they were no longer quite so ready to offer other governments special terms in order to have them subscribe to some U.S.-sponsored organization. Instead, U.S. ideas of the nature of reciprocity in international economic relations began to shift, coming to resemble more closely those of other countries. Increasingly, the executive felt the need to extract immediate benefits from specific agreements with other countries sufficient to justify each agreement. As a result, the United States was pushed farther and farther toward agreements with limited groups of countries.

Yet in making that shift, representatives of the United States have not been able to throw off all the habits and attitudes of a hegemonic power. U.S. leaders, like those of other countries, have taken it for granted that the values of their society are generally superior to the values encountered elsewhere. Unlike their counterparts, however, U.S. leaders have tended to assume that when other governments provided Americans with lesser rights than those extended to foreigners by the United States, the foreign government was being unfair. This spirit has produced the frequent allusions to level playing fields and the growing emphasis on retaliation in international negotiations.

In attempting to influence the behavior of other countries, governments accustomed to a lesser role in a world of superpowers would be inclined to move with certain restraint. Having played the role of leader for so many decades, however, the United States has found it difficult to tailor its tactics to its changed economic position. Besides, even if the United States is no longer in a position to dominate, it still exercises enough economic clout to threaten. So threats have become more common in the U.S. tactical arsenal.

Of course, threats in international economic negotiations are nothing new. In fact, before World War I, in a period when many countries followed a so-called conditional most-favored-nation policy in trade matters, the implicit threat of trade discrimination was usually the factor that brought countries to the bargaining table. Even after 1923, when the U.S. government abandoned that policy by adopting an unconditional most-favored-nation policy in foreign trade, threats continued to provide the basis for some U.S. negotiations. From the beginning, for instance, threats were the principal currency in the bilateral exchange of air traffic rights. And in the 1950s, threats began to creep back into negotiations over trade as the U.S. executive commenced its practice of persuading Japan and other countries to restrict their fast-growing exports of textiles and other products.

Since the early 1980s, the threat tactic has made its appearance in a widening range of subjects. Talk of a tit-for-tat approach has appeared not only in matters of trade but also in the licensing of foreign-owned bank offices and foreign communication carriers.[1] Moreover, the U.S. executive has been threatening to use trade restrictions to win changes from other governments in matters other than trade, including patent and insurance laws.[2]

Even the tone in which the United States has been delivering its threats has changed. Until the 1980s, U.S. negotiators from the executive branch preferred to couch their threats in terms of a congressional bugaboo, that is, what an independent Congress might take into its mind to do if the foreign government failed to meet U.S. demands. In the 1980s, to satisfy the reciprocity requirement, the president began making his threats much more directly, employing the standard metaphor of the level playing field.

Although the overt use of threats always carries elements of danger in international relations, there are various grounds on which the increased use of threats by the U.S. government can be defended. Game theorists have demonstrated, for instance, that under specified conditions, a player can use threats in ways that encourage all participants to engage in more cooperative behavior and thereby advance their collective interests.[3] Moreover, in many cases the objective of the U.S. government in employing threats against foreign governments has not been to deny foreigners access to the U.S. economy but to improve the access of Americans to foreign economies. Threats were employed, for example, in order to break down Japanese and European import barriers to U.S. farm products, to ease the entry of U.S. banks into Tokyo, and to expand the rights of U.S. computer firms in Brazil.

In making greater use of the direct threat, the U.S. government has not abandoned its participation in multilateral organizations such as the GATT and the IMF. Rather, U.S. officials were solemnly asserting in 1986 that America would pursue trade liberalization movements wherever they existed, whether in a multilateral, plurilateral, or bilateral context. If the U.S. government was weakening multilateral institutions by its use of bilateral channels and its unilateral definitions of "a level playing field," that was not its explicit intention.

What then has been its intention? In a governmental system built on checks and balances, it is pointless to attempt explaining any sequence of actions as if it resulted from the deliberations of a rational unitary actor. What one sees instead are the results of a process of hauling and pulling among the warring factions in the government, with inners-and-outers exerting fitful initiatives to confuse the pattern even further.

Accordingly, when in 1984 the U.S. government decided to make another giant push toward trade liberalization, its decision to choose the demeaned GATT as the institution through which to achieve its objectives did not represent another conscious shift in national policy. Rather, from the viewpoint of the policy entrepreneurs in the Reagan administration, the GATT seemed a useful institution for promoting the task of the moment, that of making a bold statement in favor of open markets. As a result, the GATT's members were persuaded to adopt an agenda for negotiation that represented by all odds the most formidable in the 40-year life of the agreement.

Launched in 1987, these negotiations are expected to stretch out over a half dozen years or more. As we shall presently point out, there are various reasons to doubt that the 96 members of the GATT will have sufficient common ground to generate effective agreements over the range of topics that the U.S. government hopes they will consider. Handicapped by its past history and its present structure, the GATT as an institution is unlikely to provide the fact-finding capability, the measure of authority, and the potential for compromise needed to bridge those differences. If any agreements do emerge, they likely will be limited to subsets of countries, with their application to other GATT members left in considerable doubt.

At the same time, the bilateral approach of the United States is also unlikely to provide very satisfactory results if it relies upon the use of threats. A government that hopes to promote the national interest by using threats must be in a position to choose its issues and to control its tactics in applying the threats. In the U.S. case, with several hands on the tiller simultaneously and with constant by-play between the president and Congress, the U.S. government's threats run the risk of being ill-chosen and poorly executed. The issues that the U.S. government chooses to promote through threats are likely to be selected, as they have been in the past, primarily on the basis of the energy and strength of special interest groups rather than through a rational weighing of national interests. Moreover, the administration has to reckon with the possibility that special interests in the United States supporting the threat tactic may prefer joint restrictions rather than a joint opening of markets, regardless of the effects on the national interest.

In the circumstances of the latter 1980s, an overt policy of threat is more likely to produce recrimination, retaliation, and counter-retaliation than in the past. The tendency of many Americans to see the U.S. economy as a fading giant, justified or not, is already widely shared by other countries.[4] The risk that other countries might respond defiantly to U.S. threats, even when it hurts their own interests to do so, seems especially high. There is a strong need, then, to find some other approach to the international economic problems that face the United States.

CLOUDS OVER GLOBALISM

By the 1980s, the U.S. strategy for maintaining an open market system had lost any claim to coherence. Clearly, the United States was not relying much upon the institutions it had helped create 40 years earlier to achieve that objective. The IMF, conceived in wartime, had never been allowed to exercise seriously the supervisory role over exchange rates and exchange licensing systems that its original mandate contemplated. The World Bank had quickly been relegated to an ancillary role, filing in the gaps left by other sources of public and private capital. And the GATT, flawed at birth by the uncommitted position of the U.S. Congress, was unable to add much to its one stellar achievement, reducing drastically the industrial tariffs of the United States, Europe, and Japan. The U.S. support at Punta del Este in 1986 of an ambitious new program of trade liberalization under the GATT's auspices seemed almost defiant and quixotic, exposing the GATT to the perils of an uncertain future.

Even if the United States were suddenly to renew its commitment to these global institutions, it appears unlikely that the institutions would be wholly restored to their pristine position in international economic relations. The reason is that much of the problem stems from the inherent inability of such organizations to cope with some of the changing conditions in world trade and payments.

In the field of trade, for instance, the spectacular decline in tariff rates has brought into view a variety of other trade restriction measures that previously were masked. Unlike tariffs and quotas, many of the remaining barriers are complex and subtle, varying substantially from one country to the next and deeply intertwined in domestic policies and institutions. For instance, schemes to promote laggard regions or to encourage small-scale enterprises by giving them preferences in government procurement have taken on increased importance as subtle, yet powerful, barriers to trade. So too have measures justified on the basis of health or safety, such as tamper-proof caps on drug products and safety requirements on automobiles. Because many of these measures were not explicitly designed to restrict foreign trade, it is difficult to determine how restrictive they may be and even more difficult to fashion appropriate remedies. The adjudication of disputes over such measures, it is becoming evident, requires a fact-finding capability and a degree of shared interest among governments not often found in global organizations.

Another factor contributing to the increasing complexity of international trade disputes is the growing linkage of merchandise trade with related services. Firms that sell mainframe computers or nuclear power plants, for instance, would be hopelessly handicapped if barred from assisting the buyer in installing the hardware, training operatives, and providing follow-up assistance. The performance of those functions, however, may require the entry of foreigners into the country to perform the services, or the establishment of an enterprise within the country, or both. The liberalization of trade in items such as these, therefore, often depends on policies related to the employment of foreigners or the establishment of foreign-owned enterprises, contentious issues for many of the recipient countries.

Even if the linkages to merchandise trade had not lifted the subject of services to greater prominence, the increasing role of multinational enterprises would have produced that result. Perhaps one-half of the industrial output of the noncommunist world is accounted for by firms that are affiliated in a multinational network. Enterprises of that sort build their competitive advantage partly on their ability to draw on the network's resources in other countries, including engineers, accountants, and marketing experts. The linkages between the movement of services and the establishment of foreign-owned enterprises, therefore, have become very strong.

The growth in the importance of the international movement of services has caught governments unaware. Over the decades, the ground rules that governments followed in regulating the delivery of services grew piecemeal, immune from any coherent principle. When governments turned to the problem of reducing barriers to the international movement of services, their instincts have usually led them to avoid a global approach. The diversity and complexity of national regulations in the licensing of banks, telephone companies, engineers, brain surgeons, trial lawyers, and hotels have appeared so forbidding and the attitudes of governments toward such regulations have appeared so diverse as to defy a global agreement.[5] Where broader agreements have seemed possible, as in the case of airlines and merchant shipping, the underlying principles of each such agreement have varied from one service to the next.

The changes in other areas lending themselves to international cooperation, like the areas associated with international money flows, have undergone many of the changes experienced in trade and services. In a system of fixed exchange rates such as existed among the principal currencies until 1971, the points of dispute among governments over international money flows were comparatively simple. The main concerns centered on occasional changes in exchange rates, such as Britain's revaluation of the pound in 1967, and on restrictive licensing of foreign exchange transactions, such as those applied by Japan throughout the 1950s and 1960s. These were issues of a kind that could be managed in a global organization like the IMF. Since the regime of fixed exchange rates ended in 1971, however, the monetary and fiscal policies of the major countries have become far more important to the economies of their neighbors, penetrating them more swiftly and with greater effect than in times past. With Black Monday—October 19, 1987—burned in their memories, governments have been groping to define the principles and develop the institutions capable of handling the new crop of increasingly complex and increasingly critical issues.

One obvious risk is that in seeking more effective approaches to international cooperation, the United States and other nations might withdraw too far and too fast from their support of the multilateral institutions. Even if the IMF has been dispossessed from any serious role in the management of relations between the world's principal currencies—the dollar, the yen, and the deutschemark—no alternative has yet appeared that can perform its role in riding herd on the balance-of-payment problems of the developing countries. The same can be said for the World Bank; its role in supplementing, coordinating, and rounding out the numerous bits and pieces of foreign aid scraped together by the poorest countries from bilateral sources has no obvious substitute. In addition, both institutions have made major contributions in terms of research and of counseling developing countries.

The case for continuing to support the GATT is admittedly more equivocal. A few decades ago, one might have said that the source of GATT's strength was that it separated negotiations on trade matters from all the other contentious issues involved in international economic cooperation. Today, with tariff negotiations much less important, the separation of trade issues from other issues such as rights of establishment has become a handicap rather than an advantage. And the probability seems very small that the GATT as presently constituted can effectively link such disparate issues as services, establishment rates, and information flows.

Moreover, the GATT continues to suffer from the fundamental flaw that was present at its birth. No country—certainly not the United States—is yet prepared to acknowledge that decisions reached in the GATT can have any binding effect upon its behavior. In reality, GATT rules and GATT decisions obviously do exert real influence on governments from time to time, if only by tipping the scales in the bureaucratic struggles within each government that typically precede official action.

In the U.S. case, however, Congress reserves the right to take the GATT as it chooses: to conform to the GATT's provisions, as Congress has done on two or three occasions; or to ignore such provisions, as Congress has more often been inclined to do. As a result, when parties to the GATT have found the U.S. government in violation of the agreement—as in the case of U.S. restrictions on cheese imports in the 1950s or its imposition of a discriminatory import tax on oil in the 1980s—officials in the U.S. executive branch can only shrug their shoulders and invite the injured parties to retaliate.

Yet despite the GATT's unstable foundations, it has managed to chalk up some unusual achievements. For instance, during the 1950s its members succeeded in developing and applying a remarkable set of procedures for the handling of trade complaints, procedures without precedent in international organizations. And there is some hope that the industrialized countries which are members of the GATT may be persuaded to avail themselves of these procedures more faithfully and consistently than they have in the past.[6]

Lawyers specialized in international law, aware of the critical need for more effective dispute-settling mechanisms among governments and starved for examples of such mechanisms in operation, have turned the GATT procedures into something of a legal showpiece.[7] It is ironic that an institution with such limited powers to compel governments to act should have developed such elaborate procedures for hearing and weighing complaints. But GATT's signal achievements in procedural issues alone are too important to be abandoned prematurely. Pioneer work of this sort could well prove useful as smaller groups of countries turn to some of the issues first tackled in the GATT.

In the end, however, the GATT, like the IMF and the World Bank, remains shackled by the fundamental unwillingness of most nations to cede any real power to global organizations. And in the absence of the leadership that the United States was once able to provide, it is unlikely that the other countries of the world will embrace globalism as a means of solving their foreign economic problems. That, at least, is the conclusion strongly suggested by the record to date.

THE OTHER ACTORS

With a record of over 40 years on which to draw, one can develop some broad ideas of the goals and values to which other countries are likely to respond, and the extent of their likely contribution to the strengthening of international agreements on a global scale.

The Developing Countries

When in 1945 the United States began to unveil its ideas of a postwar trading system to its neighbors in Latin America, some of the U.S. officials involved were old hands in the trade bureaucracy, whose contacts with the Latin Americans on economic matters stretched back to the years before the war. Despite their experience, the U.S. officials were carried away in the spirit of war and reconstruction by the image of a brave new world they were hoping to fashion.

To most Latin Americans, however, the idea of an open, competitive world was anathema. They saw the U.S. conception of free trade on a global basis as one that condemned them to a perpetual role as wood-hewers and water-carriers. Their reaction, therefore, was one of hostility and resistance.

The sullen response of the developing countries to the U.S. government's initiatives was intensified by the fact that some of the global institutions in the U.S. blueprint—notably the International Monetary Fund and the World Bank—had already been put in place without much advice from the developing world. The general shape of the institutions was worked out mainly between the U.S. and the U.K. representatives, Harry Dexter White and John Maynard Keynes. A system of weighted voting was implanted in the two institutions, guaranteeing that the United States and the United Kingdom in combination could veto any major policy decision. The developing countries, as some of them would put it later, had already been "marginalized."[8]

Accordingly, when the United States sought to sell its concept of a postwar economic regime, a few developing countries took the lead in an effort to produce a different balance than U.S. policymakers were earnestly promoting. Led by Brazil and India, the developing countries pushed for the proposition that under any international trade agreement, developing countries should be exempted from the general commitment to dismantle trade restrictions. U.S. negotiators, eager to find some formula that most countries would accept even if it departed substantially from their original vision, settled for the principle that the developing countries should enjoy special rights to retain trade restrictions. As the years went on, the practices and pronouncements of the parties to the GATT hardened that concession into a firm line of policy. In effect, member countries of the GATT that fell in the "developing country" category were free in practice to follow what economic practices they liked, without fear of any serious challenge in the GATT.[9]

Perhaps subsequent history would have been different if the industrialized countries themselves had adhered meticulously to the concept of open nondiscriminatory markets. But the U.S. government by the 1950s was already giving evidence of its equivocal attachment to that concept; and neither the Europeans nor the Japanese were providing better examples of unambiguous adherence.

Not surprisingly, then, the developing countries have had little faith in the idea of an open system of international economic relations in which governments would play a limited and innocuous role. Predictably, their collective initiatives have instead taken the form of a series of demands on the wealthier industrialized countries, demands for a greater voice in the governing structure of the international organizations, and for improvements in the terms by which developing countries could acquire capital, technology, or access to the markets of the wealthier countries.[10] One of their few successes in these efforts was the so-called Generalized System of Preferences, the agreement of industrialized countries in 1971 that each of them would establish its own system of tariff preferences favoring the exports of developing countries.

In their efforts to fashion a set of international economic relationships that they thought would serve their needs, developing countries also have supported the creation of a number of commodity agreements designed to generate monopoly power for them in their sales to importing countries. Even in those cases, however, the internal compulsions of the developing countries to take independent action wherever it seemed to serve their short-run interests have usually been so strong that the agreements have rarely been honored for very long. In practically all of these arrangements, some signatories could not resist breaking the monopoly price.[11] The periodic OPEC decisions of the 1970s and 1980s offered repeated illustrations of the fragile character of the agreements, as some members found ways around their price commitments and their assigned production quotas.

Regional trading agreements among developing countries have proved equally fragile. In the case of the Latin American Free Trade Association, the Andean Pact, and the East African Common Market, for example, the agreements were soon undermined by the unwillingness of some signatories to adhere to the agreed provisions.[12]

Until the 1980s, the U.S. reaction to the practices of the developing countries was usually one of acute frustration. Although the U.S. position with regard to the GATT was already marred by numerous violations, U.S. administrations from time to time invoked one provision or another of the GATT in an effort to change the trade practices of the developing countries. Observing that countries such as Brazil and Korea had attained levels of income and economic capabilities typical of some industrialized countries, the U.S. government in the 1970s questioned their continued right to the GATT's exemptions for developing countries and proposed a "graduation" process for such countries.[13] In the 1980s, the tone and tactics of the U.S. government became more threatening as it invoked various provisions of its trade laws to alter the behavior of developing countries.[14]

Although the schemes of developing countries to accelerate their industrial growth through measures inconsistent with the GATT have often ended in failure, some appear to have been resounding successes, stiffening the countries' resolve to hang on to their exemptions. Brazil's dogged attempts to build its own aviation industry provide an outstanding example of efforts of that kind.

Active state involvement in the Brazilian aeronautics industry began as early as 1941, when the Ministry of Aeronautics was created to assume control both of civil aeronautics and the Brazilian Air Force. By the 1960s, with the help of German, French, and other foreign engineers, the Brazilians succeeded in designing their first small plane. In 1968, the government created and financed EMBRAER, a state-owned enterprise designated the "national champion" of the aircraft industry. The following year, Aeronautica Macchi of Italy was persuaded to sign a licensing agreement with EMBRAER that enabled the fledgling Brazilian enterprise to gain technical expertise from the Italian designers and engineers. In 1975, EMBRAER began to produce small aircraft in Brazil under a license from Piper.

In order to generate a market for Brazilian-produced planes, however, the government had to go much further. First, it offered a series of special privileges to EMBRAER, exempting the firm from certain taxes and duties and encouraging other Brazilian corporations to invest in the company by exempting the investments from income taxes. Second, the government raised import duties on certain aircraft to as high as 50 percent and tightened the restrictions imposed on importers of aircraft. In addition, the government authorized EMBRAER to sell its planes on financial terms that its private competitors were unprepared to match. Finally, the government put its own weight behind the creation of a number of regional airlines, each of which would, of course, purchase its planes from EMBRAER.[15]

Within several years, the government's efforts had paid off. By the early 1980s, EMBRAER was producing seven types of planes, and Brazil had become self-sufficient in all but large commercial aircraft and certain sophisticated military planes. More significantly, perhaps, Brazilian planes had broken into the American market, offering a 15 to 20 seat version of its plane designed for commuter lines. By the mid-1980s, the Brazilian plane had captured about 7 percent of the domestic seat capacity in U.S. commuter planes.[16]

When developing countries have decided to increase the movement of goods or capital flowing across their borders, as many did in the 1970s, they have characteristically resorted to practices far removed from the open nondiscriminatory world that U.S. policymakers had hoped to promote through global organization. The use of various forms of selective state support has been endemic. So, too, have been various devices linking trade rights with investment rights. One favorite practice, for instance, has been the application of so-called performance requirements to the operations of foreign-owned enterprises in their territory. Under these requirements, a country such as Mexico orders the foreign owned subsidiaries in its jurisdiction to increase their exports and curb their imports; those that comply are allowed to expand their investment, production, and sales in the protected Mexican market, while others are denied that right.[17]

Sporadic efforts by the U.S. government to convince developing countries to give up their special right—to "graduate"—as their economies come to resemble those of the more industrialized nations have received only equivocal support from Europe and Japan. The Europeans have preferred to handle their problems with the developing countries through unilateral restrictions or bilateral discussions, while the Japanese have preferred to maintain a low profile on the issue. In any case, in an organization such as the GATT, whose membership consists in the main of developing countries, the graduation concept has little chance of success.

Nevertheless, the positions of developing countries have not been cast in concrete, and there has been visible movement in their policies over the past decade or two. In the 1970s, for instance, nearly all the developing countries, meeting as the Group of 77 (which eventually ballooned to over 120) or in rump gatherings in various U.N. organizations, were ready to caucus against the rich industrialized countries whenever the call went out from one of their leaders. But by the 1980s, such caucuses were becoming ceremonial and perfunctory, as the countries began to acknowledge the obvious differences among them created by varying levels of income, degree of industrialization, and extent of integration with the international economy. The developing countries attempting to open their economies to world markets, such as Singapore, were discovering how little they had in common with those opting for a more controlled economic regime. India's irritation with Pakistan, Egypt's hostility toward Libya, and Honduras's suspicions of Nicaragua were proving more potent in their policy-making than their common complaints against Europe, Japan, and the United States.

At the GATT convocation at Punta del Este in 1986, the differences among the developing countries were repeatedly in evidence. While Brazil and India continued to play their historical role as the determined leaders of the opposition to the industrialized nations, other developing countries showed an active interest in pursuing the possibilities of more open economic relations with the rest of the world.

Yet, with the possible exception of Singapore and one or two others, none of the developing countries could be said to support a concept of open competitive markets on a global scale nor to favor vesting global institutions with added powers over their national economic policies.

The Europeans

The economic ties between Europe and North America have become so pervasive and deep that there is no escaping the need to develop some structure through which to manage those relationships. At the same time, the various European national economies have gradually become so intimately entangled with one another that it is no longer very useful to think of any individual European country as an autonomous economic unit. In spite of themselves, the Europeans appear to be entrapped in a slow process that Jean Monnet, founder of the European Coal and Steel Community, used to refer to as *engrenage,* a progressive meshing of national systems.

With hindsight, one can make a case that the appearance of a European economic personality after World War II was always in the cards. Picking up on a theme that has surfaced repeatedly since the Napoleonic era, European governments have asked themselves how to survive alongside two colossi: the United States, whose economic power was becoming so great that it seemed to relegate the European economy to the role of the perpetual follower; and the Soviet Union, whose political appeal in Europe might depend on the capacity of European governments to respond to the economic demands of their electorates.

The classic response of European governments to threatened economic domination by their neighbors has been to look for partners willing to form a countervailing economic union.[18] Thus, Europe's experiences under the Marshall Plan, abetted and financed by the U.S. government, reflected its long-standing interest in the potentials of economic union. The discriminatory trade and monetary arrangements developed under the Marshall Plan had proved remarkably successful, helping the Europeans to open their borders to one another and encouraging them to discuss numerous deeper and more enduring preferential arrangements.[19] Soon thereafter, a wave of proposals for various new schemes of economic collaboration swept through the European capitals. The French initiative in 1951 for the creation of a European Coal and Steel Community, although chiefly based on a desire to prevent the resurgence of an independent Germany, nevertheless laid the groundwork for the European Economic Community that would follow eight years later. The European states that felt inhibited about joining a trading bloc that might compromise their status as neutrals—countries such as Sweden, Austria, and Switzerland—joined with others to create their own seven-country trading group but continued to link their trade intimately to the larger European group in a series of free trade agreements.

By the 1950s, therefore, the rough contours of a European economic identity were already in place. To be sure, large areas of ambiguity still remained; among them, the uncertainties created by the position of the United Kingdom, which was still finding it hard to throw in its lot irrevocably with the Europeans. Many British leaders had not reconciled themselves to the shrinking economic position of the United Kingdom. They continued to think in terms of the country's heroic role in World War II, its special place in history as a world empire, and its hostility to European Catholicism, going back nearly four centuries. But despite the British hesitation, a European economic identity was taking shape.

The willingness of the Europeans during the early postwar years to accept the nondiscriminatory approach of the GATT and the IMF, while they were beginning to think of economic union, is easy enough to understand. For some years after World War II, when Europe was cold and hungry, the United States gave it generous support. Obviously, prudence demanded that the Europeans should find some way of accommodating U.S. views, even when those views bore some of the usual signs of split personality so common to U.S. policy positions. Accordingly, the Europeans participated in building up the GATT, the IMF, and the World Bank at the same time that they were setting about to construct the elements of a European-centered economic existence, with its own trade rules and its own payment system.

Since those early days, both the European Monetary System and the European trade system have acquired a vigor and cohesiveness setting them apart from the rest of the world. Neither system is highly exclusionary or protectionist, but both place individual European states in a close lockstep when developing their relationships with non-Europeans.

For example, because the European Monetary System requires its members to alter national policies that threaten to upset the exchange rate relationships, the economic policies of the member countries have become inextricably linked.[20]

At the same time, the European Monetary System exhibits characteristics that are peculiarly European. As is so often the case, the British are half-in, half-out; although they participate in the swapping of credits among the member countries, they have refused to commit themselves to maintaining the exchange rate for sterling in any specified relationship to the other currencies in the group. As usual, the French have demanded and won some of the overt manifestations of Gallic influence; the European currency unit, not surprisingly, is dubbed the *ecu,* an obsolete French coin. As expected, it is the German currency, the deutschemark, that contributes most to the solidity and stability of the arrangement.

In the area of trade, Europe has retained remarkably open economic relationships both within Europe and with the rest of the world. The centerpiece, however, has been a tight preferential trading area created by the treaty establishing the European Economic Community and extended by a succession of weaker preferential agreements to several scores of other countries.[21] But it has remained a system based fundamentally on a European core.

Only in agriculture has the Community drawn a curtain between European and world markets. Emulating the earlier U.S. example, it followed a highly protectionist approach to agricultural products at its outset. By 1962, it had fashioned and put into effect a system that outdid the Americans in terms of controlling trade in those products.[22] The fundamental principle of the system was that internal prices of key agricultural products would be supported to the extent necessary for achieving some stated internal target prices for European farmers. To ensure that the prices were not undermined by imports, a variable levy would be imposed, sufficient to lift the landed prices of foreign products to the internal target prices. In order to enable the community's exports to be sold abroad, the exports were subsidized to the extent necessary to bring their prices down to those on world markets.[23]

Over the years, negotiations on the restrictive schemes of the United States and the EEC have been unending. An underlying tension has erupted from time to time to produce battles over issues that, to the outsider, seemed trivial for the passions they evoked. From 1962 to 1964, the United States and the European Community were locked in a so-called chicken war. In 1985, they were battling once again over the EEC's preferential treatment of Mediterranean citrus products. Then, in 1986, the Europeans' exports of pasta became the contentious issue.[24]

In all these battles, the U.S. side has exhibited its characteristic traits. The issues selected for struggle have not been based on any careful weighing of national interests, but have depended largely on the energy and strategy of the key interest groups. Moreover, the president has been obliged to conduct his international negotiations within the terms of a set of agricultural programs that were the product of some bloody congressional battles, programs that the executive branch would attempt to alter at its peril.

To make matters more difficult, the negotiators for the European Economic Community have been equally inflexible. The EEC's agricultural programs have been typically the outcome of arcane negotiations covering many aspects of the Community's operations, involving the domestic politics of France, Germany, and Britain, and producing outcomes that the various member countries usually saw as cast in concrete.[25] What has limited the eruption of overt trade warfare between the United States and Europe has been the recognition by all parties of the political gravity of such a development.

Over the years, the Europeans have also created an economic personality differing in numerous respects from the U.S. visions that originally inspired the GATT and the IMF. Some of those differences arise from the fact that most European governments allow for much more varied and more selective support of individual enterprises than does the U.S. government, mirroring the ideological differences on the two sides of the Atlantic over the appropriate role of the state and the appropriate discretionary powers of the bureaucracy.

Illustrative of these differences is the fact that state-owned enterprises have occupied a considerably larger place in European economies than in the United States. For instance, in the 1970s, state-owned enterprises accounted for more than 50 percent of the gross domestic product in the construction, manufacturing, and mining industries of France; more than 50 percent in the mining and transportation industries of Italy; and more than 75 percent in the mining industry of the United Kingdom.[26]

The existence of the state-owned enterprises promises to be a continuous source of irritation in the relations between the United States and Europe. In practice, it is difficult to deprive a state-owned enterprise of monopoly rights on its home territory and more difficult still to prevent a government from favoring enterprises owned by its own nationals in transactions conducted on its home territory. Moreover wherever such enterprises participate in international competition, there is usually a lingering suspicion—and sometimes the documented reality—of governmental subsidies influencing the sale price. In the case of the European Airbus, for instance, U.S. officials have claimed that the $10 billion in subsidies provided by the various governments to Airbus Industries has enabled the consortium to sell its aircraft at less than cost.[27]

Most European governments also have been much readier than the United States to step in with ad hoc support for a selected ailing industry or enterprise in the private sector or with aid for a lagging region; Italy's program to bolster its once-impoverished south and the various analogous programs initiated in France and Great Britain, for instance, have no counterparts in the United States.[28]

To be sure, during the 1980s, European governments were becoming somewhat less prone to engage in ad hoc undertakings. The Thatcher regime, for instance, has seemed determined to cut back the power of the state. But the gap in perception, practices, and ideologies between the two sides of the Atlantic regarding the appropriate role of government in matters affecting international trade has remained very large.

In spite of these differences, the need for joint action between the United States and Europe on numerous issues remains very strong. In addition to trade, the problems of monetary and fiscal coordination have become continuous and critical. Less obvious but no less important have been issues of jurisdictional overlap and jurisdictional conflict. Enterprises have crossed the Atlantic in both directions in such numbers and variety that the jurisdictional question has repeatedly arisen in a dozen different forms. Issues of taxation, bank safety, security controls, consumer safety, and numerous other fields continually clutter the diplomatic agenda. None can be regarded as a *causa belli*. But their inexorable growth promises to pose increasing problems in the future.

The challenge of finding an effective way for dealing with problems such as these is formidable. On neither side do governments always have control over the selection of issues they place in dispute. On the American side, special interests inside and outside the government play a heavy role in the selection. On the European side, individual countries exercise enough political and economic autonomy within the European Community to make for rigid and inflexible positions on the part of the Community. The Punta del Este proposals for GATT negotiations on services promise to highlight these difficulties as negotiators wrestle over the rules for coastwise shipping; the rights of accountants, lawyers, and doctors in foreign markets; and the appropriate coverage of patent grants.

None of these problems is likely to find its best solution through a global approach. Finding the effective institutional means for dealing with them is a challenge of the highest priority.

The Japanese

By the latter 1980s, no country had a greater stake than Japan in promoting the idea of open international markets for goods, services, and capital. Despite its history of the recent past, few countries had a better basis than Japan for claiming adherence to those pristine principles. As the 1980s approached their end, Japanese tariffs were among the lowest in the world, while Japanese restrictions on the in-bound and out-bound movements of capital and firms had been reduced to trivial levels. True, Japanese agriculture was being protected to a degree that rivaled the European Economic Community, while Japan was exploiting the restrictive provisions of the Multifibre Arrangement which shields textile manufacturers in the industrialized nations from lower-priced exports from the less developed countries as enthusiastically as the countries of Europe and North America. But on other counts, Japan was falling in rapidly with the simple concepts that had guided U.S. representatives 40 years earlier in the formulation of a postwar economic system.

Japan, it is evident, has come a long way since the 1950s when American advisers were wringing their hands over its dark and unpromising prospects. When the Japanese government agreed to join the IMF in 1952 and the GATT in 1955 it probably occurred to very few Japanese officials that the signing of these instruments might have any direct bearing on Japanese practices in the regulation of trade and capital. For one thing, Japan considered itself a developing country, and, except when they were debtors to international agencies, developing countries were free to pursue almost any reasonable course of action. Moreover, the Japanese were in balance-of-payments difficulties and seemed likely to remain so for a considerable period of time; the exceptions for countries in balance-of-payments difficulties fortified Japanese rights to independent action.

Another aspect of the economic agreements after World War II also was reassuring from the Japanese viewpoint. For the most part, the agreements were built on the assumption that the principal barriers to international movements were those imposed by governments, typically at the borders of a country. Reflecting the ethnocentricity of the Americans, accustomed to large internal markets operating under few restraints, the GATT provisions had little to say about the systems of control applied inside national borders. For a highly structured national economy such as Japan in the 1950s, with its extensive networks of internal relationships between companies and with government agencies, measures imposed by the government at the borders represented only a part of the apparatus for determining the country's behavior in international markets. What mattered much more were the lines of credit extended to enterprises, the strength of the consortia that existed for importing raw materials, the loyalties between suppliers and users of industrial materials, and other factors that were in place inside the borders of Japan. [29] Accordingly, the Japanese could comfortably accede to the GATT and other international agreements without any expectation that participation would affect their existing practices.

By the mid-1960s, however, many of Japan's starting assumptions about the impact of the GATT and the IMF on Japan's freedom of action were no longer quite as valid; by that time, Japan was neither a developing country nor a country in long-term balance-of-payments difficulties. Well before then, however, the United States and other countries had provided plenty of examples to indicate that the GATT process was tolerant of significant deviations and evasions. The U.S. government's earliest efforts to restrict Japanese exports in 1957 through "voluntary" export restrictions bewildered many Japanese at first and then placed them on guard. By 1962, the U.S. efforts to restrict its imports of textiles had blossomed into a Long-Term Arrangement (later the Multifibre Arrangement), aimed at legitimating the growing number of such coercive bilateral arrangements. Accordingly, when in the 1960s the U.S. government began to demand that the Japanese substantially liberalize their import restrictions, it was against a background in which U.S. arguments on principle had been substantially undermined.

The conventional U.S. view of Japanese trade policy, which has considerable currency in the U.S. Congress and among U.S. officials, is that the Japanese government has been engaged over the past 20 years in an elaborate process of foot-dragging, aimed at postponing the opening of Japanese markets as long as possible. The U.S. press and U.S. policymakers commonly are derisive over the official announcements of liberalizing trade measures that the Japanese government regularly issues; the usual assumption of the American public is that these announcements are simply another form of artful dodging on the part of the Japanese.

Yet, Japan has gone a long way toward dismantling the restraints that previously inhibited the movement of goods, money, and establishments across Japanese borders. In the financial field, the consequences of that retreat have been spectacular. Before 1975, Japan had in place a tightly controlled system of money flows that channelled the savings of its households smoothly and efficiently to its modern industries at bargain interest rates. To maintain that system, the Japanese authorities had developed an elaborate network of restrictions preventing the Japanese from directing their savings to other channels with higher earning possibilities, such as investments in foreign countries or investments in equity securities.[30] By the latter

1980s, practically all of those restrictions had been swept away, with only some minor remnants remaining.

Some of the pressures behind that revolution had come partly from outside Japan, as foreigners demanded greater access to Japanese capital markets. Much of the pressure came from within, as Japanese banks and other enterprises clamored for the right to lend and borrow abroad. If anyone still doubted that Japan's capital markets were intimately linked to those of the rest of the world, the stock market's extraordinary behavior in 1987 reduced those doubts.

To be sure, formidable problems still remain, inhibiting entry to Japan's markets. They are, however, of an especially difficult kind, far removed from the mandate or problem-solving capabilities of the GATT. One such problem is the propensity of the Japanese to structure their industries in vertically-integrated chains, extending from the acquisition of raw materials to the production, assembly, and even final distribution of the products involved. Even when active ownership ties do not connect the links in the chain, long-term relationships generate a pattern of behavior similar to ownership. By the latter 1980s, one could find changes in the Japanese economy representing a weakening of this tendency, but up to that time the changes were limited. As a result, foreign sellers of components often found processors and assemblers in Japan reluctant to accept their products, while foreign sellers of final products in the Japanese market commonly had difficulty in securing distribution facilities.[31]

Another factor contributing to the distinctive character of Japanese behavior in economic matters has been the relationship between business and government in Japan. Although the boundary between the public and the private spheres in Japan is fairly clear, it has nothing like the ideological or operational significance attributed to it in the United States. In Japan, interactions across the boundary are frequent and important; guidance, consultation, and support are the normal order of things, not exceptional events. In Japanese eyes, such relationships carry no pejorative overtones. As a consequence, one can readily find the Japanese government taking measures that in U.S. terms are regarded as "targeting" markets, that is, subsidizing private research and development and underwriting private market risks.[32]

In dealing with measures of this sort, U.S. negotiators have often avoided the dispute-settling facilities offered by international organizations. One reason for avoiding these organizations has been that the offending measures failed to represent clear violations of international norms. When Toshiba insists on buying its memory chips from a Toshiba affiliate, for instance, its corporate preference hardly creates a basis for crying foul.

In response, U.S. negotiators have typically used bilateral channels to press their complaints on the Japanese. These bilateral discussions have dragged on over the decades, partly because of the complex nature of many U.S. complaints and partly because of the character of the Japanese decision-making process. In Japan, most decisions on foreign economic matters require endless negotiation among rival domestic interests on both sides of the public–private frontier, generating a process that seems interminable and inconclusive to the outsider. The need of the Japanese to take the position of opponents into account in any internal policy dispute has been explained in various ways, most of them drawing on culture and history. Whatever the full explanation may be, one can identify aspects of the Japanese decision-making structure that distinguish it sharply from what one finds in the United States.

In sharpest contrast to their U.S. counterparts, the Japanese officials concerned with the formulation of economic policies both inside and outside the government usually have stable and predictable careers, characteristically within the confines of a single institution, such as a ministry or an industry trade association. As a result, any dispute within the Japanese establishment involves professionals with a long view and long memory, who expect to confront one another in a series of similar struggles over the years. Like U.S. senators who anticipate working with their colleagues for many years, Japanese bureaucrats are aware that bypassing the opposition when its guard is down is eventually likely to prove counterproductive. Consequently, every policy change is preceded by endless discussions and elaborate testing of the waters. Any effort on the part of a minister—even the prime minister—to strike out boldly in a new direction draws heavy fire from the Japanese public. Because opposing Japanese elements cannot easily be steamrollered or bypassed, some foot-draggers are likely to be involved in every major decision involving the opening of Japanese markets, a situation producing long delays and fine compromises.[33] It is hardly surprising that Americans often interpret the process as a systematic effort to stall and mislead U.S. negotiators.

In the end, however, the economic ties binding Japan and the United States are so large as to compel both sides to continue searching for common ground. Even though Japan's stake in finding that common ground is at least as great as that of the United States, it is unlikely to contribute much to the search; as in the past, Japan's contributions are likely to be reactive, lacking in initiative, responding to the demands of others. The country's endemic need for internal consensus will continue to contribute to an appearance of deliberate vacillation. Its representatives rarely will be empowered with the authority and flexibility that international initiatives require if they are to have half a chance of a successful launching. The asymmetry in Japan's relationship with the United States is bound to continue, pitting U.S. innovators without staying power against Japanese negotiators without the ability to move more than a few steps at a time.

THINKING IN PARTS

By economic interest and by ideological preference, Americans have a major stake in maintaining a system of open markets in the world. If institutions organized on a global basis could be counted on to contribute substantially to that objective, they would clearly be the preferred medium through which the U.S. objectives should be pushed. But our reading of the events of the past 40 years points to the conclusion that under present circumstances, organizations with a global membership operate under severe limitations in addressing the problems associated with maintaining open markets.

Yet while global organizations are relatively ineffectual, unilateral measures are downright perilous. The United States cannot altogether rule out the use of threats and tit-for-tat in its efforts to open up foreign markets, but it must also recognize that its domestic system of checks and balances hinders its ability to select and prosecute such threats with the care they demand. And the United States must realize that any unsubtle or extensive use of threats is likely to produce bitter reactions, hurtful to all parties involved.

Recognizing the limitations of the global approach and the dangers of the unilateral approach U.S. policymakers have been engaged in a kind of Darwinian adaptation to their new international environment. They have moved toward agreements that narrow the number of countries involved and widen the subject areas for negotiation. Like any such adaptation, opportunism has played a role, as targets for their new approach have unexpectedly arisen. The oil crisis of 1973, for instance, created one such opportunity, leading to the establishment of the International Energy Agency under the auspices of the OECD. The debt crises of the developing countries in the early 1980s produced other opportunities, generating novel responses in the Club of Paris, the informal committee representing governmental creditors of the developing countries, and the Club of London, the committee representing private bank creditors. The wild gyrations of the dollar throughout the 1980s generated still other responses, strengthening the experience of the industrialized countries with the ad hoc coordination of monetary policy.

At the same time, these opportunistic responses have entailed some obvious dangers.

One such danger has been that countries joined together in small groups will dump their collective problems on the shoulders of outsiders. The prewar cartels in commerce and industry, the postwar phenomenon of OPEC, and the agriculture policies of the European Economic Community offer striking illustrations of such policies. On the other hand, as numerous scholars have pointed out, agreements that are less than global in their scope need not be exclusionary in structure or destructive to outsiders.[34] Some agreements among smaller groups may deal with problems whose solutions simply do not much affect outsiders, as in the case of bilateral tax treaties or other agreements attempting to reconcile conflicts in national jurisdiction. Some may be open-ended and nonexclusionary, inviting other adherents who may find it in their interest to join; an agreement on trade in services, for instance, is likely to involve only a limited number of signatories at the outset but could readily admit other nations. Some agreements may even entail commitments that are moderately helpful to outsiders, as illustrated by the OECD codes that seek to define the norms of behavior on the part of multinational enterprises.

Another risk associated with agreements among smaller groups of countries is that the agreements may prove to be ineffectual, lacking any substantial capacity for finding the facts or applying the moral suasion that larger groups have been known to exercise. Clearly, agreements among small groups of countries do entail such risks. Bilateral treaties of investment have been notorious in their failure to influence the signatory countries whenever issues of real substance arose between them. And agreements among OECD countries typically have been quite ineffectual, notwithstanding that OECD membership has been limited to the industrialized countries.

Limited membership, however, may also open up new opportuni-

ties for creating more effective methods of enforcement. It is clear
by now that neither the U.S. government nor other governments
have any desire to vest much power in global organizations, with
their characteristically heterogeneous mix of countries covering different interests and different ideologies. Where smaller groups of
countries are involved, however, governments may be willing to arm
international institutions with more effective executorial powers than
has been the case in the past. The experience of the European Court,
operating without the proverbial division of marines to enforce the
provisions of the European Community, offers strong evidence that
international institutions can operate effectively among small groups
of like-minded nations.[35] Even the French government, notorious for
its stiff-necked approach to issues of sovereignty, has bowed to its
authority more often than it has resisted it.

Americans, it is true, have usually bridled at the idea of allowing
multilateral institutions to settle international disputes. Their resistance has stemmed in part from the assumption that when such institutions gain power, they reduce the ability of groups within each
country to protest and reverse the actions of their own governments.
Because this is a right that rates especially high in the U.S. value
system, Americans will have a difficult time facing up to the need
for more effective international machinery to handle disputes. It is
an issue that must be dealt with if more effective international cooperation is to be achieved.

A movement to smaller groups offers still another opportunity
that is not usually available in global organizations, namely, the opportunity to link different issues for negotiation effectively. Global
organizations with real substantive responsibilities tend to be narrow
in their scope, inhibiting the linkage of negotiations on different subjects. But where a smaller number of countries are concerned, the
problems of creating such linkages appear less formidable.

Linking different subjects in a common negotiation does not always add to the prospects for a constructive and successful outcome.
The Law of the Sea negotiations, for instance, foundered on the fact
that the negotiators tried to link issues of peaceful passage, jurisdictional limits, and marine research to the problems of creating a deep-
sea mining authority; in the end, the unwillingness of the United
States to agree to the terms of a mining regime stopped the ambitious
effort in its tracks.[36]

On the other hand, there are instances in which some kind of linkage is indispensable to any international negotiation, so that conces-

sions in one area can be traded for those in another.[37] That has been the essential principle leading GATT negotiators in the past to stretch the coverage of their tariff negotiations as widely as they could, a maneuver that has contributed to the success of the negotiations.

Linked negotiations might also provide new opportunities for dealing with difficult problems in other fields, such as lightening the debt load of the developing countries. There is widespread agreement that lightening the servicing load of the debtor countries would be beneficial not only for them but for the creditor countries as well;[38] the problem has been to find a palatable way of producing the result. Although a dozen ingenious schemes to that end have been proposed, most of them seem to have placed the burden of concessions on the creditor countries alone.[39] None of the schemes has yet embraced the possibility of linking the debt issue with other issues in agreements that might appear more balanced. Moreover, because the schemes have been confined to the handling of the debt issue alone, the possibility of distinguishing between the treatment accorded different countries has been limited. The result has been the creation of a stultifying impasse relieved only by short-run improvisations, threatening to both debtor and creditor countries.

The situation is a classic one for considering the possibilities of linkage, by folding the debt problem into a negotiation that includes other elements in the complex relations between some creditor and debtor countries. It is difficult to say whether that could be done while maintaining a common front among creditor nations, such as has been more or less maintained through the IMF, the Club of Paris, and the Club of London. That uncertainty, however, ought not to deter policymakers from exploring the possibilities of linkage as a means of breaking the dangerous impasse that isolation of the debt issue has helped to maintain.

In departing from a global approach, however, the United States and other countries run the risk of losing their way, of growing uncertain where their various agreements may be taking them. In the U.S. case, it is possible to identify some fixed preferences of the electorate that are so strong and continuous as to offer useful landmarks by which policymakers can navigate. Except in emergencies, Americans prefer to constrain the power of government and to limit the choices of its bureaucracy. In spite of the protectionist surge of the 1980s, they are more comfortable with the idea of open global markets than of heavy restriction at national borders. In moving to a pattern of smaller agreements, the challenge for U.S. policymakers will be never to lose sight of those objectives as they move from one issue to the next, and constantly to search for larger patterns of cooperation that might contribute to those ends.

CONCLUSION

As distances shrink and national economies become increasingly sensitive to outside forces, the need for cooperation in international economic affairs continues to grow. A strong case can be made for the view that if more cooperation is needed, bold undertakings based on large propositions have a better chance of surviving than cautious incremental steps. The picture we have just painted, however, suggests that the conditions for creating such undertakings are not yet present. Instead, any cooperation likely to emerge will involve smaller groups of countries, joined together by a common sense of promise or threat. This is a time, therefore, for exploring a new terrain, for analyzing opportunities aggressively as they arise, and for groping toward new patterns of cooperation.

The U.S. establishment that is involved in international economic policy-making is less than ideally suited for engaging in such a process. Our final chapter, therefore, considers what can be done to improve the country's capacity for exploring the landscape, for exploiting targets of opportunity, and above all for learning from its experiences.

8

Preparing for the New Game

ELEPHANTS WON'T FLY

IN PROPOSING HOW the United States should ready itself for the new game, one has to resist making proposals that ask elephants to fly. The American people have built strong institutions and developed strong values over the years. Those institutions and values have been associated far more often with success than with failure. It would be hard to find much public support for radical change.

Two convictions in particular show no sign of losing popular support among Americans. One is the support for diffusing the power of the national government by maintaining the existing system of checks and balances and by holding the bureaucracy under a tight rein. The other, related to the first, is the principle of protecting the rights of special interest groups to challenge and modify the actions of the government.

U.S. policymakers have run into serious domestic obstacles whenever they have attempted to implement policies that appeared either to cede too much discretionary power to government agencies or to place particularly heavy burdens on well-defined interest groups. The efforts of the U.S. government to restrict oil imports in the 1950s and 1960s and to limit capital flows in the 1960s provide telling indications of the resistance that ambitious actions at odds with American values are likely to produce. In both instances, the original restrictions were chiselled back bit by bit in the years following their enactment until they lost all their substantive bite.

The same basic American values suggest why any extensive effort to apply the tit-for-tat approach in U.S. relations with other countries is likely to miscarry. To put that approach into actual operation, one must be willing to place considerable power and discretion in the hands of the bureaucrats, permitting them to assess the merits of individual cases. With time, Congress is sure to grow more and more uncomfortable about leaving such powers in the hands of executive agencies, and will begin to increase its own efforts at oversight and second-guessing.

In addition, as the economic interests of the United States have become more deeply intertwined with those of other countries, a policy of tit-for-tat has begun to approach the practice of self-flagellation. Ironically, the United States cannot punish Japanese exporters without improving the position of Japanese interests already located in the United States. And it cannot punish Mexico without endangering American interests, including investment interests, export interests, and the interests of retirees. With any injured interests readily able to gain access to the U.S. political process, the chances are that any prolonged effort on the part of the U.S. government at applying the tit-for-tat approach would be blocked by the mounting protests of the affected U.S. interests.

In the decades to come, there is little reason to suspect that the U.S. political system will be tolerant of any greater bureaucratic discretion or government intervention than it has in the past. The challenge for U.S. policy makers, therefore, is to formulate foreign economic policies that will allow the country to adapt to the new international game without greatly modifying its own traditional values.

THE EXECUTIVE AND THE CONGRESS

One area in which constructive change may be possible without sacrificing basic values involves the relationships between the executive and the legislative branches in the formulation and execution of foreign economic policies.

Widening the Fast Track

One of the predictable recommendations in any proposal to improve the relations between the executive and Congress is a suggestion for better communication and coordination between the branches. There is a strong temptation to look for a mechanism in which the main lines of trade policy, monetary policy, fiscal policy, and establishment policy will have been jointly explored between the branches in an effort to identify the key assumptions, establish the principal goals, and iron out the gross inconsistencies. But it is difficult to conceive of an executive branch and a legislative branch so structured that they would be capable of an effective dialogue on such wide-ranging issues.

More limited steps for improving communication between the branches, however, should not be ruled out. For example, the concept of the "fast track," whose application to international trade issues is described in Chapter 3, could be extended in one form or another to other problems in foreign economic relations.

With the authority to conduct foreign economic policies divided between the executive and the legislative branches, the challenge for the executive branch has been to carry the legislators along in international negotiations whose results they have the power to veto, and to ensure that the legislative branch would honor those agreements in its subsequent enactments. Aware that congressional commitment is critical to the outcome, the executive branch has usually engaged in some measure of consultation with key congressmen and representatives of special interest groups. The scope and intensity of those consultations have varied with the personalities and politics of different administrations, as well as with the nature of the subject matter. But the consultations have rarely been sufficient to give Congress a sense of having been effectively involved.

The problem has been exacerbated since the latter 1960s by the growing importance of foreign economic policies to the American public. Responding to the burgeoning demands of constituent groups as well as to their own perceptions of appropriate balance, members of Congress have sought to maintain their influence in various ways. To build congressional influence, committees of Congress began creating more elaborate legislative histories for the laws that they enacted, hoping thereby to influence the executive agencies and the courts in the administration of the laws. These measures, however, have failed to produce the kind of responsiveness from the executive branch that Congress hoped for, and legislators have turned to other devices. They have introduced provisions in the trade laws that give special interest groups much broader opportunities and stronger powers to compel the executive to impose new barriers to trade. They have amended the foreign aid laws to require many more formal findings of the president in connection with the distribution of foreign aid. They have experimented with the enactment of various veto schemes aimed at blocking objectionable actions by the executive, including vetoes by a single house of Congress.[1] When in 1983 an adverse Supreme Court decision cast a pall on the constitutionality of the veto measures, several hundred statutes already contained provisions of this sort.

Yet, none of these measures has checked the increasing tension between Congress and the executive. On the contrary, the efforts of Congress to hold the executive to closer account have actually increased the number of instances in which the executive was formally obliged to decide the merits in individual cases. The president, for example, has been authorized to extend or withhold most-favored-nation tariff concessions from communist countries on his own, judging whether or not these states have violated certain basic standards of human rights. The president's finding in 1985 that the shoe industry should not receive added protection from foreign imports and his finding in 1987 that Guatemala was entitled to a continuation of foreign aid despite its poor record in protecting human rights are further illustrations of the counterproductive effects of congressional efforts to curb the apparent discretion of the president.

Many members of Congress are already aware that some of their efforts to participate in the country's foreign economic affairs have been costly and unproductive. That realization opens up the possibility of considering other approaches. One of these is to extend the fast-track procedure beyond matters of international trade to other aspects of international economic policy. The fast-track approach to international trade negotiations was created as a response to the divided authority of Congress and the executive on trade issues. It will be remembered that in the 1960s the administration decided that the time had come for GATT members to try to reduce their nontariff barriers to trade. In the case of the United States, such measures are characteristically imposed by statute and can only be altered by statutory changes. With Congress in control of U.S. trade legislation, other governments were unlikely to negotiate seriously with representatives of the executive branch on such matters unless the concurrence of the Congress could be assured. To deal with that problem, counsel for the relevant congressional committees, after a number of false starts, worked out the ingenious fast-track provisions described in Chapter 3, provisions that proved indispensable in allowing the president to engage in serious negotiations with foreign countries.

Implicit in the fast-track approach is a bargain between the executive and Congress that alters the traditional position of each branch, and modifies the sequential process through which checks and balances would ordinarily be exercised. Under the fast track provisions, the relevant interest groups are brought into the negotiating process from the start, and route their concerns through the executive, while Congressional representatives look on. In turn, Congress agrees to limit the exercise of its powers after the negotiations are completed, promising expeditious action and confining its action to either acceptance or rejection of the negotiated agreements.

In application, the fast track is not very fast. It demands slow, tortuous, and difficult consultations among the executive, the Congress, and representatives of the interest groups. Only the last stage is fast, that is, the stage at which the Congress is invited to ratify the results of the negotiation. First applied in negotiations under the Trade Act of 1974, it became widely recognized in the following years that some such procedure, difficult as it might be, was almost indispensable for effective international negotiations on a wide range of trade issues.

The idea of early and continuous cooperation between the Congress, the executive, and domestic interest groups in the formulation of new policies is hardly radical. The novel aspect of the fast-track provisions has only been the degree to which the process has been formalized, with the obligations of both sides specifically defined.

Like any proposal for closer cooperation between Congress and the executive, a wider use of the fast-track approach in other fields of foreign economic policy is bound to stir apprehension in various quarters. Members of Congress will wonder if they are giving up too much power. Others in the executive branch and elsewhere will wonder if they are setting the fox among the chickens, giving the special interests greater control over decisions that ordinarily require a disinterested view. Anyone who has tracked the country's agricultural policies over the past few decades, produced in a setting in which consultation was close and intimate, will recognize that these are not empty worries. But for the most part, the experience under the 1974 act with the fast-track approach indicates that extensive consultation with special interest groups and Congress in some circumstances can produce constructive results.

Experience with the fast track provision has served to reaffirm what close students of congressional behavior have typically insisted: that no one can easily predict the behavior of the typical member of Congress simply by identifying the special interests in the legislator's district.[2] Special interests affect that behavior in predictable ways, but they are far from determining it.[3]

Contrary to popular impression, most members of Congress understand the perils of creating a foreign economic policy that is based simply on the demands of special interests. Indeed, many wish wistfully that they could find some way of fending off such pressures. Most legislators do not relish being caught between conflicting forces in their districts or being pushed into supporting a position that they know could be hurtful to U.S. interests. The complexity of congressional reactions can be glimpsed in the fact that even though Congress has regularly enacted laws obliging the United States to violate the terms of the GATT, individual legislators have regularly expressed considerable interest in the possibility of strengthening the powers of the institution.

A striking reaffirmation of the ambivalence of the Congress on matters of foreign trade appears in the history of the 1988 omnibus trade bill. Throughout its legislative life, as it tracked its way through the House and the Senate, the bill was widely regarded as a strongly protectionist measure. In the bill's final form, however, the observer from Mars would be hard put to decide whether its trade-liberalizing features were weaker or stronger than its restrictive features. As usual, the president was given added authority to negotiate trade liberalizing measures with other countries. And, as usual, he was directed to make the executive branch even a little more available to complaining special interests.

Congress may very well be amenable to a wider use of the fast-track process, especially if an acceptable structure can be developed to implement the process and if that structure will insulate individual congressmen from some of the pressures coming from special interest groups. One has to acknowledge, however, that relying on the fast-track approach may not prove an unmixed blessing for U.S. negotiators. It may, for instance, weaken the efficacy of the bugaboo tactic so frequently used by negotiators from the executive branch—that is, invoking a threatened action from Congress in order to wring a concession from a foreign negotiator. The strength of that weapon depends, of course, on how anxious others may be to reach agreement with the United States; at a certain point, the independence of Congress becomes a reason for others to refuse to come to the bargaining table rather than a reason for conceding a contested point. With the decline in the relative strength of the U.S. economy, therefore, the congressional bugaboo can easily turn from a strength to a handicap. In any event, the fast-track approach, retaining the requirement for a final affirmative blessing from Congress over measures agreed among the negotiators, continues to have some of the characteristics that have made the congressional bugaboo tactic useful to negotiators.

At the same time, one also has to realize that the case for closer cooperation between the executive branch, Congress, and domestic interests on foreign economic policies varies considerably from one area of policy to the next. The executive branch is likely to resist collaboration, for instance, in those policy areas in which domestic groups have not yet developed a set of clearly defined interests, or in which the executive has traditionally reigned unchecked. With the increase in the importance of the foreign sector as a potential stimulant or constraint on the performance of the U.S. economy, however, the areas of foreign economic policy that will escape the attention of interest groups and the Congress seem destined to shrink. Even the field of monetary policy, heretofore the unchallenged domain of the Federal Reserve Board, has begun to draw attention from Congress, reflecting a heightened interest on the part of constituents and the early signs of public mobilization around given positions. A symptom of the trend is the inclusion of a provision in the 1988 trade bill directing the executive to negotiate with foreign governments over the revaluation of their exchange rates.[4] Accordingly, earlier and more continuous contact between the Congress and the executive as a prelude to international negotiations is likely to become desirable even in fields in which the Congress has traditionally been relatively passive.

If consultations with Congress and interest groups are greatly increased, the importance of linking issues in appropriate bundles for negotiation will also become much more critical. Our recommendation has been that the U.S. policymakers should feel free to consider linking issues that heretofore have been dealt with in watertight compartments, such as issues of trade, investment, and foreign debt. The content of these bundles, however, may prove critical not only in the success of negotiations with other countries but also in the outcome of negotiations inside the U.S. establishment. The lesson offered by the Law of the Sea negotiations is obvious. Ideally, no such package should be vulnerable to a special interest group whose power is so great that it gives the group the ability to veto the whole package.[5]

Improving Consulting Capabilities

The prospect of conducting international negotiations on a bundle of issues under fast-track authorization assumes that the executive branch and Congress have some capability for integrating their views within each of their respective branches and for consulting with one another on the issues. In the U.S. system, that is a very strong assumption. The obvious fact is that neither body is well designed to handle sustained consultation with the other, especially when the consultations involve a package of issues.

One can only go a little way in improving that ability. Party identification counts, as demonstrated by the Reagan administration's problems in communicating with a Democratic Congress. So does personality. But structure is not irrelevant. And the predominant trends in the structures of both the executive and Congress in the 1970s and 1980s have exacerbated the problems of consultation, especially of consultation over a package of issues.

On the congressional side, the sharp increase in the number of congressional subcommittees claiming an interest in international economic issues has been a major source of difficulty. Not long ago, one could speak of the agricultural policy of a given Congress. Today, one is obliged to speak of its sugar policy, its peanut policy, or its wheat policy as if they were unrelated issues. The result has been to relegate individual members of Congress to small areas of specialization, and to reduce the likelihood that any general policy on agriculture will emerge.

There are some small signs that this trend has begun to affect senior congressmen and senators with a sense of frustration and impotence. In recent years, a number of incumbents have declined to stand for reelection even though they occupied safe seats, claiming that they were no longer able to get anything done in Congress.[6] If this sense of dissatisfaction becomes sufficiently acute at a time when Congress is being invited to enlarge its participation in the conduct of foreign economic policies, the change could open the way to some overhauling of the unwieldly structure through which Congress performs its foreign economic policy role.

At the same time, questions also arise about the ability of the executive branch to carry out its part of any new cooperative arrangement. This is the kind of subject that commands instant attention in the incestuous communities inside Washington's Beltway and along the Charles, probably out of proportion to its intrinsic importance.

Still, such discussion has occasionally produced significant changes in structure. In the field of trade, for instance, the displacement of the State Department as the lead agency in the 1960s and the establishment of the Office of the Special Trade Representative were steps in an effort to reflect the growing interaction between domestic and foreign economic policy. In other areas of foreign economic policy, the question of identifying a lead agency in the executive branch has generated less struggle. In monetary and banking matters and in issues involving developing country debt, the Treasury Department has usually taken the lead as a matter of course. In matters of jurisdictional conflict, specialized U.S. agencies such as the SEC or the Antitrust Division of the Justice Department have often taken over.

If future negotiations are to link disparate issues more closely than in the past, some integrative mechanism will have to be maintained inside the executive branch that can ride herd on the negotiations. Admittedly, the creation of any new interagency hybrid is likely to cause some rumblings of discontent within the executive branch. But if the president genuinely favors such a mechanism, the rumblings are not likely to present insuperable problems.

ADJUSTING COSTS AND BENEFITS

If, as we suggest, future agreements may bundle various economic issues into one agreement package, then a larger domestic question will inevitably need to be addressed: How can the costs and benefits be redistributed within the U.S. economy so that no sector of the economy is asked to bear a substantial burden for the rest? For instance, if an agreement with Japan increased the rights of U.S. banks to enter the Tokyo market in return for increasing the rights of Japanese shipping lines to carry U.S. oil, the domestic problem of assuaging U.S. maritime interests would still remain. How to deal with such formidable opposition?

In situations in which the economy as a whole is likely to benefit from a national policy at the expense of some group within it, the remedy that economists and political scientists usually propose is side payments to the injured group. In the U.S. culture, however, side payments as a form of indemnity usually carry pejorative overtones. They smack of discrimination and they add authority to the bureaucratic machinery that must identify the worthy recipients. The tendency of Congress, therefore, has been to weigh down any programs of side payments with numerous guidelines and limitations, making them unwieldly as instruments for internal adjustment. How badly such schemes can misfire is illustrated by the trade adjustment programs of the various trade acts, which degenerated from a concept for the retraining and redeploying of workers to a program that simply offered a few more weeks of unemployment benefits.

The challenge in this instance will be to provide side payments that do more than pay the rent and grocery bills during a few more weeks of idleness. Signs of a more positive approach appeared in some of the provisions of the 1988 trade bill, which envisaged more emphasis on genuine retraining programs and proposed that enterprises should only receive trade protection if they were prepared to use the period of protection in ways that benefited the economy as a whole. But thinking and experimenting on this line of policy have barely begun.

For the United States the problem of redistributing the costs and benefits of an open economy has taken on a special importance, extending beyond the problems of individual equity.

In the U.S. economy, open borders appear to be most advantageous for those at the high end of the country's income distribution, with less clear-cut benefits for the rest. It is the business managers, bankers, technicians, academics, accountants, and lawyers that benefit most obviously from the globalization of manufacture and services. And it is the unskilled and semiskilled workers, including workers in the mass-producing industries of the country, that feel the first effects of foreign competition. During the 1980s, the distribution of family income in the United States tended to become more dispersed, a phenomenon that some observers attributed to the progressive opening up of the economy.[7] Whether or not they were right, the prospect of a widening of the income gap threatens the political ability of the country to embrace the globalization process.

The problem is exacerbated by the presence in the United States of a large mass of workers untrained for anything more than the most unskilled and undemanding kind of work and unlikely to upgrade their skills as new opportunities arise. In Europe, that position has been occupied principally by foreign workers, many of whom could be shipped home if necessary; but in the United States, most in the unskilled pool are permanent U.S. residents.

In attempting to analyze the causes of the problem, social scientists usually point to fundamental factors that can be changed only slowly—such as the high fertility rates of poor, uneducated adolescent mothers, the shocking inadequacies of educational facilities at the preschool and elementary school level in some areas, and the dominance of languages other than English in many urban communities. With the continued globalization of business, the problems of untrained workers with limited capacities for adaptation threaten to worsen, at least when compared with the lot of other Americans. Problems such as these demand long-term remedies of a kind that goes well beyond the scope of this study. In the long run, the failure to deal with them could generate major pressures against the maintenance of an open national economy.

STAFFING THE EXECUTIVE BRANCH

At least as important as improving the coordination between the various branches of government and redistributing costs and benefits is the pressing need to rebalance the roles of political appointees in the U.S. executive branch in relation to career civil servants. By the 1980s, the composition of the U.S. officials in the formulation and execution of international economic policies had become so heavily dominated by political appointees as to represent a major handicap for the United States.

In spite of the extensive professionalization of U.S. personnel in the past half century, the American public still seems prepared to accept Andrew Jackson's conviction that any citizen—in the modern variant, any lawyer or businessman—can manage the affairs of the executive branch, including its foreign economic policies. As long as the U.S. government conducted its foreign economic policies and its international economic negotiations from an unambiguous position of strength, and as long as the country enjoyed the obvious ability to accept a wide range of outcomes, it may not have mattered very much whether Andrew Jackson was right or wrong. Today, however, the U.S. public must adjust to the unfamiliar fact that it has a much greater stake riding on the proper formulation and execution of the country's foreign economic policies.

The need to increase the relative weight of the professionals in the executive branch will prove especially strong if the fast-track principle is to be applied over a wider range of negotiations and if the typical negotiation is to cover a larger bundle of issues. In that case, the executive branch will have to manage two especially complex sets of negotiations in tandem: one inside the U.S. system, the other with foreign governments. As the experience of the 1974 trade act demonstrated, the management of the negotiating process within the U.S. system demands a very high degree of expertise in the executive branch and requires officials with the personal skills to interact with Congress and special interest groups.

It is in the negotiations with other countries, however, that the professional capabilities of the U.S. side will be most severely tested. In an historical turnabout, U.S. negotiators will be obliged to study the values and institutions of other countries with the same care that other countries have characteristically applied in the past to the study of U.S. institutions. For once, it will be essential for U.S. negotiators to explore questions of history, personality, language, and culture that previously they could afford to disregard, and to understand the internal negotiating structures of the other countries as well as they know their own.

Finally, if the United States is to learn from its experiences in the changed international environment that it now confronts, a core of officials must exist that is capable of carrying the lessons of that experience from one administration to the next. Otherwise, the new departures that we have recommended in these pages will turn into aimless wanderings.

Today, the executive office of the president has no enduring core of officials capable of drawing on the experiences of the past. Each new administration faces empty file cabinets when it arrives and leaves empty file cabinets when it departs. By contrast, it is sobering to recall the introductory remarks with which Vice Minister Makoto Kuroda, for many years Japan's leading trade negotiator, was introduced at a dinner in Cambridge in 1987. "My job of introduction," said the chairman, "is very simple indeed. After graduating from Tokyo University in 1955, Minister Kuroda joined MITI. He has been there ever since."

THE U.S.–CANADIAN FREE-TRADE AGREEMENT

By coincidence, as this book was receiving its final touches, a test appeared of some of the propositions offered in the preceding pages in the form of an agreement to create a free trade area between the

United States and Canada.[8] The agreement, negotiated over a period between 1984 and 1987, incorporated to a remarkable extent the various features that we deem essential for U.S. patterns of cooperation in the future.

In some respects, the negotiations presented fewer difficulties than one might ordinarily expect for foreign economic issues. The two governments were in continuous contact for many decades over a wide variety of issues. The bureaucrats in each camp had a very considerable understanding of the political and economic problems of the other, thereby avoiding many of the problems of acute cultural dissonance. On the other hand, the continuous and intimate contact across the border tended to politicize some of the key issues in one country or the other, for example, the issue of lumber imports from Canada to the United States and the issue of threatened U.S. dominance of the mass media in Canada. In most respects, however, the agreement provided a remarkable opportunity to test the validity of many of the key propositions offered in this chapter.

The agreement was negotiated under a fast-track dispensation contained in the 1984 trade act, thereby making the U.S. proposals credible in the eyes of the Canadian negotiators. It incorporated a variety of subjects: not only provisions for the eventual elimination of tariffs but also provisions on the cross border sale of energy, practices in government procurement, the establishment of financial services, the regulation of agriculture, and various other subjects—enough, in short, so that the interests affected by the treaty were sufficiently numerous and diverse to prevent any of them from dominating the legislative process. Despite foot-dragging on the U.S. side, the agreement contained special provisions with regard to the settlement of disputes that commanded the respect of the two parties. Because the agreement required ratification by the U.S. Congress under the fast-track procedures, the risk that Congress would subsequently enact legislation in violation of its terms was much reduced.

The story of how the U.S. Congress came to grant the executive the authority to negotiate with the Canadians also highlights some of the points we made earlier about the domestic components of any international negotiation. When the Reagan administration first discussed the idea of a free trade agreement with Canada, it encountered serious opposition from key U.S. senators. For the first time in 50 years, Congress seemed prepared to deny the president the authority to negotiate with other countries for a more liberal trading regime.[9]

Part of the reluctance of Congress was due, no doubt, to a growing desire to exhibit some measure of independence in the formulation of trade policies. More importantly, however, the idea of a U.S.-Canadian free trade agreement was anathema to the U.S. lumber industry, which had been lobbying intensively for several years to win protection against imported Canadian softwoods.[10] By 1986, the lumber industry had already gained several powerful supporters in Congress, including some members of the Senate Finance Committee. The executive's eagerness to begin negotiations under the fast-track provisions previously enacted in the 1984 trade act gave the lumber industry and its supporters the leverage they were seeking.

It soon became clear to the White House and to the Office of the Special Trade Representative that any congressional action with respect to the fast track provisions hinged on a resolution of the softwood question. Ultimately, a bargain seems to have been struck: The Commerce Department revised an earlier ruling making the U.S. lumber industry eligible for relief from low-priced Canadian imports, and, almost at the last moment, the administration was allowed to go ahead with its negotiations. By dealing with Congress and special interest groups from the earliest stages of the negotiating process, the executive had found a means of accommodating its most powerful source of opposition and was able to build a feasible basis for moving ahead.

On the whole, the agreement eventually reached by the U.S. and Canadian negotiators in October 1987 appears to satisfy the concept of a trade-creating arrangement that is open-ended in intent. Some provisions, such as one with respect to automobiles assembled in Canada, were obviously drafted in an different spirit, being aimed at preventing Japanese exporters from using their access to Canada as a means of penetrating the U.S. market. Other provisions exempting certain cultural areas from the provisions of the agreement reflect Canada's deep-seated concern for preserving its national identity. But on the whole, the agreement appears to be trade-creating both in intent and in likely effect.

The agreement also takes the first tentative steps toward the regulation of trade in services. Banking facilities, insurance companies, and securities firms are all promised easier access to and more favorable treatment in markets that lie across the border. In addition, separate "understandings" have been reached that will allow telecommunications and computer services from one country to compete on an equal basis with local firms in the other, will permit businessmen to cross the border without any prior approval or permission, and will allow architects licensed in one country to be automatically certified in the other.

What remained to be tested on both sides of the border was the reaction of the respective legislatures. Would the diversity of issues covered by the agreement as well as its limited geographic scope prove advantageous in securing its ratification? Would the momentum generated by the agreement offer the needed insulation to members of Congress in holding off special interests that stood a chance of losing benefits under the agreement's terms? As this book went to the printer, the issue was still in doubt. Whatever the outcome might be with regard to this particular agreement, however, it was evident that circumstances were pushing the United States to a new stage beyond the postwar period of globalism.

OVER TIME AND SPACE

While readying the United States for more effective participation in international affairs, one can easily be overcome at times by a sense of futility. Since the 1960s, the U.S. government's ability to lead other countries in any new initiatives has visibly declined. The Atlantic alliance has lost some of its cohesiveness, weakened not only by a U.S. propensity to go it alone but also by a new air of openness and accommodation from the Kremlin. The concept of a Pacific community in which the U.S. government might take a leading role has remained feeble and amorphous, strained by the disputes between the United States and Japan. The wide gap between the United States and the developing countries of Latin America, Asia, and Africa, has shown signs of widening further during the 1980s. The projections of political scientists and commentators on the future position of the United States in international relations have ranged from the lugubrious to the downright alarmist.[11] Without a leader such as the United States, some political scientists have been unsure if any substantial group of countries could be persuaded to cooperate on any economic subject of significance.

Our review of the record of governments in addressing common economic problems, however, suggests that their capacity for agreement is not nearly so limited. In the latter 1980s, practically all countries were conscious of the decline in their ability to control their boundaries; if nothing else had pushed them to that conclusion the stock market gyrations of October 1987 had succeeded in making the point. Almost all were troubled by the inadequacies of their international economic relations. In spite of the increasing peevishness and querulousness of the interchanges on economic issues, international consultations on such issues were continuing to rise in variety and frequency. Despite the decline in the power of the United States to persuade or coerce, the usual menu of issues covering trade, money, and investment was being supplemented and enriched by discussions regarding consumer protection, environmental control, securities regulations, bank safety, and scores of other novel subjects. The basis for global actions on pressing issues may have declined, but the possibility of measures of more limited scope seems on the increase.

In any case, the next major phase in the development of international economic policy, when it occurs, is unlikely to be built on the ideas and blueprints of an innovative leader. Instead, it is likely to be conceived and developed by a number of nations, reflecting a mélange of national experiences and ideologies. That assumption explains why our emphasis in these chapters has been on processes, institutions, and basic aims, rather than on the substance of the new arrangements.

The most difficult challenge of all for U.S. policymakers may be to define the role that the United States will play in constructing the new arrangements. The country's ideology, built on a century of economic growth in relative isolation from Europe, still radiates a basic assurance regarding the superiority of the U.S. economic system. The three decades of economic leadership that followed World War II have only served to reaffirm among Americans the superiority of U.S. economic values. The doubts and misgivings that some Americans have been expressing in the 1980s regarding U.S. foreign economic policies have not yet fostered much tolerance for the disparate views of other governments on international economic relations. A capacity for listening and learning has still to be developed.

Notes

CHAPTER 1 A New Game

1. "Poll Shows Southern Support for Import Limits," *New York Times,* March 6, 1988, p. 34.

2. For statistics on the declining costs of various transportation and communications media, see Richard N. Cooper, "How Open is the U.S. Economy?" in R. W. Hafer, ed., *The United States as an Open Economy* (Lexington, MA: Lexington Books, 1986), pp. 3–24.

3. Quoted in Jeffrey A. Frieden, *Banking on the World: The Politics of American International Finance* (New York: Harper & Row, 1987), p. 115.

4. Federal Technology Transfer Act of 1986 (PL 99–502, October 20, 1986), Sec. 12.

5. Omnibus Trade Bill of 1987 (HR 3, July 21, 1987), Sec. 1401.

6. For instance, the Fair Export Financing Act of 1986 (Senate Bill S2246, March 25, 1986), Sec. 2.

CHAPTER 2 Looking Back

1. In "Foreign Affairs and the Constitution," *Foreign Affairs* (Winter 1987/88), p. 310.

2. The dominant philosophical view, of course, places principal emphasis on the interest of the sovereign. See Niccolo Machiavelli, *The Prince,* translated by Leo Paul S. Alvarez (Dallas: University of Dallas Press, 1980), p. 88; Thomas Hobbes, *Leviathan,* edited by Michael Oakeshott (New York: Collier Books, 1962), esp. pp. 80–86, 129–133.

3. Grotius and Rousseau are perhaps the first to exhibit some sensibility to

the possibility that the responsibilities of the state should include the prosperity as well as the protection of its members. See Jean-Jacques Rousseau, *The Social Contract,* translated by Maurice Cranston (Hammondworth, England: Penguin Books, 1968), pp. 59–63, 130, 140; and Hugo Grotius, *The Rights of War and Peace* (Westport: Hyperion Press, 1979), p. 113. Not until Locke, however, does economics assume a more central role. See John Locke, *The Treatises of Government* (New York: Cambridge University Press, 1960), pp. 395–409.

4. Daniel Boorstin, *The Discoverers* (New York: Random House, 1983), pp. 665–666.

5. These developments are summarized in Walter Lefeber, "The 'Lion in the Path': the U.S. Emergence as a World Power," *Political Science Quarterly,* vol. 101, no. 5 (1986), pp. 710–718.

6. This so-called "doctrine of primary jurisdiction" has been variously interpreted; but deference to the agencies' "expertness" was the general rule in the 1950s and 1960s. At one point, in 1959, the Supreme Court went so far as to claim that even the remotest possibility of conflicting jurisdiction between the courts and the agencies was sufficient to limit the jurisdiction of state courts. See Louis L. Jaffe, "Primary Jurisdiction," *Harvard Law Review,* vol. 77, no. 6 (1964), pp. 1037–1070.

7. For a review of the Administrative Procedures Act and its subsequent implementation, see Howard Ball, ed., *Federal Administrative Agencies* (Englewood Cliffs, NJ: Prentice-Hall, 1984), and Robert E. Litan and William D. Nordhaus, *Reforming Federal Regulation* (New Haven: Yale University Press, 1983).

8. One observer has noted that some judges today see themselves as "warriors in the fight to limit discretion" on the part of administrative agencies. See Donald L. Horowitz, "The Courts as Guardians of the Public Interest," *Public Administration Review,* vol. 37 (March/April 1977), pp. 148–153. Reprinted in Ball, ed., *Federal Administrative Agencies,* pp. 250–257.

9. See Samuel P. Huntington, *American Politics: Promise of Disharmony* (Cambridge: Belknap Press, 1981), pp. 207–214. Also Thomas E. Cronin, "A Resurgent Congress and the Imperial Presidency," in Charles W. Kegley, Jr., and Eugene R. Witkopf, eds., *Perspectives on American Foreign Policy* (New York: St. Martin's Press, 1983), pp. 320–345; and Dom Bonafede et al., "The President vs. Congress: The Score since Watergate," *National Journal,* vol. 8, no. 22 (May 27, 1976), pp. 730–748.

10. See Allen Schick, "Let the Sunshine In," in Ball, ed., *Federal Administrative Agencies,* pp. 292–297.

11. In the landmark *Chadha* decision on June 23, 1983, the Court ruled that statutory provisions requiring the president or his subordinates to submit proposed legislation to Congress for potential veto had impermissably altered the constitutional process. Two weeks after, the Court also ruled

legislative vetoes unconstitutional in the Natural Gas Policy Act of 1978 and in the Federal Trade Commission Improvements Act of 1980. See Robert S. Gilmour and Barbara Hinkson Craig, "After the Congressional Veto: Assessing the Alternatives," *Journal of Policy Analysis and Management,* vol. 3, no. 3 (Spring 1984), pp. 373–392.

12. Quoted in Walter Salant, "The Collected Writings of John Maynard Keynes," *Journal of Economic Literature,* vol. 18, no. 3 (September 1980), pp. 1056–1062.

13. For a description of the growth of federal agencies, see Ball's chapter, "Growth of Federal Agencies," in Ball, ed., *Federal Administrative Agencies,* pp. 5–56. For the growth in congressional committees, see George Goodwin, Jr., *The Little Legislatures* (Amherst, MA: University of Massachusetts Press, 1970), p. 10; also, Roger H. Davidson, "Subcommittee Government: New Channels for Policy Making," in Thomas E. Mann and Norman J. Ornstein, eds., *The New Congress* (Washington, DC: American Enterprise Institute, 1981), pp. 99–131; and Lawrence D. Dodd and Richard L. Schott, *Congress and the Administrative State* (New York: John Wiley, 1979).

14. From 1933 to 1965, for instance, the average term of cabinet secretaries was only 40 months. See Roger B. Porter, *Presidential Decision Making* (Cambridge, Eng.: Cambridge University Press, 1980), p. 21.

15. A book that describes the influence of six such executive policymakers is Walter Isaacson and Evan Thomas, *The Wise Men: Architects of the American Century* (New York: Simon & Schuster, 1986).

16. See Albert O. Hirschman, "The Principle of the Hiding Hand," *The Public Interest,* vol. 6 (Winter 1967), pp. 10–23.

17. See, for instance, Hugh Heclo, *A Government of Strangers* (Washington, DC: The Brookings Institution, 1977), pp. 84–112.

18. For a description of Kennedy's personal involvement with and commitment to the Alliance for Progress and the Trade Act of 1962, see Bruce Miroff, *Pragmatic Illusions: The Presidential Politics of John F. Kennedy* (New York: David McKay, 1976), pp. 110–142; James MacGregor Burns, *John F. Kennedy: The Promise and the Performance* (New York: DaCapo Press, 1975), pp. 294; 268–271; and Theodore C. Sorenson, *Kennedy* (New York: Harper & Row, 1965), pp. 410–412; 533–537.

19. Cases decided by the Supreme Court include: Panama Refining Co. v. Ryan, 293 U.S. 399 (1935); Schechter Poultry Corporation v. United States, 295 U.S. 495 (1935); Youngstown Sheet and Tube Company v. Sawyer, 343 U.S. 579 (1952); Missouri v. Holland, 252 U.S. 416 (1920); U.S. v. Curtiss Wright Export Corp., 299 U.S. 304 (1936).

20. An interesting example is described in Diana Crane, "Transnational Networks in Basic Science," in Robert O. Keohane and Joseph S. Nye,

Jr., eds. *Transnational Relations and World Politics* (Cambridge: Harvard University Press, 1972), pp. 235–251.

21. For two conflicting views on the capture phenomenon, see Theodore J. Lowi, *The End of Liberalism* (New York: W.W. Norton, 1969), pp. 102–124; and James Q. Wilson, "The Politics of Legislation," in James Q. Wilson, ed., *The Politics of Regulation* (New York: Basic Books, 1980) pp. 75–120.

22. One study cites an initial propensity of each new administration to avoid cooperative undertakings and to take unilateral action on foreign economic problems, a propensity that eventually gives way during the course of that administration to a willingness to participate in joint ventures with other countries. See C. Fred Bergsten, "America's Unilateralism," in C. Fred Bergsten, Etienne D'Avignon, and Isamu Miyazaki, eds., *Conditions for Partnership in International Economic Management,* Report to the Trilateral Commission, 1986, pp. 3–14.

23. See, for instance, John Zysman, "The French State in the International Economy," in Peter J. Katzenstein, ed., *Between Power and Plenty* (Madison, WI: University of Wisconsin Press, 1978), p. 275, passim; James M. Laux, "Managerial Structures in France," in Harold F. Williamson, ed., *Evolution of International Management Structures* (Newark, DE: University of Delaware Press, 1975), pp. 100–101.

24. See, for instance, John Zysman, "The French State in the International Economy," in Katzenstein, ed., *Between Power and Plenty,* pp. 257, 265.

25. For a hint that France's disappointing military performance may have contributed to this persistent preoccupation, see Donald J. Harvey, "Contemporary Concepts of French Strategy," in Edward Mead Earle, ed., *Modern France: Problems of the Third and Fourth Republics* (Princeton: Princeton University Press, 1951), p. 424; and Richard D. Callener, "The Military Defeat of 1940 in Retrospect," in Earle, ed., *Modern France,* pp. 405–420.

26. This question is raised by Ralf Dahrendorf, *Society and Democracy in Germany* (New York: W. W. Norton, 1967), esp. pp. 17–26.

27. See for instance, Georg H. Küster, "Germany," in Raymond Vernon, ed., *Big Business and the State* (Cambridge, MA: Harvard University Press, 1974), p. 86; John S. Odell, *U.S. International Monetary Policy* (Princeton: Princeton University Press, 1982), p. 231; and "Bonn Balks at Spurring Economy," *New York Times,* July 3, 1986, p. D1.

28. See, for instance, Richard E. Neustadt, "White House and Whitehall," *The Public Interest,* no. 2 (Winter 1966), pp. 55–69.

29. *New York Times,* November 25, 1987, p. 27.

30. See, for instance, Richard J. Samuels, *The Business of the Japanese State* (Ithaca, NY: Cornell University Press, 1987), esp. pp. 285–290.

CHAPTER 3 **The Politics of International Trade**

1. For an historical analysis of U.S. tariff policy, see Samuel F. Bemis, *A Diplomatic History of the United States* (New York: Holt, 1955); Sidney Ratner, *The Tariff in American History* (New York: Van Nostrand, 1972); F. W. Taussig, *Tariff History of the United States,* 8th ed. (New York: Putnam, 1931); E. Stanwood, *American Tariff Controversies* (New York: Houghton Mifflin, 1983); E. E. Schattschneider, *Politics, Pressures, and the Tariff* (New York: Prentice-Hall, 1935).

2. See, for instance, F. W. Taussig, *State Papers and Speeches on the Tariff* (Cambridge: Harvard University Press, 1982), pp. 1–107, which reproduces Hamilton's 1789 "Report on Manufacturing."

3. Ibid., pp. 252–316, 317–385.

4. The post-Civil War record indicates that the only downward revisions in tariff rates (the Wilson tariff act in 1894 and the Underwood tariff act in 1913) were passed by Democratic congresses. See Don D. Humphrey, *American Imports* (New York: Twentieth Century Fund, 1955), pp. 72–104.

5. See Stephen Lande and Craig VanGrasstek, *The Trade and Tariff Act of 1984* (Lexington, MA: Lexington Books, 1986), p. 4.

6. For an account of the struggle, see Henry Cabot Lodge, *The Senate and the League of Nations* (New York: Charles Scribner, 1952), pp. 96–227; also Melvyn Dubofsky et al., *The United States in the Twentieth Century* (Englewood Cliffs, NJ: Prentice-Hall, 1978), p. 138.

7. Bernhard Ostrolenk, *The Surplus Farmer* (New York: Harper, 1932), pp. 67–68; also Sidney Ratner, *The Tariff in American History* (New York: Van Nostrand, 1972), pp. 46–57; and Richard N. Cooper, "Trade Policy as Foreign Policy," Discussion Paper no. 1160, Harvard Institute of Economic Research, Cambridge MA, June 1985, p. 61.

8. These episodes are summarized in an unpublished manuscript by Edward M. Graham, "Organized Labor and U.S. International Economic Policy, 1881–1981," Part 1, undated, University of North Carolina, Chapel Hill, N.C. This portion of the manuscript relies mainly on the following sources: American Federation of Labor, *Report of the Proceedings of the Convention* for 1881 and subsequent years; Samuel Gompers, *Seventy Years of Life and Labor,* vol. 1 (New York: E. P. Dutton, 1925); Simeon Larson, *Labor and Foreign Policy: Gompers, the AFL, and the First World War 1914–1918* (Raleigh, NJ: Fairleigh Dickinson University Press, 1974); William Green, "Labor and International Industry" and E. Guy Talbot, "Transplanted American Industry" in *The American Federalist,* vol. 35 (January 1928), pp. 19–20 and 30–31 respectively; Mira Wilkins, *The Maturing of Multinational Enterprise* (Cambridge, MA: Harvard University Press, 1974), chapter 2, pp. 49–163; E. E. Schattschneider, *Politics, Pressures, and the Tariff: A Study of Free Private Enterprise in Pressure Politics, as Shown in the 1929–1930 Revision of the Tariff* (New York: Prentice-

Hall, 1935), pp. 3–9; U.S. Congress, House of Representatives, Committee on Ways and Means, *Hearings on H.R. 2667 (Tariff Readjustment),* vol. 4 (Washington, DC: U.S. Government Printing Office, 1929), pp. 2869–2870; U.S. Congress, Senate, Committee on Finance, *Hearings on H.R. 2667,* vol. 2 (Washington, DC: U.S. Government Printing Office, 1929), pp. 15–16, 102–103, and 480–483.

9. See, for instance, James T. Patterson, *Congressional Conservatism and the New Deal* (Westport, CT: Greenwood Press, 1967), pp. 32–76, 128–187; Alan Brinkley, *Voices of Protest: Huey Long, Father Coughlin and the Great Depression* (New York: Alfred A. Knopf, 1982), passim; Edgar E. Robinson, "An Unaccustomed Road," in Morton Keller, ed., *The New Deal* (Huntington, NY: Robert E. Krieger Publishing, 1977), pp. 30–35.

10. For background on both the AAA and the NRA, see James D. Magee, *The National Recovery Program* (New York: F. S. Crofts, 1934), pp. 28–40; and William Lewin, ed., *A Documentary History of American Economic Policy since 1789* (Chicago: Aldine Publishing, 1961) pp. 342–385.

11. See, for instance, Barbara Hinckley, *The Seniority System in Congress* (Bloomington, IN: University of Indiana Press, 1977), p. 41.

12. See William R. Allen, "The International Trade Philosophy of Cordell Hull, 1907–1933," *American Economic Review,* vol. 63, no. 1 (March 1953), pp. 101–116.

13. Another hypothesis, more recently formulated, is that by the 1930s certain key sectors of the business community had become proponents for multinationalism and thus for free trade. See Thomas Ferguson, "From Normalcy to New Deal," *International Organization,* Winter 1984, pp. 41–94.

14. William Diebold, *The End of the I.T.O.,* Essays in International Finance, no. 16 (Princeton, NJ: Princeton University, International Finance Section, October 1952). Reprinted by University Microfilms International, Ann Arbor, MI, 1979, p. 7; Don D. Humphrey, *American Imports* (New York: Twentieth Century Fund, 1955), p. 114.

15. See Richard N. Gardner, *Sterling-Dollar Diplomacy in Current Perspective* (New York: Columbia University Press, 1980), pp. 56–68; also James Reston, "Pact with Britain Sets Free Trade as Basis of Peace," *New York Times,* February 25, 1942.

16. *Havana Charter for an International Trade Organization,* March 24, 1948. Department of State publication 3206. (Washington, DC: U.S. Government Printing Office, 1948).

17. See Frank A. Weil and Norman D. Glick, "Japan—Is the Market Open? A View of the Japanese Market Drawn from Corporate Experience," *Law and Policy in International Business,* vol. 2, no. 3 (1979), pp. 845–902.

18. Malcolm S. Salter, Alan M. Webber, and Davis Dyer, "U.S. Competitiveness in Global Industries: Lessons from the Auto Industry" in Bruce M. Scott and George C. Lodge, eds., *U.S. Competitiveness in the World Economy* (Boston: Harvard Business School Press, 1985), p. 192.

19. *The Economist,* "The War of Tomorrow's Worlds," August 24, 1985, pp. 69-70.

20. Raymond F. Hopkins and Donald J. Puchala, *Global Food Interdependence: Challenge to American Foreign Policy* (New York: Columbia University Press, 1980), p. 48.

21. According to some estimates, the dollar's high value has been responsible for as much as one-half to two-thirds of the current trade deficit. See *Congressional Quarterly Weekly Report,* September 28, 1985, p. 1909.

22. In a poll of business leaders conducted in 1986, for instance, only 10 percent of the respondents cited the budget deficit as the most important concern facing American business. When asked to choose the biggest weakness in meeting foreign competition, their answers focused on high labor cost, unions, and management complacence. See *New York Times Business Magazine,* December 7, 1986, p. 22.

23. Raymond A. Bauer, Ithiel de Sola Pool, and Lewis Anthony Dexter, *American Business and Public Policy* (New York: Atherton Press, 1963), pp. 94, 143.

24. The decline in party labels as a predictor can be seen in the congressional voting record on trade bills. In 1962, the Trade Expansion Act passed the Senate 78-8: Rep. 22-7; Dem. 56-1. In the House, the bill passed 256-91: Rep. 78-56; Dem. 178-34. In 1974, the Trade Act passed the Senate 77-4: Rep. 32-1; Dem. 45-3. In the House, it passed 323-36: Rep. 147-11; Dem. 176-25. In 1979, the Trade Agreements Act passed the Senate 90-4: Rep. 38-1; Dem. 52-3. In the House, it passed 395-7: Rep. 148-2; Dem. 247-5. Adapted from various volumes of *Congressional Quarterly Almanac.*

25. See Lande and VanGrasstek, *The Trade and Tariff Act of 1984,* p. 135.

26. The first signs of declining Republican partisanship are recounted in Pietro S. Nivola, "The New Protectionism: U.S. Trade Policy in Historical Perspective," *Political Science Quarterly,* no. 4 (1986), pp. 586-590. For an argument that the Republican party was becoming more interested in a world perspective as early as the 1930s, see Ferguson, "From Normalcy to New Deal."

27. See, for instance, the Republican party platform of 1892 in *National Party Platforms,* vol. 1, 1840-1956, compiled by Bruce Johnson (Urbana: University of Illinois Press, 1978), p. 94.

28. Based on data in U.S. Department of Commerce, *U.S. Direct Invest-*

ment Abroad, 1982 Benchmark Survey Data (Washington, DC: U.S. Government Printing Office, 1985), p. 153.

29. Similar observations have been made, for example, by Bauer, Pool, and Dexter, *American Business and Public Policy,* pp. 91-94, 112-115.

30. See, for instance, "Adjustment Assistance to Firms under the Trade Act of 1974—Income Maintenance or Successful Adjustment," U.S. General Accounting Office, Report to the Congress (Washington, DC: U.S. Government Printing Office, 1978); and Steve Charnovitz, "Worker Adjustment: The Missing Ingredient in Trade Policy," *California Management Review,* vol. 28, no. 2 (Winter 1986), pp. 156-170.

31. Experiences under the program are summarized in Robert Z. Lawrence and Robert E. Lipton, *Saving Free Trade* (Washington, DC: The Brookings Institution, 1986), pp. 51-62; see also Richard M. Cyert and David C. Mowery, eds., *Technology and Employment: Innovation and Growth in the U.S. Economy* (Washington, DC: National Academy Press, 1987), pp. 146-151.

32. That proposition has had wide currency. See Richard N. Cooper, "Trade Policy as Foreign Policy," Discussion Paper no. 1160, Harvard Institute of Economic Research, Cambridge, June 1985; also I. M. Destler, "Protecting Congress or Protecting Trade?" *Foreign Policy* no. 62 (Spring 1986), pp. 96-107.

33. Bauer, Dexter, and Pool, *American Business and Public Policy,* pp. 353, 373-374, 398.

34. This conclusion was widely shared by persons who studied congressional behavior in trade matters. See, for instance, George P. Shultz and Kenneth W. Dam, *Economic Policy Beyond the Headlines* (Stanford: Stanford Alumni Association, 1977), p. 148; also Robert Pastor, *Congress and the Politics of U.S. Foreign Policy 1929-1976* (Berkeley: University of California Press, 1980), p. 122; and Bauer, Dexter, and Pool, *American Business and Public Policy,* p. 34.

35. *Economic Report of the President,* 1973, p. 295.

36. Bank for International Settlements, *Annual Report,* 1963, p. 106.

37. Pastor, *Congress and the Politics of U.S. Foreign Policy,* pp. 136-165; also Gilbert H. Winham, "Robert Strauss, the MTN, and the Control of Faction," *Journal of World Trade Law,* vol. 14.5 (September/October 1980), pp. 377-397.

38. *The Tokyo Round of Multilateral Trade Negotiations,* reported by the Director-General of GATT (Geneva: GATT, 1979), pp. 49-88; also see the *Annual Report of the President of the United States on the Trade Agreements Program, 1979* (Washington, DC: U.S. Government Printing Office, 1979), pp. 39-75.

39. Mentioned in Winham, "Robert Strauss, the MTN, and the Control

of Faction," p. 394. Strauss is also given high praise in I. M. Destler, "Trade Consensus, SALT Stalemate: Congress and Foreign Policy in the 1970s," in Thomas E. Mann and Norman J. Ornstein, eds., *The New Congress* (Washington, DC: American Enterprise Institute, 1981), pp. 354–357.

40. On Strauss, see I. M. Destler, *American Trade Politics: System Under Stress* (Washington, DC: Institute for International Economics, 1986), pp. 91–93; Robert Shogan, *Promises to Keep: Carter's First Hundred Days* (New York; Thomas Y. Crowell, 1977), p. 273.

41. See *The Economist,* "Rewriting GATT's Rules for a Game that Has Changed," September 13, 1986, pp. 63–66.

42. *New York Times,* October 2, 1985, p. B6; April 9, 1987, p. B10.

43. "What the Agreement Represents to Ottawa and Washington," *New York Times,* October 5, 1987, p. D5.

44. On cheese, Defense Production Act of 1951, Section 4; on textiles, Agricultural Act of 1956, Section 204; on oil, Mineral Leasing Act of 1920, Section 28(u) as amended in 1973.

45. The theme of protectionism for Congress is best described in Destler, *American Trade Politics,* esp. pp. 57–86.

46. Ibid., pp. 27–28.

47. Gary C. Hufbauer and Howard F. Rosen, *Trade Policy for Troubled Industries* (Washington: Institute for International Economics, 1986), pp. 5–28; Lande and VanGrasstek, *The Trade and Tariff Act of 1984,* pp. 95–106.

48. Cited in Jack Behrman, *Survey of U.S. International Finance* (Princeton, NJ: Princeton University Press, various issues—1951, 1952, 1953).

49. Walter Adams and Joel B. Dirlam, "The Trade Laws and Their Enforcement by the International Trade Commission," in Robert E. Baldwin, ed., *Recent Issues & Initiatives in U.S. Trade Policy* (Washington, DC: National Bureau of Economic Research Conference Report, 1984), pp. 128–153.

50. Lande and VanGrasstek, *The Trade and Tariff Act of 1984,* p. 104.

51. See Department of Commerce, 19 Code of Federal Regulations, Part 353, Section 353.6, reported in *Federal Register,* vol. 45, no. 26 (Wednesday, February 6, 1980), p. 8191.

52. Lande and VanGrasstek, *The Trade and Tariff Act of 1984,* pp. 107–139; Carl J. Green, "Legal Protectionism in the United States and its Impact on United States–Japan Economic Relations," unpublished manuscript prepared for the Advisory Group on United States-Japan Economic Relations, July 1980, passim.

53. Alan H. Rugman and Andrew D. H. Anderson, *Administered Protection in America* (London: Croom Helm, 1987), pp. 19–20.

54. See Robert V. Guido and Michael F. Morrone, "The Michelin Decision: A Possible New Direction for U.S. Countervailing Duty Law," *Law and Policy in International Business,* vol. 6, no. 1 (Winter 1974), pp. 237–266; and Rugman and Anderson, *Administered Protection,* pp. 56–98.

55. See United States, International Trade Commission, *Operation of the Trade Agreements Program,* 37th report (Washington, DC: USITC Publication 1871, June 1986), pp. 11–12.

56. See Nivola, "The New Protectionism," p. 573.

57. Lande and VanGrasstek, *The Trade and Tariff Act of 1984,* p. 144.

58. Ibid., pp. 143–145.

59. Trade and Tariff Act of 1984, P.L. 98–573, October 30, 1974, sec. 803.

60. "U.S. Plans Tariffs to Punish Europe," *New York Times,* Nov. 27, 1987, p. D2.

61. A game-theoretic basis for a tit-for-tat policy in the trade context is explored in Catherine L. Mann, "Protection and Retaliation: Changing the 'Rules of the Game,'" in *Brookings Papers on Economic Activity,* no. 1 (1987), pp. 311–335.

62. Reported in International Monetary Fund, *Exchange Agreements and Exchange Restrictions* (Washington, DC: International Monetary Fund, 1986), p. 259.

63. Fair Export Financing Act of 1986 (Senate Bill S2246).

64. *New York Times,* "U.S. Fights France on Export Credit," November 13, 1985, p. D17.

65. *New York Times,* "The Ex-Im Bank's Tricky Tactics," February 2, 1986, Sec. 3, p. 4.

66. See Export-Import Bank of the United States press release, March 19, 1986 and May 15, 1986.

67. See *Operation of the Trade Agreements Program,* United States International Trade Commission, USITC Publication 1871, June 1986.

68. "American Treasury Market," *The Economist,* December 20, 1986, pp. 110–112.

69. "Conferees Bar Japanese Bidding on Government's Works Projects," *New York Times,* December 18, 1987, p. A30.

CHAPTER 4 The Politics of Foreign Exchange

1. *World Financial Markets,* Morgan Guaranty Trust Co., various issues.

2. See, for instance, J. Henry Richardson, *British Economic Foreign Policy* (New York and London: Garland Publishing, 1983), p. 49.

3. See Robert Craig West, *Banking Reform and the Federal Reserve 1863–1923* (Ithaca, NY: Cornell University Press, 1977), pp. 116–135; Albert Fishlow, "The Debt Crisis in Historical Perspective," in Miles Kahler, ed., *The Politics of International Debt* (Ithaca, NY: Cornell University Press, 1986), p. 80.

4. J. Z. Rowe, *The Public-Private Character of United States Central Banking* (New Brunswick, NJ: Rutgers University Press, 1965), pp. 51–66; C. H. Kisch and W. A. Elkin, *Central Banks* (London: Macmillan, 1928), pp. 28–9.

5. For comparative studies of the various central banking systems, see Derek H. Aldcroft, *From Versailles to Wall Street 1919–1929* (Berkeley: University of California Press, 1977); Benjamin M. Rowland, *Balance of Power or Hegemony: The Interwar Monetary System* (New York: New York University Press, 1976); C. H. Kisch and W. A. Elkin, *Central Banks* (London: Macmillan, 1928).

6. Charles P. Kindleberger, *A Financial History of Western Europe* (London: George Allen & Unwin, 1984), pp. 334, 385–386.

7. See Barry Eichengreen and Richard Portes, "Debt and Default in the 1930s: Causes and Consequences," Harvard Institute of Economic Research, Discussion Paper No. 1186, Oct 1985.

8. Fishlow, "The Debt Crisis," p. 76.

9. For comparative data, see Ibid., pp. 72–77.

10. Judith C. Kooker, "French Financial Diplomacy: The Interwar Years," in Benjamin M. Rowland, ed., *Balance of Power or Hegemony,* p. 104; Charles O. Hardy, *Credit Policies of the Federal Reserve System* (Washington, DC: Brookings Institution, 1932), p. 106.

11. From Barry Eichengreen, "International Coordination in Historical Perspective" in W. H. Buiter and R. C. Marston, eds., *International Economic Policy Coordination* (Cambridge, Eng.: Cambridge University Press, 1984) p. 168; and Benjamin M. Rowland, "Preparing the American Ascendency: The Transfer of Economic Power from Britain to the United States, 1933–1944," in Benjamin M. Rowland, ed., *Balance of Power or Hegemony,* pp. 195–207.

12. See Robert J. A. Skidelsky, "Retreat from Leadership: The Evolution of British Foreign Economic Policy, 1870–1939," in Benjamin M. Rowland, ed., *Balance of Power or Hegemony,* pp. 175–189.

13. For a more extended treatment of the background discussions that preceded the U.S. proposal, see Edward M. Bernstein, "Reflections on Bretton Woods," unpublished paper, May 10, 1984, pp. 1–4.

14. See Richard N. Gardner, *Sterling-Dollar Diplomacy in Current Perspective* (New York: Columbia University Press, 1980), pp. 71–77.

15. John S. Odell, *U.S. International Monetary Policy* (Princeton:

Princeton University Press, 1982), pp. 93–96. The original formulation appears in Robert Triffin, *Gold and the Dollar Crisis* (New Haven: Yale University Press, 1960).

16. Odell, *U.S. International Monetary Policy,* pp. 130–145.

17. Margaret Garritsen de Vries, *The International Monetary Fund, 1972–1978,* vol. 2, "Narrative and Analysis" (Washington, D.C.: The International Monetary Fund, 1985), pp. 871–883.

18. Peter B. Kenen, *The International Economy* (Englewood Cliffs, NJ: Prentice-Hall, 1985), pp. 497–498.

19. See, for instance, Sherman J. Maisel, *Managing the Dollar* (New York: W.W. Norton, 1973), chapter 9. See also Odell, *U.S. International Monetary Policy,* p. 182, and George N. Halm, ed., *Approaches to Greater Flexibility of Exchange Rates: The Burgenstock Papers* (Princeton, NJ: Princeton University Press, 1970).

20. For instance, Odell, *U.S. International Monetary Policy,* pp. 183–199.

21. Cited in Ibid., p. 245.

22. Ibid., pp. 247–248; Robert Solomon, *The International Monetary System, 1945–1981* (New York: Harper & Row, 1982), p. 191; Henry Brandon, *The Retreat of American Power* (New York: Dell Publishing, 1973), p. 229.

23. Solomon, *International Monetary System,* pp. 189–193.

24. Ibid., p. 189.

25. Brandon, *Retreat of American Power,* pp. 230–236.

26. *New York Times,* March 12, 1973, pp. 1, 47; For an in-depth analysis of the negotiations of this period, see Odell, *U.S. International Monetary Policy,* pp. 313–326.

27. International Monetary Fund, *Exchange Arrangements and Exchange Restrictions,* (Washington, DC: International Monetary Fund, 1986), p. 5.

28. International Monetary Fund, Annual Report 1972, p. 36.

29. Guido Garavoglia, "From Rambouillet to Williamsburg: A Historical Assessment," in Cesare Merlini, ed., *Economic Summits and Western Decision-Making* (New York: St. Martin's Press, 1984), pp. 38–39.

30. See Robert Putnam, "The Western Economic Summits: A Political Interpretation," in Merlini, ed., *Economic Summits,* pp. 43–49.

31. Solomon, *International Monetary System,* pp. 349–350.

32. Adam Smith, *Paper Money* (New York: Summit Books, 1981), p. 123.

33. See Adam Smith, *Paper Money,* p. 123; Richard N. Cooper, *The Economics of Interdependence* (New York: McGraw-Hill, 1968), p. 119.

34. For instance, Cooper, *Economics of Interdependence,* pp. 139–147; Beth M. Farber, "International Banking Facilities: Defining a Greater Presence in the Eurodollar Market," *Law and Policy in International Business,* vol. 13, no. 4 (1981), pp. 997–1046.

35. "Foreign Bonds in Japan," *The Economist,* Nov. 22, 1986, p. 78.

36. On the competition factor, see Rimmer de Vries, "Global Capital Markets: Issues and Implications," Marcus Wallenberg Papers on International Finance, Georgetown University, vol. 1, no. 4 (October 1986), pp. 17–18.

37. An informed guess, based on surveys made in the United States, United Kingdom, Japan, and Canada would put the daily foreign exchange figure at $200 billion. The trade figure is calculated from world trade aggregates reported in the United Nations *Statistical Yearbook.*

38. See Jack M. Guttentag and Richard J. Herring, "Disaster Myopia in International Banking," Essays in International Finance Series, No. 164 (Princeton, NJ: Princeton University Press, September 1986).

39. See, for instance, Miles Kahler, ed., *The Politics of International Debt* (Ithaca, NY: Cornell University Press, 1986); Alizali F. Mohammed, "The Debt Problem," in Michael Posner, ed., *Problems of International Money, 1972–1985* (Washington, DC: International Monetary Fund, 1986), pp. 113–138; Brian Kettell and George Magnus, *The International Debt Game* (London: Graham & Trotman, 1986); George C. Abbott, *International Indebtedness and the Developing Countries* (London: Croom Helm, 1979); Darrell Delamaide, *Debt Shock* (New York; Doubleday, 1984); John H. Makin, *The Global Debt* (New York: Basic Books, 1984).

40. Kettell and Magnus, *The International Debt Game,* p. 49.

41. Ibid., pp. 49–50.

42. See, for instance, "Report on International Developments in Banking Supervision," Report No. 5, Committee on Banking Regulations and Supervisory Practices, Basle, September 1986.

43. "12 Nations Ask Banks to Build Cash Reserves," *New York Times,* December 11, 1987, p. A1.

44. International Monetary Fund, *Exchange Arrangements and Exchange Restrictions* (Washington: International Monetary Fund, 1985), p. 512.

45. Ibid., p. 315.

46. See *Washington Post,* September 22, 1981, p. 1; *Washington Post,* September 30, p. 3.

47. Benjamin J. Cohen, "Debt and U.S. Policy," in Miles Kahler, ed., *The Politics of International Debt* (Ithaca, NY: Cornell University Press), p. 143; and Garritsen de Vries, *The IMF,* vol. 2, p. 186.

48. For a good description of conditionality, see Margaret Garritsen

de Vries, *The International Monetary Fund, 1972–1978,* vol. 1, "Narrative and Analysis" (Washington, DC: The International Monetary Fund, 1985), pp. 482–507; also Manuel Guitan, "Economic Management and International Monetary Fund Conditionality," in Tony Killick, ed., *Adjustment and Financing in the Developing World* (Washington, DC: The International Monetary Fund, 1982) pp. 73–104.

49. See Alexis Rieffel, "The Role of the Paris Club in Managing Debt Problems," Essays in International Finance Series, No. 161 (Princeton, NJ: Princeton University Press, December 1985); and Charles Lipson, "International Debt and International Institutions," in Miles Kahler, ed., *The Politics of International Debt* (Ithaca, NY: Cornell University Press, 1986), pp. 220–235; K. Burke Dillon and Gumersindo Oliveros, "Recent Experience with Multilateral Official Debt Rescheduling," *World Economic and Financial Surveys* (Washington, DC: International Monetary Fund, February 1987), pp. 3–13.

50. See Margaret Garritsen de Vries, *Balance of Payments Adjustment, 1945 to 1986: The IMF Experience* (Washington, DC: International Monetary Fund, 1987), pp. 243–254.

51. "Bank Proposes a Way to Ease Debt Crisis," *New York Times,* December 30, 1987, p. D6; "Lessons Found in Mexico Debt Plan," *New York Times,* March 5, 1988, p. 46.

52. One recent work argues that the autonomy of the Federal Reserve Bank is unique within the U.S. political system, and defines its position as "the crucial anomaly at the core of representative democracy." See William Greider, *Secrets of the Temple: How the Federal Reserve Runs the Country* (New York: Simon & Schuster, 1987).

CHAPTER 5 The Politics of Multinational Enterprises

1. For an account of the extent of that dominance, see *Transnational Corporations in World Development, Fourth Survey* (New York: Centre on Transnational Corporations, United Nations, 1988).

2. See, for instance, Mark Casson, ed., *The Growth of International Business* (London: George Allen & Unwin, 1983); John H. Dunning, ed., *The Multinational Enterprise* (London: George Allen & Unwin, 1971); and Raymond Vernon, *Storm Over the Multinationals* (Cambridge: Harvard University Press, 1977).

3. See Kurt Rudolf Mirow and Harry Maurer, *Webs of Power* (Boston: Houghton Mifflin, 1982), pp. 15–23.

4. 40 STAT. 516–518 (1918), 15 U.S.C. 61–65 (1952). See also Kingman Brewster, Jr., *Antitrust and American Business Abroad* (New York: Arno Press, 1976), p. 24.

5. American Banana Co. vs. United Fruit Co., 213 U.S. 347, 355–57 (1909).

6. Ibid., see also William W. Bishop, *International Law: Cases and Materials* (Boston and Toronto: Little, Brown, 1971), p. 567.

7. See various issues of *The Congressional Record:* Senate, April 29, 1938, vol. 83, part 6, pp. 5992–5996; Senate, June 9, 1938, vol. 83, part 8, pp. 8595–8596; Senate, March 31, 1941, vol. 87, part 3, pp. 2698–2706; and Appendix, July 12, 1939, vol. 84, part 13, p. 3199.

8. See Mirow and Maurer, *Webs of Power,* pp. 24–25; George W. Stocking and Myron W. Watkins, *Cartels in Action* (New York: The Twentieth Century Fund, 1947), p. 92.

9. See, for instance, Thurman W. Arnold, "Cartels or Free Enterprise?" Public Affairs Pamphlet No. 103 (New York, Public Affairs Committee, 1945).

10. Mirow and Maurer, *Webs of Power,* p. 30.

11. See, for instance, the Economic Cooperation Agreement between the United States and the United Kingdom, article II, T.S. No. 1795 (July 6, 1948).

12. See, for instance, the Italo-American commercial treaty of 1948, 63 STAT. pt. 2, 2255, 2282, T.S. No. 1965, article XVIII (3) (July 26, 1949); and the Japanese-U.S. Treaty of Friendship, Commerce, and Navigation, 4 U.S.T. 2063, T.I.A.S. 2863 (April 2, 1953).

13. U.S. Circuit Court of Appeals, 2nd circuit, 1945.

14. See A. H. Hermann, *Conflicts of National Laws with International Business Activity* (London: Contemprints, 1982), p. 46.

15. See Raymond Vernon, *Storm over the Multinationals,* pp. 96–101; also see, for instance, "Brazil: A New Brand of Imperialism," *Business Week,* August 11, 1973, p. 52.

16. Hermann, *Conflicts of National Laws,* pp. 45–57, 76–88. He notes, for instance, that although several European countries have borrowed provisions from U.S. antitrust law, extraterritorial application of national antitrust laws still leads to the most severe conflicts between nations. See also Joel Davidow, "International Antitrust Codes: the Post-Acceptance Phase," *The Antitrust Bulletin,* Fall 1981, p. 588.

17. See, for instance, "Restrictive Business Practices of Multinational Enterprises," Report of the Committee of Experts on Restrictive Business Practices (Paris: OECD, 1977), pp. 55–62.

18. See, for instance, Davidow, "International Trust Codes," p. 570.

19. See Karen J. Hladik, *International Joint Ventures* (Lexington, MA: Lexington Books, 1985) pp. 39–63; also *Transnational Corporations in

World Development, Fourth Survey, Centre on Transnational Corporations.

20. Raymond Vernon, *Manager in the International Economy,* 4th ed. (Englewood Cliffs, NJ: Prentice-Hall, 1981), p. 121.

21. For an extended discussion of the capital restriction program, see Brian Tew, *The Evolution of the International Monetary System, 1945–1977* (New York: John Wiley, 1977), pp. 116–119.

22. For a comprehensive survey of the U.S. policy-making process in U.S.–USSR relations, see Joseph S. Nye, Jr., ed., *The Making of America's Soviet Policy* (New Haven: Yale University Press, 1984). For a treatment of the economic dimension, see Marshall Goldman and Raymond Vernon, "Economic Relations" in that volume.

23. The 1979 Amendments to the Export Administration Act did contain some specific procedural steps that the executive was to take in connection with the imposition of export controls, such as a calculation of the likely impact on U.S. exports. These provisions, however, had little effect on presidential discretion. See Homer E. Moyer, Jr. and Linda A. Mabry, "Export Controls as Instruments of Foreign Policy: The History, Legal Issues and Policy Lessons of Three Recent Cases," *Law and Policy in International Business,* vol. 15, no. 1 (1983), pp. 137–138.

24. Moyer and Mabry, "Export Controls," pp. 69–92.

25. The case is described in "U.S. Officials Split," *New York Times,* September 29, 1987, pp. A1, D6.

26. "Congressional Conferees Clear Majority of Big Trade Bill, but Veto is Possible," *Wall Street Journal,* April 1, 1988, p. 3.

27. That general rule has several very important exceptions. See H. David Rosenbloom, "Tax Treaty Abuse: Policies and Issues," *Law and Policy in International Business,* vol. 15, no. 3 (1983), pp. 763–831.

28. Model Double Taxation Convention on Income and Capital, Report of the OECD Committee on Fiscal Affairs (Paris: Organization for Economic Cooperation and Development, 1977), p. 8.

29. For a more detailed analysis of the differences between the U.S. and the OECD model treaties, see Harry A. Shannon III, "Comparison of the OECD and U.S. Model Treaties for the Avoidance of Double Taxation," *The International Tax Journal,* vol. 12, no. 4 (Fall 1986), pp. 265–292.

30. As of 1987, the United States had bilateral tax treaties in effect with over 80 countries, including all of the members of the OECD.

31. See for instance, "Calling Britain's Bluff," *The Economist,* August 2, 1986, p. 65.

32. See A. W. Granwell, B. Hirsh, and D. R. Milton, "Worldwide Unitary Tax: Is it Invalid under Treaties of Friendship, Commerce, and Navi-

gation?'' *Law and Policy in International Business,* vol. 8, no. 4 (1986), pp. 713–715.

33. The relationship between the state and big business has spawned numerous studies, all of which have been highly controversial. The classic works include: V. I. Lenin, *Imperialism: The Highest Stage of Capitalism* (New York: International Publishers, 1939; reprinted in 1977); Harry Magdoff, *The Age of Imperialism* (New York: Modern Reader Paperbacks, 1969); Joseph Schumpeter, ''Imperialism,'' in *Social Classes and Imperialism: Two Essays by Joseph Schumpeter* (New York: Meridian Books, 1955); Robert Gilpin, *U.S. Power and the Multinational Corporation* (New York: Basic Books, 1975); Stephen D. Krasner, *Defending the National Interest* (Princeton, NJ: Princeton University Press, 1978).

34. For a similar generalization on this key question, see Stephen D. Krasner, *Defending the National Interest,* passim, esp. pp. 53–71, 119–128.

35. See, for instance, Ralph W. Hidy and Muriel E. Hidy, *History of the Standard Oil Company (New Jersey): Pioneering in Big Business 1862–1911* (New York: Arno Press, 1955), pp. 686–698.

36. Federal Trade Commission, *The International Petroleum Cartel,* published as Committee Print No. 6 of the U.S. Senate Select Committee on Small Business, 83rd Congress, 2nd Session, (Washington, DC: U.S. Government Printing Office, 1952; reprinted by Arno Press, New York, 1976, pp. 38–56); Louis Turner, *Oil Companies in the International System,* 3rd ed. (London: George Allen & Unwin, 1983), pp. 26–34.

37. The story is told at length in Irvine H. Anderson, Jr., *The Standard-Vacuum Oil Company and United States East Asian Policy 1933–1941* (Princeton: Princeton University Press, 1975), passim.

38. Krasner, *Defending the National Interest,* p. 178; Michael B. Stoff, *Oil, War and American Security* (New Haven: Yale University Press, 1980), p. 63.

39. Lorenzo Meyer, *Mexico and the United States in the Oil Controversy, 1917–1942* (Austin, TX: University of Texas Press, 1977), pp. 180–185, 220–224.

40. Scholars seem to disagree as to which segments of the oil industry were most responsible for undermining the project. The traditional accounts assign that role primarily to Socal and Texaco, then the only partners of ARAMCO, who were said to have refused to allow even minority government ownership in the company. See Krasner, *Defending the National Interest,* pp. 188–197. Recent research, however, suggests that Ickes may have bowed to pressures from Exxon and Mobil, which at the time had not yet acquired an interest in Saudi oil. See Irvine H. Anderson, *Aramco, The United States and Saudi Arabia* (Princeton: Princeton University Press, 1981), p. 56; also Robert O. Keohane, ''State Power and Industry Influ-

ence: American Foreign Oil Policy in the 1940s," *International Organization,* vol. 36, no. 1 (Winter 1982), pp. 170–173.

41. Robert O. Keohane, *After Hegemony: Cooperation and Discord in the World Political Economy* (Princeton: Princeton University Press, 1984), pp. 173–177; Krasner, *Defending the National Interest,* pp. 195–205. See also Stoff, *Oil, War and American Security,* pp. 184–195.

42. U.S. Federal Trade Commission, *The International Petroleum Cartel* (Washington, DC: U.S. Government Printing Office, 1952; reprinted by Arno Press, New York, 1976).

43. See Craufurd D. Goodwin, "Truman Administration Policies toward Particular Energy Sources," in Craufurd D. Goodwin, ed., *Energy Policy in Perspective* (Washington, DC: The Brookings Institution, 1981), pp. 119–127.

44. Numerous accounts of this episode are available. See, for instance, statements of Richard Funkhouser, E. L. Shafer, and H. W. Page in "Multinational Companies and United States Foreign Policy," testimony before the Church Committee, 93rd Congress, Part 7, pp. 170–171, 244–253, 294–303; also David Wise and Thomas Ross, *The Invisible Government* (New York: Random House, 1964); and Andrew Tully, *CIA: The Inside Story* (New York: William Morrow, 1962).

45. Goodwin, "Truman Administration Policies," pp. 114–115.

46. Shoshana Klebanoff, *Middle East Oil and U.S. Foreign Policy* (New York: Praeger, 1974), p. 95.

47. Klebanoff, *Middle East Oil,* p. 95; George Stocking, *Middle East Oil: A Study in Political and Economic Controversy* (Kingsport, TN: Vanderbilt University Press, 1970), pp. 157–158.

48. William J. Barber, "The Eisenhower Energy Policy: Reluctant Intervention," in Goodwin, *Energy Policy in Perspective,* pp. 227–228.

49. Ibid., p. 230.

50. Ibid., p. 257.

51. Ibid., pp. 254–255.

52. James L. Cochrane, "Energy Policy in the Johnson Administration: Logical Order versus Economic Pluralism," in Goodwin, ed., *Energy Policy in Perspective,* p. 375.

53. Klebanoff, *Middle East Oil,* p. 130.

54. Keohane, *After Hegemony,* p. 171.

55. P. H. Frankel, "Oil Supplies During the Suez Crisis—On Meeting a Political Emergency," *Journal of Industrial Economics,* vol. 6, no. 2 (February 1958), p. 96. Frankel was the United Kingdom's leading independent oil analyst at the time.

56. Frankel and Keohane, cited in earlier footnotes, place somewhat dif-

ferent interpretations on the Suez affair, with Keohane claiming to see substantially more cooperation and coordination between the U.S. government and the oil companies than does Frankel.

57. The crisis is fully described in Raymond Vernon, ed., *The Oil Crisis,* (New York: W.W. Norton, 1976), especially pp. 39–58, 159–202.

58. Stobaugh, "The Oil Companies in the Crisis," in Vernon, ed., *The Oil Crisis,* p. 189; also "Report by the Commission on the Behavior of the Oil Companies in the Community during the Period from October 1973 to March 1974," Commission of the European Communities, Brussels, December 1975, pp. 48–55, 59–66.

59. The incident is recounted in Mira Wilkins, "The Oil Companies in Perspective," in Raymond Vernon, ed., *The Oil Crisis,* pp. 167–168; see also an interpretation of that incident in Krasner, *Defending the National Interest,* pp. 258–269.

60. From *Survey of Current Business* (Washington, DC: United States Department of Commerce, Bureau of Economic Analysis), various issues.

61. See, for instance, C. Fred Bergsten, Thomas Horst, and Theodore H. Moran, *American Multinationals and American Interests* (Washington, DC: The Brookings Institution, 1978), p. 31.

62. See Pamela B. Gann, "The U.S. Bilateral Investment Treaty Program," *Stanford Journal of International Law,"* vol. 21 (Fall 1985), pp. 373–457; Raymond Vernon, "Codes on Transnationals: Ingredients for an Effective International Regime," in John H. Dunning and Nikoto Usui, eds., *Structural Change, Economic Interdependence and World Development* (London: Macmillan Press, 1987), pp. 227–240.

CHAPTER 6 The Politics of U.S. Foreign Aid

1. While the percentage of respondents who claim to be in favor of U.S. foreign aid varies with the exact wording of the question, surveys since the mid-1950s usually show between 40 to 50 percent of the population supporting U.S. aid programs abroad. For survey data and information, see William G. Mayer, "The Ideological Explanation, Part 2: Foreign Policy," unpublished Ph.D. dissertation, Harvard University, 1988, Table 10. When respondents were asked whether to increase or decrease U.S. spending on foreign aid, however, a majority usually favored decreasing it.

2. Foreign Assistance Act of 1961, as amended by the International Narcotics Control Act of 1985, P.L. 99–83, Title VI, Sec. 601, August 8, 1985.

3. See U.S. President, *Third Report to Congress on Assistance to Greece and Turkey,* for the period ended March 31, 1948, pp. 40, 61; cited in W. A. Brown and R. Opie, *American Foreign Assistance* (Washington, DC: The Brookings Institution, 1973), pp. 129–130.

4. Secretary of State George C. Marshall's Address at Harvard Commencement, June 5, 1947, reprinted in Stanley Hoffmann and Charles Maier, eds., *The Marshall Plan: A Retrospective* (Boulder, CO: Westview Press, 1984).

5. Quoted in James P. Warburg, *Put Yourself in Marshall's Place* (New York: Simon and Schuster, 1948), p. 46.

6. President's Committee on Foreign Aid, *European Recovery and American Aid: A Report* (Washington, DC: U.S. Government Printing Office, 1947).

7. See Robert A. Packenham, *Liberal America and the Third World* (Princeton: Princeton University Press, 1973), p. 34.

8. Representative works include: Joseph Marion Jones, *The Fifteen Weeks* (New York: Harcourt, Brace & World, 1964); H. B. Price, *The Marshall Plan and its Meaning* (Ithaca, NY: Cornell University Press, 1955); Edward S. Mason, *Foreign Aid and Foreign Policy* (New York: Harper & Row, 1964), esp. pp. 8–25; and Brown and Opie, *American Foreign Assistance.* There are, of course, exceptions to this otherwise universal praise. For a classical revisionist account, see Joyce and Gabriel Kolko, *The Limits of Power: The World and the United States, 1943–1954* (New York: Harper & Row, 1972), esp. chapter 17, "The Failure of the Marshall Plan, 1949–1950." For an interesting interpretation that draws upon the Kolkos's work yet makes a radically different point, see Tyler Cowen, "The Marshall Plan: Myths and Realities," in Doug Bandow, ed., *U.S. Aid and the Developing World: A Free Market Agenda* (Washington, DC: The Heritage Foundation, 1985), pp. 61–74.

9. The most recent example was President Reagan's Caribbean Basin Initiative, which called for a "major economic aid program for Central America similar to the Marshall Plan," *New York Times,* March 6, 1983.

10. Charles L. Mee, *The Marshall Plan: The Launching of the Pax Americana* (New York: Simon & Schuster, 1984), p. 77; Hadley Arkes, *Bureaucracy, the Marshall Plan and the National Interest,* (Princeton, NJ: Princeton University Press, 1972), p. 26; and John Gimbel, *Origins of the Marshall Plan,* (Stanford, CA: Stanford University Press, 1976), p. 4.

11. See Mee, *The Marshall Plan,* pp. 217–220.

12. Ibid., p. 245.

13. For good historical accounts, see Alonzo L. Hamby, *Beyond the New Deal: Harry S. Truman and American Liberalism* (New York: Columbia University Press, 1973), esp. pp. 317–372; Jonathan Daniels, *The Man of Independence* (Port Washington, NY: Kennikat Press, 1950), pp. 368–369; and Robert P. Morgan, *Science and Technology for International Development: An Assessment of U.S. Policies and Programs* (Boulder, CO: Westview Press, 1984), p. 105. For a contrasting view that sees Truman's idea

of an expanded Marshall Plan as nothing but a "public relations gimmick," see Louis J. Halle, *The Society of Man* (New York: Harper & Row, 1965), pp. 21–30.

14. In one letter, Truman recounts "dreaming of TVAs in the Euphrates Valley and the Danube. . . . When they happen, when millions and millions of people are no longer hungry and pushed and harassed, then the causes of war will be less by that much." HST Memoirs, II, 227–239, cited in Hamby, *Beyond the New Deal,* p. 371.

15. See, for instance, Jonathan Daniels, *The Man of Independence* (Port Washington, NY: Kennikat Press, 1950), p. 368.

16. See the testimony of Secretary of State Dean Acheson in *Act for International Development,* Committee on Foreign Relations, U.S. Senate, Hearings, 81st Congress, 2nd Session, March 30 and April 3, 1950, p. 5; also Packenham, *Liberal America,* p. 43.

17. Packenham, *Liberal America,* p. 43.

18. Congress added to the bill a provision that the United States should also improve the climate for private foreign investment and provide needed capital investment. See Brown and Opie, *American Foreign Assistance,* p. 395.

19. Public Law 165, 82nd Congress, 1st Session (1951).

20. See Brown and Opie, *American Foreign Assistance,* pp. 523–524.

21. Public Law 165.

22. See Price, *The Marshall Plan,* p. 168.

23. Cited in Jerome Levinson and Juan de Onis, *The Alliance That Lost Its Way* (Chicago: Quadrangle Books, 1970), p. 41.

24. The proceedings of the conference are recorded in *Journal of International Affairs,* vol. 9, no. 2, 1955.

25. Levinson and de Onis, *The Alliance,* p. 41.

26. See, for instance, U.S. Congress, Senate, Special Committee to Study Foreign Aid Program, "The Objectives of United States Economic Assistance Programs," prepared for the Committee by the Center for International Studies, Massachusetts Institute of Technology, in *Compilation of Studies and Surveys,* 85th Congress, 1st Session, July 1957, p. 1.

27. See, for instance, Max F. Millikan, "The Political Case for Economic Development Aid," in Robert A. Goodwin, ed., *Why Aid?* (Chicago: Rand McNally and Company, 1963).

28. Max F. Millikan and Walt W. Rostow, *A Proposal: Key to an Effective Foreign Policy* (New York: Harper, 1957), pp. 3–4.

29. For further elaboration of the critique of the Millikan-Rostow thesis, see Arthur Schlesinger, Jr., "The Alliance for Progress: A Retrospective," August 1974, p. 22 of an unpublished manuscript.

30. See U.S. Congress, Senate, Special Committee to Study the Foreign Aid Program, *Foreign Aid Program, Compilation of Studies and Surveys,* 85th Congress, 1st Session, July 1957.

31. The best example of support for the private approach is U.S. President, The President's Citizen Advisors on the Mutual Security Program, *Report to the President,* 1957.

32. Levinson and de Onis, *Alliance That Lost Its Way,* p. 48.

33. Operation Pan America was proposed by President Kubitschek of Brazil in August 1958. For a full text, see Pan American Union, "Operation Pan America and the Work of the Committee of 21," August 1960, pp. 1–3.

34. In the view of one author, public support for humanitarian objectives in the early 1970s can be explained as part of a larger popular outpouring against the disparity between American ideals and institutions. See Samuel P. Huntington, *American Politics: The Promise of Disharmony* (Cambridge, MA: Harvard University Press, 1981), pp. 167–220.

35. Packenham, *Liberal America,* p. 87; Robert Pastor, *Congress and the Politics of U.S. Foreign Economic Policy* (Berkeley: University of California Press, 1980), pp. 273–278.

36. For an in-depth study of the new program, see Agency for International Development, *Implementation of 'New Directions' in Development Assistance,* Report to the Committee on International Relations on Implementation of Legislative Reforms in the Foreign Assistance Act of 1973.

37. See *Congressional Quarterly Almanac,* vol. 29, 1973, p. 823, discussion of House Report 93–388.

38. Pastor, *Congress and the Politics of U.S. Foreign Economic Policy,* p. 267; taken from *Development Co-Operation, 1984 Review* (Paris: Organization for Economic Cooperation and Development, 1984), Table II.I.8.

39. See Foreign Assistance Act of 1962, amendment to subsection (e) of Section 620 of Foreign Assistance Act of 1961.

40. Pastor, *Congress and the Politics of U.S. Foreign Economic Policy,* p. 291; and *Congressional Record,* October 2, 1962, pp. 21615–16.

41. The Hickenlooper amendment was invoked against Ceylon in 1963. See Richard P. Lillich, "Requiem for Hickenlooper," *American Journal of International Law,* vol. 69 (January 1975).

42. Pastor, *Congress and the Politics of U.S. Foreign Economic Policy,* pp. 298–299.

43. Ibid., pp. 297–301.

44. Ibid., p. 264.

45. Public Law 480, the Agricultural Trade and Development and Assistance Act of 1954.

46. Section 620(a) of Foreign Assistance Act of 1969.

47. For these "additionality" requirements, see statement of William S. Gaud, U.S. Congress, Joint Economic Committee, "A Review of Balance of Payments Policies," Hearings before the Subcommittee on International Exchange and Payments, 91st Congress, 1st Session, January 13, 1969, p. 92; also Judith Tendler, *Inside Foreign Aid* (Baltimore: Johns Hopkins University Press, 1975), pp. 45–46.

48. John W. Sewell and Christine E. Contee, "U.S. Foreign Aid in the 1980s: Reordering Priorities," in John W. Sewell et al., eds., *U.S. Foreign Policy and the Third World: Agenda, 1985–86* (New Brunswick, NJ: Transaction Books, 1985), p. 109; "Foreign Aid by U.S. is Tied to Exports," *New York Times,* Nov. 24, 1984, p. 1.

49. The Trade and Development Enhancement Act of 1983, P.L. 98–181, November 30, 1983.

50. In 1987, the authority was being used only with respect to U.S. agricultural exports to Egypt. See Elliot Berg, "The Effectiveness of Economic Assistance," in John Wilhelm and Gerry Feinstein, eds., *U.S. Foreign Assistance: Investment or Folly* (New York: Praeger, 1984), pp. 187–219; Mark Lundell, "The Economic Assistance of Some Other Major Donors," in Wilhelm and Feinstein, eds., *U.S. Foreign Assistance,* pp. 269–303; and Sewell and Contee, "U.S. Foreign Aid in the 1980s," in Sewell et al., eds., *U.S. Foreign Policy and the Third World,* p. 109.

51. Robert L. Paarlberg, *Fixing Farm Trade: Policy Options for the United States* (Cambridge, MA: Ballinger Publishing, 1988), p. 94.

52. See Foreign Assistance Act of 1961, Sec. 620(b); reappears as Sec. 620(f) in Foreign Assistance Act of 1962.

53. See Herbert Feis, *Foreign Aid and Foreign Policy* (New York: St. Martin's Press, 1964), pp. 168–169.

54. Senate Joint Resolution 156, December 18, 1975.

55. Foreign Assistance Act of 1961, as amended in 1976, Section 116 (a); see also Thomas M. Franck and Edward Weisband, *Foreign Policy by Congress* (Oxford: Oxford University Press, 1979), p. 88.

56. For Argentina, see *New York Times,* March 1, 1977, p. 6; for Uruguay and Nicaragua, *New York Times,* April 6, 1977, p. 3.

57. Amendment to HR 7355, Department of Defense Appropriations, Fiscal Year 1983, December 8, 1982.

58. International Security and Development Cooperation Act of 1985, P.L. 99–83, August 8, 1985.

59. "I.M.F. Plans $8 Billion African Help," *New York Times,* December 24, 1987, p. A3.

60. See Sewell and Contee, "U.S. Foreign Aid in the 1980s," in Sewell

et al., eds., *U.S. Foreign Aid Policy and the Third World,* pp. 97–98; Carol Lancaster, "The Budget and U.S. Foreign Aid: More Tough Choices?" *Policy Focus* (Washington, DC: Overseas Development Council, 1986, no. 2), pp. 4–6; Agency for International Development, "A.I.D. Policy Guidance on Implementing A.I.D. Privatization Objectives," PD–14, June 16, 1986.

61. In 1986, automatic cuts took over $600 million from congressionally appropriated aid programs. See Lancaster, "More Tough Choices," p. 2; "Grudmanned," *The Economist,* September 27, 1986, pp. 27–28.

62. See the Commission on Security and Economic Assistance, "Report of the Commission on Security and Economic Assistance to the Secretary of State," (Washington, DC: United States Government Printing Office, 1983), p. 22.

63. Based on data reported in the annual publication of the Agency for International Development, entitled *Overseas Loans and Grants.*

64. Anglo–Irish Agreement Support Act of 1986, P.L. 99–415, September 19, 1986.

65. International Security and Development Cooperation Act of 1985, P.L. 99–83, August 8, 1985.

CHAPTER 7 **Prospects for International Cooperation**

1. See, for instance, Tatsuhiro Shukunami, "The Race for Value-Added Services: Changes and Opportunities in the U.S., Japan, and the U.K.," (Cambridge, MA: Center for Information Policy Research, 1987), research draft, p. 118.

2. See "Reagan Moves against Trading Partners," *New York Times,* September 8, 1985, p. 1; "President is Attempting to Dismantle Barriers Built Up Over Years," *New York Times,* September 8, 1985, p. 20; *Operation of the Trade Agreements Program,* 38th Report, 1986 (Washington, DC: United States International Trade Commission, 1987), pp. 4–40, 4–45; *Exchange Arrangements and Exchange Restrictions,* Annual Report, 1986 (Washington, DC: International Monetary Fund).

3. For instance, when actors expect future encounters with each other, it is possible to evoke cooperative behavior by making threats of retaliation in the future for present uncooperative behavior. See Robert Axelrod, *The Evolution of Cooperation* (New York: Basic Books, 1984), esp. pp. 126–154.

4. See, for instance, Alan J. Stoga, "If America Won't Lead," *Foreign Policy* no. 64 (Fall 1986), pp. 79–97; for a similar observation regarding the U.S. stature in military matters, see William K. Domke, Richard C. Eichenberg, and Catherine M. Kelleher, "Consensus Lost? Domestic Politics and the 'Crisis' in NATO," *World Politics,* vol. 39, no. 3 (April 1987),

pp. 382–407; for an opposing view that debates the decline in the power of the United States, see Bruce Russett, "The Mysterious Case of Vanishing Hegemony," *International Organization,* no. 39 (Spring 1985), pp. 207–231.

5. See Jagdish N. Bhagwati, "Trade in Services and the Multilateral Trade Negotiations," *The World Bank Economic Review,* vol. 1, no. 4 (September 1987), pp. 549–569; and George C. Lodge, *U.S. Competitiveness in the World Economy* (Boston: Harvard Business School Press, 1985).

6. For some imaginative proposals to that end, see the recommendations in *The Uruguay Round of Multilateral Trade Negotiations Under GATT* (Washington, DC: Atlantic Council, 1987). The report is the product of a committee of distinguished U.S. experts, chaired by John M. Leddy.

7. See, for instance, William J. Davey, "Dispute Settlement in GATT," *Fordham International Law Journal,* vol. 11, no. 51 (Fall 1987), pp. 51–109; Robert Hudec, "The GATT Legal System: A Diplomat's Jurisprudence," *Journal of World Trade Law* (September–October 1970), pp. 615–665.

8. For greater detail about how U.S. and U.K. negotiators worked out the Bretton Woods accords, see Richard N. Gardner, *Sterling Dollar Diplomacy in Current Perspective* (New York: Columbia University Press, 1980), pp. 110–144.

9. See, for instance, Diana Tussie, *The Less-Developed Countries and the World Trading System* (New York; St. Martin's Press, 1987), passim.

10. For a summary of the provisions supported by developing countries, see David B. H. Denoon, ed., *The New International Economic Order* (New York: New York University Press, 1979), pp. 3–31.

11. See, for instance, Mohammed E. Ahrari, *OPEC: The Failing Giant* (Lexington, KY: The University Press of Kentucky, 1986), pp. 171–177; James Mwandha et al., *Coffee: The International Commodity Agreements* (Brookfield, VT: Gower Publishing, 1985), p. 113.

12. See Miguel S. Wionczek, *Economic Cooperation in Latin America, Africa, and Asia* (Cambridge, MA: MIT Press, 1969), pp. 8–9; for analysis of the individual associations, see G. Aforka Nweke, "The Organization of African Unity and Intra-African Functionalism," *The Annals of the Academy of Political and Social Science,* vol. 489 (January 1987), pp. 133–147; *The Economist,* "Africa: Not Our Fault," July 27, 1985, pp. 26–27; John David Edwards, *Economic Ideology and Economic Integration in Latin America,* Ph.D. dissertation, University of Virginia, 1974 (Ann Arbor, MI: University Microfilms), pp. 136–268; *Regional Industrial Cooperation: Experiences and Perspectives of ASEAN and the Andean Pact* (Vienna: United Nations Development Organization, 1986), pp. 44–95.

13. Isaiah Frank, "The 'Graduation' Issue for LDCs," *Journal of World Trade Law,* vol. 13 (1979), pp. 289–302.

14. See Art Pine, "U.S. Preparing to Restrict Imports from Brazilians," *Wall Street Journal,* May 15, 1986, p. 32; David Hoffman, "U.S. to Prepare Trade Action against Brazil: White House Council Orders Move Following Refusal to Ease Import Restrictions," *Washington Post,* May 15, 1986, p. E-1.

15. See Ravi Ramamurti, *State-Owned Enterprises in High Technology Industries* (New York: Praeger, 1987), pp. 175–211.

16. *A Competitive Assessment of the U.S. General Aviation Industry,* U.S. Department of Commerce, International Trade Administration, Trade Development Office of Aerospace (Washington, DC: U.S. Government Printing Office, 1986), p. 45.

17. *Incentives and Performance Requirements for Foreign Direct Investments in Selected Countries,* U.S. Department of Commerce, Industry and Trade Administration (Washington, DC: U.S. Government Printing Office, 1978); and U.S. Labor-Industry Coalition for International Trade, *Performance Requirements: A Study of the Incidence and Impact of Trade Related Performance Requirements* and *An Analysis of International Trade Law* (Washington, DC: March 1981), pp. 5–7.

18. The classic account of Europe's propensity to form economic unions is Jacob Viner, *The Customs Union Issue* (New York: Carnegie Endowment for International Peace, 1950), esp. pp. 15–40, 82–108.

19. See, for instance, Lord Franks, "Lessons of the Marshall Plan Experience," in *From Marshall Plan to Global Interdependence* (Paris: OECD, 1978), pp. 18–26; and Lincoln Gordon, "Lessons from the Marshall Plan: Successes and Limits," in Stanley Hoffman and Charles Maier, eds., *The Marshall Plan,* pp. 57–58.

20. See, for instance, Horst Ungerer, *The European Monetary System: The Experience, 1979–1982* (Washington, DC: International Monetary Fund, 1983); Jacques van Ypersele, *The European Monetary System: Origins, Operation, and Outlook* (Brussels: Commission of the European Communities, 1984).

21. Gardner Patterson, "The European Community as a Threat to the System," in William R. Cline, ed., *Trade Policy in the 1980s* (Washington, DC: Institute of International Economics, 1982), pp. 223–257.

22. John W. Evans, *The Kennedy Round in American Trade Policy* (Cambridge: Harvard University Press, 1971), pp. 82–85.

23. For information on the goals and policies of Europe's common agricultural policy, see Stuart Holland, *Uncommon Market* (New York: St. Martin's Press, 1980), pp. 27–33; Leon N. Lindberg and Stuart A. Scheingold, *Europe's Would-Be Policy* (Englewood Cliffs, NJ: Prentice-Hall, 1970), pp. 141–155.

24. See for instance, *GATT Activities,* yearly reports that include a listing of disputes before the GATT. For a more in-depth treatment of the "chicken war," see Evans, *The Kennedy Round,* pp. 172–180; and William R. Cline, "Reciprocity: A New Approach to World Trade Policy?" (Washington, DC: Institute for International Economics, 1982), p. 22.

25. Patterson, "European Community as Systemic Threat," pp. 224–230.

26. See Mary Shirley, "Managing State-Owned Enterprises," World Bank Staff Working Papers, no. 557 (Washington, DC: The World Bank, 1983), p. 8.

27. William G. Miller, "The Dogfight over the Airbus," *The Boston Globe,* January 2, 1988, p. 13.

28. For national examples, see Alberto Martinelli, "The Italian Experience: A Historical Perspective," in Raymond Vernon and Yair Aharoni, eds., *State-Owned Enterprises in Western Europe* (London: Croom-Helm, 1981), pp. 85–97; Jean-Pierre Anastassopoulos, "The French Experience: Conflicts with Governments" in Vernon and Aharoni, eds., *State-Owned Enterprises,* pp. 99–116; and Michael Beesley and Tom Evans, "The British Experience: The Case of British Rail," in Vernon and Aharoni, eds., *State-Owned Enterprises,* pp. 117–132.

29. See Yoshi Tsurumi, *The Japanese are Coming* (Cambridge, MA: Ballinger Publishing Company, 1976), pp. 16–69; Chalmers Johnson, *MITI and the Japanese Miracle* (Stanford, CA: Stanford University Press, 1982), pp. 189–241.

30. See Yoshio Suzuki, *Money and Banking in Contemporary Japan* (New Haven: Yale University Press, 1980), pp. 59–61; Terutomo Ozawa, *Multinationals, Japanese Style* (Princeton, NJ: Princeton University Press, 1979), pp. 11–14; Eisuke Sakakibara et al., *Japanese Financial System in Comparative Perspective,* paper prepared for the Program on U.S.–Japan Relations, Center for International Affairs, Harvard University.

31. See Frank A. Weil and Norman D. Glick, "Japan—Is the Market Open? A View of the Japanese Market Drawn from Corporate Experience," *Law and Policy in International Business,* vol. 2, no. 3 (1979), pp. 845–902; Gary R. Saxonhouse, "The Micro- and Macroeconomics of Foreign Sales to Japan," in Cline, ed., *Trade Policy in the 1980s;* and Rosalie L. Tung, *Business Negotiations with the Japanese* (Lexington, MA: Lexington Books, 1984), pp. 34–37.

32. See Weil and Glick, "Japan—Is the Market Open?"; Chalmers Johnson, *MITI and the Japanese Miracle: The Growth of Industrial Policy, 1925–1975* (Stanford, CA: Stanford University Press, 1982), pp. 83–156; Organization for Economic Cooperation and Development, *The Industrial Policy of Japan* (Paris: OECD, 1972), pp. 49–63; and Ezra F. Vogel, *Japan as No. 1* (Cambridge: Harvard University Press, 1979), p. 241.

33. See Rosalie L. Tung, *Business Negotiations with the Japanese* (Lexington, MA: D. C. Heath, 1984) pp. 47–49. Also Vogel, *Japan as No. 1,* pp. 94–95.

34. For a game-theoretic analysis, see, for instance, Robert Axelrod and Robert O. Keohane, "Achieving Cooperation Under Anarchy: Strategies and Institutions," *World Politics,* vol. 38, no. 5 (October 1985), esp. pp. 234–238.

35. See Lionel N. Brown and Francis G. Jacobs, *The Court of Justice of the European Communities* (London: Sweet Maxwell, 1983).

36. See James K. Sebenius, *Negotiating the Law of the Sea* (Cambridge, MA: Harvard University Press, 1984) pp. 71–109.

37. For a technical discussion of linkage and side payments see, for instance, C. R. Plott and M. E. Levine, "On Using the Agenda to Influence Group Decisions: Theory, Experiments, and an Application," California Institute of Technology Working Paper No. 66, November 1974; and Ernst B. Haas, "Why Collaborate? Issue Linkage and International Regimes," *World Politics,* vol. 32, no. 3 (April 1980), pp. 357–405.

38. See, for instance, Jeffrey D. Sachs, "International Policy Coordination: The Case of the Developing Country Debt Crisis," Working Paper Number 2287 (Cambridge, MA: National Bureau of Economic Research, 1987), pp. 45–56.

39. See, for instance, Martin Feldstein et al., "Restoring Growth in the Debt-Laden Third World," No. 33 of the Triangle Papers, Task Force Report, Chapter 4. Presented to the Trilateral Commission, San Francisco, March 1987.

CHAPTER 8 **Preparing for the New Game**

1. See *Congressional Quarterly Almanac,* vol. 39 (1983), pp. 566–567; Robert S. Gilmour and Barbara Hinkson Craig, "After the Congressional Veto: Assessing the Alternatives," *Journal of Policy Analysis and Management,* vol. 3, no. 3 (Spring 1984), pp. 373–392; and Robert S. Gilmour, "The Congressional Veto: Shifting the Balance of Administrative Control," *Journal of Policy Analysis and Management,* vol. 2, no. 1 (Fall 1982), pp. 13–25.

2. See Robert A. Pastor, *Congress and the Politics of U.S. Foreign Economic Policy, 1929–1976* (Berkeley: University of California Press, 1980), pp. 4–5; I. M. Destler, *American Trade Politics: System Under Stress* (Washington, DC: Institute for International Economics, 1986), pp. 12–36; Lewis Anthony Dexter, "The Representative and his District," in Robert Peabody and Nelson W. Polsby, *New Perspectives on the House of Representatives* (Chicago: Rand McNally, 1969), pp. 3–29; John W. Kingdon, *Congressmen's Voting Decisions* (New York: Harper & Row, 1973), pp.

139–146; R. Kent Weaver, "The Politics of Blame Avoidance," Brookings Discussion Papers in Governmental Studies, no. 8 (Washington, DC: Brookings Institution, 1987).

3. See Robert E. Baldwin, *The Political Economy of U.S. Import Policy* (Cambridge, MA: MIT Press, 1985), p. 49.

4. Omnibus Trade and Competitiveness Act of 1987; Title IV of the Trade and International Economic Policy Reform Act of 1987, Part 4.

5. For an in-depth analysis of the negotiations, see James K. Sebenius, *Negotiating the Law of the Sea* (Cambridge: Harvard University Press, 1984).

6. See "Harried Lawmakers Find Congress 'Too Chaotic'," *New York Times,* January 13, 1988, p. A15.

7. The relationship between globalization and the income gap is still hotly debated. See, for instance, "Growing Gap: U.S. Rich and Poor Increase in Numbers; Middle Loses Ground," *Wall Street Journal,* September 22, 1986, p. 1.

8. For an official summary of the agreement's provisions, see Office of the United States Trade Representative, "Summary of the Agreement," press release, October 15, 1987; for a scholarly review of the underlying issues, see Robert M. Stern et al., eds., *Perspectives on a U.S.–Canadian Free-Trade Agreement* (Washington, DC: Brookings Institution,1987).

9. See Clyde Farnsworth, "Twelve Senators Opposing Reagan on Canada Trade," *New York Times,* April 17, 1986, p. D5. According to the provisions of the 1984 trade act, the executive was required to notify Congress whenever it commenced international negotiations under the fast-track process; Congress then had the power to disapprove of the use of the fast-track mechanism within 60 days of the executive's announcement.

10. For a detailed analysis of the U.S.–Canadian lumber controversy, see Joseph P. Kalt, "The Political Economy of Protectionism: Tariffs and Retaliation in the Timber Industry," Harvard University, Kennedy School of Government, Energy and Environmental Policy Center, Discussion Paper E–87–03, March 1987.

11. See, for instance, Robert Gilpin, "American Policy in the Post Reagan Era," in *Daedalus,* vol. 116, no. 3 (Summer 1987), pp. 33–67.

Index